# *Let Your Voice Be Heard!*
## *Songs from Ghana and Zimbabwe*

# *Let Your Voice Be Heard!*
## *Songs from Ghana and Zimbabwe*

Call-and-response, Multipart and Game Songs

Arranged and Annotated for Grades K-12

by Abraham Kobena Adzinyah, Dumisani Maraire and
Judith Cook Tucker

*Musical Transcriptions by Judith Cook Tucker*

### *SONGS FROM SINGING CULTURES*
### *VOL. I*

**World Music Press**
multicultural materials for educators
P.O. Box 2565, Danbury, CT 06813

"Zangaiwa Chakatanga Pano" and "Chawe Chidyo Chem'chero" from : *African Story-Songs: Told and Sung by Dumisani Maraire.* Copyright © 1969 University of Washington Press, Seattle, WA. Used by permission.

These arrangements of: "Sorida;" "Vamuroyi Woye;" "Chatigo Chinyi;" "Cho Kurima Woye;" "Vamudara;" "Wai Bamba" © 1986 Dumisani Maraire. "Chiro Chacho" © 1977 Minanzi Marimba Ensemble, used by permission.

These arrangements of: "Kye Kye Kule;" "Ɔboɔ Asi Me Nsa;" "Bantama Kra Kro;" "Sansa Kroma;" "Pɛtɛ Pɛtɛ;" "Kyerɛm;" "Wɔnfa Nyɛm;" "Meda Wawa Ase;" "Ɔkwan Tsen Tsen," © 1986 A. Kobena Adzinyah.

Thank you to the owners or custodians of art & photos which appear by permission: A.K. Adzinyah: 13,22,39,70,76,96; D. Maraire: 55,87; J.C.Tucker :iii,16,32,90,103,105; Hoa-Qui: 52, Cooperation:88 (thanks to Lawrence Hill); John Chernoff, University of Chicago Press from *African Rhythm and African Sensibility:* 4,89 © 1979; Thomas Stewart in Paul Berliner's *Soul of Mbira*, Univ. of California Press, 93 © 1981; Phyllis Tarlow: illustration of African percussion instruments between pp.xiv and xv ©1987 and 93 (illus. of axatse); map of Africa adapted from one in *The Africans*, Random House, 1982, A Karl/ J. Kemp ©1982; Saki Mafundikwa, cover illustration and drawing of Vamudara found between pp.84 and 85 © 1986. We have made a sincere effort to locate all permission holders for the photos and artwork in these pages. Any ommission is unintentional and will be rectified in future printings if the authors are contacted through the publisher.

### Let Your Voice Be Heard! Songs from Ghana and Zimbabwe.

## World Music Press

Multicultural Materials for Educators
P.O. Box 2565
Danbury, CT 06813    (203) 748-1131

Limited first printing; 1984 as *Songs from Singing Cultures*
Revised, expanded and printed in present form: July 1986 First printing
Second printing August 1987

### Library of Congress Cataloging in Publication Data

Let your voice be heard! :Songs from Ghana and Zimbabwe
    (Songs from singing cultures ; v. 1)
    For 1-4 voices.
    Words in the Akan and Shona languages; also
printed as texts with English translations and extensive background notes.
    Includes index.
    Bibliography; p.
    1. Folk-songs, Akan--Ghana. 2. Folk-songs, Shona--
Zimbabwe. I. Adzinyah, Abraham Kobena, 1939-
II. Maraire, Dumisani, 1943-    . III. Tucker, Judith
Cook, 1947-    . IV. Title: Songs from Ghana and Zimbabwe.
V. Series.
M1830.L47 1986              86-751979
    ISBN 0-937203-00-9 (pbk)
    ISBN 0-937203-04-1 (spiral bdg.)
    ISBN 0-937203-03-3 (cassette companion  tape)

Cover Design and Illustration by Saki Mafundikwa
Music Engraving by Music Art. Co. 276 W. 43 St., NY, NY 10036
Printed by BookCrafters

# About the Authors

Abraham Kobena Adzinyah has taught West African music at Wesleyan University (CT) since 1969. He is a Fanti, born in the village of Gomoa Aboso in the southern central part of Ghana, not far from the coast. His grandfather and father, with whom he studied from the time he was a young boy, were master drummers, and the entire family was well-versed in the musical and cultural traditions of the Akan people. He studied for five years at the School of Music, Dance and Drama, Institute of African Studies (University of Ghana in Legon), after which he was made master drummer of the Ghana Dance Ensemble. In this role he toured throughout the world. He has taught on all levels at numerous elementary and high schools and colleges, including summer institutes for teachers, and has performed widely at concerts and festivals throughout the United States and Canada. He is director of the "Talking Drums" highlife and traditional West African music and dance group, and a member of the Canadian contemporary percussion group "Nexus." Mr. Adzinyah holds a B.A. from Goddard College (VT) and M.A. in music from Wesleyan University.

Dumisani Maraire was born at Chakohwa Village, Chimanimani District of Manicaland province, in the eastern area of Zimbabwe. He was raised in a Christian home, in a musical family with a tradition of singing every night. He began performing when he was a boy of twelve, adding guitar as accompaniment by age fourteen. Although some of his relatives were involved in traditional music, he did not delve into it until 1963 when, under the guidance of ethnomusicologist Robert Kauffman, he entered a Methodist Church program focused on the composing of African hymns for the church services. In 1966 he entered the Kwanongoma College of Music, and began playing the nyunga nyunga mbira and marimba, developing a repertoire of traditional music as well as Western. Since 1968 he has taught at numerous schools and colleges in the United States, first as a visiting artist, then as program coordinator and lecturer at Evergreen State College, (WA) and lecturer in the Ethnomusicology Department at the University of Washington, Seattle. In 1977 he founded the Maraire School of African Music in Seattle. He has led and toured widely with several traditional music groups, including the Minanzi Marimba Ensemble, the Maraire Marimba Ensemble, and Spirit of Mbira, has recorded several albums of traditional and original compositions, published articles on African music, and contributed 80 hymns to various church hymnals. He has held positions in the Department of Recreation, Ministry of Youth, Sport and Recreation in Zimbabwe. As a Staff Development Fellow, Mr. Maraire is presently back in the United States working toward a Ph. D. in Ethnomusicology at the University of Washington.

Judith Cook Tucker grew up in New Rochelle, New York. Her mother had worked as a music teacher in the New York City schools, touring throughout the school system with a group of children demonstrating international folk dance and song. As a result, Tucker was exposed from birth to music from many cultures and in many languages. She studied classical piano and flute, folk guitar, built dulcimers and performed original and traditional folk music for many years as a solo and member of folk groups. Always most interested in participatory music making, Tucker was strongly influenced by Pete Seeger and the Weavers' enthusiastic and successful use of ethnic material, and has been the recipient of several grants to bring multicultural music into schools, libraries and community settings. She regularly serves as a clinician at in-service workshops, conferences and summer institutes for teachers who want to increase their repertoire of ethnic materials. School choirs throughout the United States have performed her compositions influenced by traditional music of many cultures. She works directly with choral groups as a composer-in-residence. She received a BA in Journalism and Anthropology from New York University (1969), and an M.A.L.S. with a concentration in World Music for the classroom from Wesleyan University (CT) in 1983.

# Table of Contents

# List of Transcriptions

# List of Illustrations

## LIST OF MAPS

# A Note on the Transcriptions

As many musicologists have noted, transcribing African music is a frustrating and extremely difficult job if the transcriber uses Western notation, as we have. African vocal performance practices include slides, slurs, notes which are only slightly flatted or sharped, whistles, yodels and nuances of syncopation and timbre which create obvious problems if one attempts to notate each phrase of a particular performance perfectly, according to Western practices. Therefore, we have chosen to present a slightly edited version of some of the more complex songs, pared down to an unadorned foundation of core parts to increase the chances of being used successfully by teachers in school and community settings. The only unusual symbols you will see are↓ or ↑ to indicate a note should be sung a bit flat or sharp (or in the neighborhood of the written tone but not necessarily fully on top of it), ⅃ which stands for a note of indefinite pitch, and x after a note which indicates the voice should should be allowed to drop or slide off the pitch.

Percussion accompaniments have similarly been selected from the possibilities offered by the original context, and reduced to a core of parts which will add drive and excitement to the arrangements but will still be within the grasp of the students' abilities and the school's instrumentarium.

Each song is presented in its original language. Below each line is a transliteration. The literal translation follows, and also a more general or expanded translation if the words contain multiple meanings or levels of meaning. Teaching suggestions are found in the "Notes on Use" sections.

It is important to note that these transcriptions present the songs as "frozen" at one point in time, in one particular configuration of parts, and with one specific melodic and rhythmic form. In actual practice, it would be unlikely to find a song or drumming, singing and dancing ensemble from Ghana or Zimbabwe performed in precisely the same way each time, or in such rigid fashion that the rhythm of every note or phrase would fall precisely within regularly divided measures. Do not, therefore, take the time signatures and bar lines as laws to be followed without question. They are present in the transcriptions as an organizational aid, but once the pieces have been learned and are sung up to tempo, allow the phrases to become more fluid, and delineations more blurred.

# Key to Pronunciation

I. WORDS IN AKAN: Vowels (approximate)

a = as in <u>hat</u> or <u>far</u> (**ah** in transliteration)
e = as <u>a</u> sound in <u>late</u> or <u>i</u> in <u>hit</u>, (**ay** or **ih** in
     transliteration)
i = as <u>ee</u> sound in <u>flee, tree</u> (**ee** in transliteration)
o = as in <u>boat, goat</u> or <u>u</u> sound in <u>putt</u> (**oh** or **uh** in
     transliteration)
u = as in <u>fumes</u> (**oo** in transliteration)
ε = as <u>e</u> sound in <u>red, get</u> (**eh** in transliteration)
ɔ = as <u>o</u> sound in <u>lost</u> or <u>aw</u> in <u>raw</u> (**aw** in translit.)

## Consonants

x     = as <u>h</u> in <u>hot</u>
dw    = as <u>j</u> in <u>jump, with lips quite rounded</u>
gy    = as <u>j</u> in <u>jump</u>
ky    = as <u>ch</u> in <u>check, chair</u>
ny    = as <u>ny</u> in <u>canyon</u>, (<u>y</u> is often less obvious)
kp    = as <u>k</u> simultaneously with <u>p</u>, (<u>p</u> is most obvious)
dz    = combination of <u>d</u> and <u>z</u> sounds
ts    = combination of <u>t</u> and <u>s</u> sounds, <u>s</u> is most obvious)
r     = slightly rolled

(Adapted from W.K. Amoaku, **African Songs and Rhythms for Childhood**, (New York:Schott, 1971), p.9; and Abraham Kobena Adzinyah, **Acquisition of Musical Knowledge by Traditional Musicians of Akan Society**, (M.A. thesis, Wesleyan University, 1978), p. v.)

II. WORDS IN SHONA: Vowels (approximate)

a = as in <u>father</u> (**ah** in transliteration)
e = as in <u>take</u>   (**ay** in transliteration)
i = as in <u>feet</u>   (**ee** in transliteration)
o = as in <u>go</u>     (**oh** in transliteration)
u = as in <u>blue</u>   (**oo** in transliteration)

## Consonants

b     = implosive when used initially
d     = implosive when used initially
dh    = as English <u>d</u>
dz    = combination of <u>d</u> and <u>z</u> sounds
zh    = approx. as soft <u>g</u> in <u>orange</u>
n(di) = velar stop as in <u>ng</u> in <u>hung</u>
dy    = as <u>j</u> in <u>job</u>
r     = rolled

(Adapted from Paul Berliner, **The Soul of Mbira**, (Berkeley: University of California Press, 1981), p. xi.)

# Preface

Here are nineteen game songs, story songs and multipart recreational songs representing the Akan people of Ghana, West Africa and the Shona of Zimbabwe in south central Africa. The individual songs were selected from our personal repertoires, keeping in mind the teacher who is interested in using ethnic materials in the music class or with a school chorus. Our many years of teaching and performing the traditional music and dance of Africa has shown us there is a great deal of interest and excitement in this art form which is an intrinsic part of the total fabric of African culture. Although the African musical heritage has been maintained by word of mouth over the centuries, we have become actively involved in presenting it in a form that will encourage non-Africans, accustomed to learning from written materials, to become acquainted with our music, use it, and thus grow to love the richness of our cultures.

We first taught Judith Cook Tucker these songs and discussed their meanings and traditional context when she was conducting research for her master's degree at Wesleyan. We all then took the resulting thesis and revised and rewrote the entire manuscript cooperatively, making alterations or additions within our own areas of expertise. Her role was primarily as a bridge between ourselves--African traditional musicians--and our target audience of teachers and ethno-musicologists.

We present these songs in authentic settings with notes on translation, transliteration, musical structure, performance practice, and how to introduce them to your students. Many are transcribed here for the first time. Those few which might appear elsewhere are presented in this book as personal or regional variants. We have used every one with students of all ages and know they can be an exciting tool to intercultural understanding and personal growth. We also hope that such a collection will help to dispel the widely held and unfortunate stereotype that African music making is limited exclusively to drumming and "unintelligible chants." These songs range from games which even a kindergarten child can quickly master to four-part songs which will be a challenge to a high school chorus.

Children in Ghana and Zimbabwe learn about their culture and at the same time develop the coordination and sensitivity needed to master complex rhythm patterns, movement and part-singing by learning game songs and story songs, and by imitating adult music making overall. Similarly, you and your students can gain the skills you'll need to tackle the more difficult songs by learning each in the order presented in the book. You might find that working with the companion tape (which places the learning experience in the more traditional aural/oral context) makes dealing with unfamiliar languages and rhythms easier and clarifies nuances of pronunciation, rhythm and melody which are impossible to notate.

We have tried to keep the spirit within each song alive just as we have tried to communicate relevant information accurately and clearly. We offer them in friendship. This music is for all people.

Abraham Kobena Adzinyah<br>Dumisani Maraire

**Note:** Akan and Shona words appear in boldface the first time they are used in a section. If they are used more than once, they will no longer be in boldface type. All words in boldface are explained in the glossary.

# Acknowledgements

*First and foremost I thank my father, my mother, my brothers and my sisters with whom I share the gift of musical ability, and my wife for her support.*

*I wish to thank Kwabena Nketia for making it possible for me to come to the United States, for encouraging me over the years in my studies and work, and for acting as a second father to me.*

*Thank you also to A.M. Opoku, former artistic director of the Ghana Dance Ensemble for introducing me to the art forms of different ethnic groups of Ghana.*

*And thank you to my colleagues who encouraged me with my studies and my work here in the United States.*

*Abraham Kobena Adzinyah*


*I would like to extend my deepest gratitude to my brother, the late Nkosana Maraire, who gave me encouragement to go into music seriously. He was always there supporting me, strengthening my resolve when I was not sure of the path I should take.*

*Robert Kauffman was the first man to actually get me involved in working with traditional music, in 1963, and I owe him grateful thanks for his influence and guidance, and for his devotion to the music of Zimbabwe.*

*Thank you to Robert Garfias, who helped me in my understanding of ethnomusicology and for encouraging me to write and publish in the past as well.*

*I appreciate the wonderful start I had in my parents' home, which was frequently filled with the sound of the whole family singing hymns. My mother and father gave me my first training in singing and harmony, and I thank them.*

*Finally, I thank my wife and family for their assistance and support of my performing, and most importantly, for keeping the spirit going.*

*Dumisani Maraire*


*Grateful thanks to: Barbara Potter and Abraham Kobena Adzinyah in their role of faculty supervisors for the master's thesis which is the foundation of this book; Maxwell Amoh, who carefully read through all of the Ghanaian material and brought the spelling of Akan words into line with the Fanti dialect; Alan Thrasher, now at the University of British Columbia, for clarifying my thinking about how non-Western music can be introduced to teachers so they will be inspired to integrate it into their curriculum; the staff and faculty at Wesleyan in both the Graduate Liberal Studies Program and the World Music Department, including Freeman Donkor, Mark Slobin, Judith Gray, Tom Ross (who introduced me to the music of Zimbabwe) and Mara Capy, as well as Phyllis Bruce who nudged me in the direction of making my thesis something that would have practical applications in the "real world."*

*Thank you to Pete Seeger in his many guises and the Weavers for a lifetime of ideas and influences.*

*Thanks and love to my parents and sister, my husband and children for supporting and encouraging me musically, financially and emotionally in countless ways through several years of creative juggling, to Jeanette Hyer and Martha Tucker for the gift of time to work.*

*Finally, heartfelt appreciation to Abraham Kobena Adzinyah and Dumisani Maraire for sharing with me their expertise in performance and their extensive knowledge of and love for their musical and cultural heritage, and for their enthusiastic cooperation on this project.*

*Judith Cook Tucker*

"It is the *process* of music making that is valued as much as, and sometimes more than, the finished product. The value of music, is, I believe, to be found in terms of the human experiences involved in its creation."

–John Blacking in *How Musical is Man?*

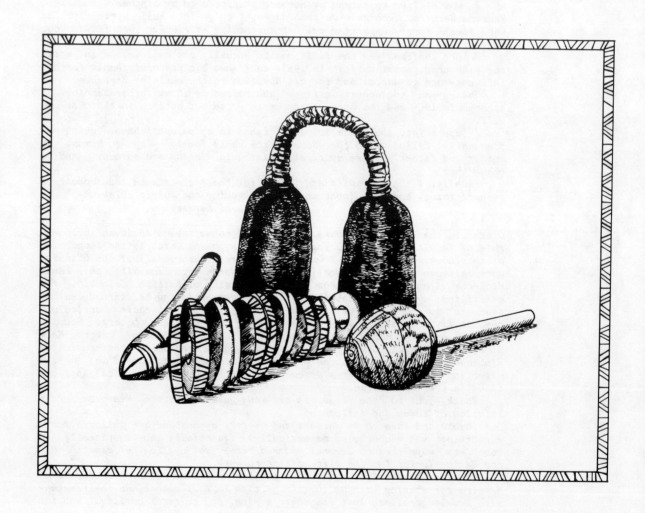

# Map of Africa

AFRICA
▲
1986

Adapted from: David Lamb, THE AFRICANS, Random
House, 1982.

## GHANA IN BRIEF

Ghana is the oldest independent black African nation. It gained independence from British colonial rule under the leadership of Kwame Nkrumah in 1957, and then had several bloodless coups which placed alternately military and civilian leaders in power. Currently, the head of the government is Flight Lt. Jerry Rawlings and a council of seven.

Ghana's area is 92,000 square miles, bounded on the west by the Ivory Coast, on the north by Burkina Faso, and on the east by Togo. The population of almost twelve million is 99% Ghanaian with only a sprinkling of permanent residents originally from other countries, including India, the middle east and the United States. The largest ethnic groups are the Ashanti and Ewe. The Fanti are next largest with 10.5% of the total population. English and 50 tribal languages are spoken!

The climate is equatorial, with an average temperature of 80 degrees Farenheit, and two seasons - wet and dry. The majority of the people are farmers of various sorts, growing yams, cassava, millet, maize, plantains, peanuts, palm nuts, tomatoes, onions and rice for their own needs. In the coastal areas fishing has traditionally been the chief occupation. The Ghanaian coast is pounded by a rough Atlantic surf, yet fishermen negotiate the waves in dugout canoes in their search for herring, eels, sole, mackerel, snapper and other fish. The cocoa farmers supply about 30% of the world's demand for the bean, in both raw and processed forms. Copra (from coconut), tropical hardwoods, kola nuts, oils and rubber are also exported, and cotton textiles, glass products and a variety of building materials including bricks and cement are produced for use within the country. Modern factories and mills for processing raw materials are increasing in number, and the population of the cities has grown to over 25% in response to the new jobs. Local breweries supply palm wine, a tart drink from the fermented sap of the palm tree, and **pito**, a thin, slightly sour beverage made from water and ground millet which has been brewed for only three days. Ghanaians like to gather at local palm wine and pito bars after work or when they find themselves with a few free hours. These open-air cafes feature socializing, talk of work, politics, upcoming festivals and singing, and are not really bars in the sense of heavy drinking and rowdy behavior as one might find in American "beer joints." Perhaps the most common dish eaten is **fufu**, balls made of mashed, boiled and pounded yams, cassava, plantain and/or cocoyam. The balls are frequently dipped into stews or soups made with tomatoes, onions, hot chili peppers, chopped ground nuts (peanuts) and a small amount of fish, chicken or meat.

Crafts include pottery making, wood carving, gold and metal work and making the traditional **kente** and **adinkra** cloths used in the **ntama**, a garment made of a large rectangle of cloth wrapped around the body in special ways. Men sometimes throw the last section of cloth over one shoulder, leaving the other shoulder bare. Women often fold the cloth and wear it as a wrapped skirt with a traditional blouse or **kaba**. Patterns woven and stamped on the fabric are symbolic and in many cases are tied to particular rituals, and are therefore worn only when particular dances or ceremonies call for them.

Missionaries introduced Ghanaians to Christianity, and today about 42 percent are Protestant or Catholic, about 12 percent are Moslem (mainly in the northern areas), but about 46 percent still practice traditional religions. Some Christian Ghanaians also maintain traditional beliefs and observe ancient rites alongside those introduced by the missionaries.

There are several fine schools, and the colleges include the University of Ghana at Legon, with courses in social studies, arts, agriculture, sciences, law and medicine, and the University of Science and Technology at Kumasi.

Ghanaians take pride in their traditions and in their steady evolution into a modern nation. An important symbol seen throughout Ghana is **san kɔfa**--the bird which looks backwards, with its head turned and beak poking into its feathers. "San kɔfa" stands for "Go back and take it," indicating how people rush forward to grasp the good things in life, but forget that there are equally good things they have left behind. They are advised to go back for them, for "the past experience is a guide for the future."

# Map of Ghana

*Adapted from: Dennis M. Warren,* The Akan of Ghana. *Accra: Pointer Ltd.,1973.*

# ZIMBABWE IN BRIEF

Zimbabwe, (formerly Rhodesia) gained independence from Great Britain in 1980, and now has a bicameral Parliamentary Democracy with seats for 100 blacks and 20 whites in the government led by Prime Minister Robert Mugabe.

Zimbabwe (the name means "houses of stone" after the ruins of an ancient state in the south east which was a major trading area between the ninth and thirteenth centuries) is located in the south central part of Africa, with Zambia to the north, Mozambique to the east, Botswana to the southwest and South Africa to the south. The population is over seven million living in a area of 150,803 square miles (about the same size as California). Ninety-six percent are Africans, with the largest ethnic groups being the Shona and Ndebele. The Shona are Bantu-speaking peoples living in the area between the Zambezi and Limpopo Rivers in Zimbabwe, although there are also some Shona in Mozambique and Zambia. Shona dialects include Karanga, Zezuru, Manyika and Ndau.

Unlike Ghana, which is not very mountainous, Zimbabwe's terrain ranges from a low of 2,000 feet above sea level, to a high (Mount Inyangani) of 8,500 feet, although most of it is a fairly level plateau about four thousand feet above sea level. The climate is moderate, with temperatures during the day varying from about 70 to 90 degrees Fahrenheit (unlike Ghana's highs of over 100 degrees). At night it is even cool. There are two seasons, a wet (November until April) and a dry (May to November).The temperate climate combined with some very interesting and beautiful natural and historic spots, including the ruins of Zimbabwe and the dramatic Victoria Falls with its curtain of mist and rainbows make it a popular tourist stop.

The three main religions practiced are Christianity, Islam and Hinduism, although many Christians also practice the traditional religions as well, striving to establish and maintain contact with the spirits of dead ancestors out of respect and also for aid with present problems. The mbira is often played as part of religious rites, as well as recreationally.

Although sixty-five percent of Zimbabweans work in some agricultural area, including growing tobacco, tea, cotton, wheat, maize, peanuts and cattle, (making Zimbabwe fairly self-sufficient in terms of its food needs) industries are growing and more people are working in textile mills, food processing plants, engineering and metal foundries. Mining of minerals is centered mainly around gold, tin, coal, copper, silver and iron. The existence of so many metals had a profound effect on the development of tools, weapons and even musical instruments (the **mbira** for example, with its hammered metal keys). It has also had an effect on the lifestyles of the people, because many Africans have left their homes in the countryside to work in city jobs related to mining and manufacturing, and in some cases men have had to leave their families  at home in the villages and live in rough barracks-style  housing  provided by industry.  Some have  found  city living to be a destructive experience,  and their tales often find  their way into music as they gather in the  beer  parks after long days of work to socialize,  sing and dance.  It is not  unusual to hear the sounds of pop music from other parts of  Africa  and rock from the West alongside  or  alternating with the most ancient, traditional songs and instruments such as the musical bow,  flutes, pipes, and hand-flutes. Although Zimbabwe, like Ghana, is struggling to balance the modern and the traditional, interest in and popularity of older forms of instruments,  music,  games,  storytelling,  work and  social songs  is  growing,  aided in part by courses in  traditional music offered at the Kwanongoma College of Music,  founded in 1960 in Bulawayo to teach European and African music.  Graduates of the college are teaching on all levels throughout the country,  exposing their students to the treasures  contained within their traditions.

# Map of Zimbabwe

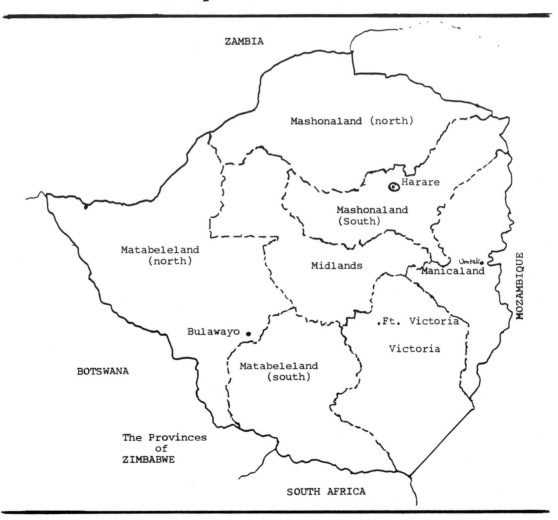

-xix-

# Introduction

This group of songs from the repertoires of Abraham Kobena Adzinyah and Dumisani Maraire is an attempt to meet the growing interest in and need for curriculum materials in the African tradition, a need which has often been expressed by ethnomusicologists, African scholars and African and American educators alike. There are so many Americans of all ages and of non-European backgrounds who find the music programs in American schools largely irrelevant. Multi-ethnic education is "concerned with modifying the total educational environment," according to James Banks, "so that (it) is more reflective of the ethnic diversity of American society." (1977:p.3) Alexander Ringer, writing on the application of Kodaly's insights and techniques to the American educational scene, says:

> In order to give young blacks, Mexican-Americans, Puerto Ricans, or...American Indians a truly meaningful musical education the schools will have to apply ... insights gained from the study of their indigenous background...to maximize the vast as yet untapped educational potential...embedded in the totality, rather than a mere segment of America's...musical resources.(1972:p.151)

Kwasi Aduonum, a Ghanaian musician, scholar and music educator, states in his doctoral dissertation that curriculum resources are "scanty." He notes:

> The lack of materials drawn from African culture and suitable for elementary or secondary school students underlines the continuing need for well-prepared materials on a variety of African musics and for personnel specifically trained to function effectively with such music. (1980:p.9)

J. H. Kwabena Nketia of Ghana, ethnomusicologist and one of the foremost scholars of African musical traditions, writes:

> If intercultural studies are to make headway in the general field of music education, a lot of ground work must be done in different cultures, in the preparation of curricular materials. Although there is a growing accumulation of materials on African...musical culture, field field recordings and ethnomusicological descriptions of music do not constitute curricular materials until they are properly sorted out and systematized for instructional purpose. (1978:p.111)

Additionally, much of American popular music has its

roots in African soil. The more students learn about African vocal and instrumental musical structure, composition techniques and performance practice, the more they will recognize and understand the links to American jazz, blues, soul, rock and disco music.

The integration of African music in the activities of daily life gives it an intensity and importance which is rarely communicated in Western music. Adzinyah holds that "the African community is held together with musical bonds." His and Maraire's lifetime of musical experiences in Ghana and Zimbabwe illustrate what many writers have noted, that music surrounds an African from the moment of birth, through all stages of growth, courting, marriage, work, religious and recreational celebrations, illness, business matters and family history, and, finally, at funerals. As John Chernoff observes, this functional integration of music and culture in Africa creates a situation whereby "the study of African music can reveal a great deal about the nature of culture and community life." (1979:p.36)

African songs are an archive of cultural values, history and societal expectations. Children's game and story songs contain proverbs and teachings which will guide the child's behavior in his or her community. According to Chernoff:

> The development of musical awareness in Africa constitutes a process of education: music's explicit purpose in the various ways it might be defined by Africans, is, essentially, socialization. An individual learns the potentials and limitations of participation in a communal context dramatically arranged for the engagement, display and critical examination of fundamental cultural values. (1979:p.154)

It is widely accepted in Africa that if "you can speak you can sing." Francis Bebey notes:

> Any individual who has the urge to make his voice heard is given the liberty to do so; singing is not (generally) a specialized affair. Anyone can sing and, in practice, anyone does....This is the essence of the collective aspect of African music; no one is ruled out because he is technically below par. (1975:p.115)

This is not to say that cantors or lead singers who are acknowledged as experts and play specific roles in certain songs do not exist. There are definitely individuals and even groups who sing parts requiring a high level of expertise and ability. But within the context of most African vocal music there is also ample room for participation by those with less polish but equal motivation.

While Westerners strive for perfect technique and accurate note reading, and listen silently to performances of folk music, Broadway show tunes and opera alike, Africans structure their music in such a way so as to maximize participation possibilities for all levels of expertise. Referring to the Venda people in southern Africa, John Blacking writes:

> It is the process of music making that is valued as much as, and sometimes more than, the finished product. The value of music is, I believe, to be found in terms of the human experiences involved in its creation. (1973:p.50)

Singing call-and-response and multipart songs is an experience centered more around human relationships which happen to be expressed musically than around accurate and repetitive rendering of musical manuscripts. The fact that the resulting sounds are rich, interesting and exciting is a wonderful bonus. African music offers a collective, community experience on many levels. It "includes structures within easy reach of all which allow for group learning and spontaneous participation," (Nketia 1980:p.158), and it accepts and incorporates individual efforts. Chernoff believes "perhaps the most fundamental aesthetic in Africa (is) that without participation there is no meaning...." (1979:p.23)

There are many children and adults in America who have never had an opportunity to make music in a situation where free expression is encouraged and individual contributions, no matter how small, are welcomed as an exciting addition to the total creation. On the contrary, it is not difficult to find adults who were told as children they had a tin ear or could not sing, and were instructed to only mouth the words to songs. In workshops offered for such "non-singers," it is not unusual for participants to be deeply moved as they sing the melody of a simple childhood folksong for the first time in their lives. Participation in musical activity is not only a pleasant way to spend time-- it is a necessity for psychological and even physical health for many people.

It is our hope that this collection will serve as a resource for music specialists who previously have found materials in the African tradition to be unavailable, inaccessible or difficult to use, not authentic, or simply scanty. All of the songs, games and stories included here have been classroom tested with exciting results. We found that students developed a love for the music, and an interest in exploring African cultures further. African music is not for those of African extraction only. It is, rather, music to share with the world, with all who would experience the fellowship of cooperative music making. We hope the process rather than product or goal orientation will encourage hesitant singers to find their voice, plunge headlong into learning the short repeated phrases which abound in most of these songs, and boldly join the singing community. We offer these pieces as a starting point on a joyous and challenging adventure. Allow yourself and your students the freedom to improvise and experiment with vocal parts and with body percussion, percussion instruments and movement. These songs are not artifacts from dead cultures. They are living bridges to vital parts of the global community. You can be sure that while Akan children in Ghana and Shona children in Zimbabwe learn to master and respect tradition as they take part in games, folktale parties and singing, they are also developing the ability to improvise, innovate and create. In this spirit, take a breath, open your mouth, and **let your voice be heard!**

Chernoff photo;*African Rhythm and African Sensibility*, Univ. of Chicago Press, c 1979.

Young Ewe Borborbor dancers sing as they come out to dance

# Chapter I:

# Game Songs

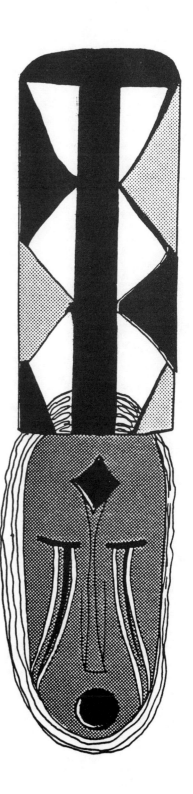

# Game Songs

Children around the world share a love of games played as part of or accompanied by chants, songs and motions. They will spend many hours involved in circle games with chants; counting games played to silly songs; jump rope and ball bouncing chants; clapping games with intricate arm, hand and finger motions; or games naming animals, people and things. Typically children learn these songs directly from each other, not from adults, and often each family, clique, neighborhood, village or region uses distinctive variants or secret verses. Game songs are the child's special domain.

African children are no exception to this world-wide tradition. By the age of four or five they join in on circle games of all sorts; counting games using fingers, stones or sticks; handclapping, rhythm and name games, and dances requiring special motions. The authors have observed basic differences, however, in the content and purpose of American children's games and those played by children in Ghana and Zimbabwe.

American game songs might give practice in counting, reciting the alphabet and ordering lists alphabetically. On occasion, recitation of academic subject material may be worked into a chant, but the abundance of "silly" words (such as "amalama kumalama kuma la vista") which have no meaning to the participants, good-natured teasing chants and action songs seems to indicate they are primarily for exercise and fun. American elementary school teachers occasionally appropriate game songs as a tool to enchance rote learning, but it can be fairly said that most American adults do not invest them with any deeper importance.

Many African game songs, on the other hand, embody moral teachings and cultural values, proverbs, tribal and family history, teach the individual's role in society, offer practical hints for daily life, and create opportunities to practice complex rhythms on "found" instruments or their bodies. They increase coordination, train the child's voice to be flexible, and give the children experience in projecting feelings to an audience through the medium of music. By the age of six, children in Ghana and Zimbabwe are eased into participation in music and dance during actual festivals and over time become perfectly comfortable with performing in front of hundreds or thousands of people. The first ingredient in the recipe for "no stage fright" is a good dose of participation in game songs.

These differences in the role game songs play may be a reflection of oral versus written traditions in communicating important societal information to young people. Francis Bebey writes:

> African musical education is a school in the broadest sense...a comprehensive preparation for that strange adventure upon which (the child) is about to embark - life....The musical games played by children are never gratuitous; they are a form of musical training which prepares them to participate in all areas of adult activity -- fishing, hunting, grinding maize, attending weddings, funerals, dances, and by necessity, even fleeing from wild animals. (1975:p.8)

By the age of five, children in Ghana and Zimbabwe participate in games that are inspired by (or actually based on ) traditional rhythm patterns which are used by adult ensembles. They sing corrective songs with good-natured teasing that directs the child toward appropriate and acceptable behavior, and they even begin to make their own instruments and attempt to copy older children and adults with mini-ensembles. Many game songs include sounds imitative of bird and animal noises. Stretching to create hoots, howls, growls and snarls trains a child's voice in various levels, gradually develops and improves their singing ability, and increases their musical resources.

Handgames such as "Sorida" from Zimbabwe and "Nsa Ni O" from Ghana offer crossrhythms to be learned and mastered. The child sings in one rhythm and uses another in the motions. Stone passing games like "Ɔboɔ Asi Me Nsa" from Ghana frequently begin slowly and increase in speed. This gradual acceleration helps develop coordination and steadiness in maintaining an even beat no matter how fast the chant is sung. Such games also provide an opportunity for practice of polyrhythms. Some of the chants actually employ the exact pattern the bell (which is seen as the time keeper) uses in drumming ensembles. Other game songs require call-and-response singing of two parts, which may be in harmony as they overlap, or of alternating sections of group and solo singing.

It is easy to see that game songs, although "child's play" throughout much of the world, are serious business in Africa. Their hours of fun serve as a training ground for musical and social skills which later will be essential as a youth seeks to become a full member of society.

# Sorida

## A Shona Handgame Song

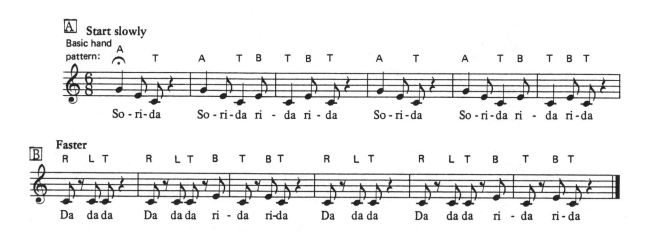

## Version "A"

```
A    T    A    T   B T B T
SO-RI-DA, SO-RI-DA, RI-DA RI-DA        (repeat)

R   L   T   R   L   T   B T B T
DA-DA-DA, DA-DA-DA, RI-DA RI-DA        (repeat)

A    T    A    T   B T B T
SO-RI-DA, SO-RI-DA, RI-DA RI-DA        (repeat)
```

## Version "B"

```
A    T    A    T   F T F T
SO-RI-DA, SO-RI-DA, RI-DA RI-DA        (repeat)

P   S   T   P   S   T   F T F T
DA-DA-DA, DA-DA-DA, RI-DA RI-DA        (repeat)

A    T    A    T   F T F T
SO-RI-DA, SO-RI-DA, RI-DA RI-DA        (repeat)
```

*(Substitute "E" for "F" in above; then switch unexpectedly by calling out "Arms!" or "Elbows!" or "Backs!"*

# Sorida

A:  SORIDA, SORIDA, RI-DA, RI-DA (two times)
soh-ree-dah, soh-ree-dah, ree-dah, ree-dah

B:  DA-DA-DA, DA-DA-DA, RI-DA, RI-DA (two times)

(Form:  AA-BB ending with the word "Sorida" sung three times as in first measures)

## TRANSLATION

"Sorida" is a term of greeting in the Shona language, similar in use to "jambo" in Swahili, or perhaps "shalom" in Hebrew.

## EXPLANATION

This is an example of a handgame that can be done quite simply for the youngest child, but can easily be increased in complexity to challenge a player of any age.  In addition to being tremendous fun, likely to precipitate great hilarity, handgames like "Sorida" give practice in coordination and train participants to sing in one rhythm and move the arms and hands in a complementary rhythm.

## NOTES ON USE

Mai Chi Maraire, who is an early-childhood-education specialist, sings a very simple version using only standard handclaps and a circular arm motion. (Version A on transcription.)
For older children a more complex version is more exciting.  Noted as version B (below), this particular configuration involves clapping both the front and back of the partner's hands, touching palms to partner's elbows, and forearms to forearms. Speed up for extra excitement.

### VERSION A
(Partners sit or stand facing each other.)
KEY: A= hands swept apart in upward circular motion
     T= clap own hands together
     B= partners hit back-of-right to back-of-right hands
     L= partners hit left palms across
     R= partners hit right palms across
### VERSION B
KEY: (additional motions):
     P= hold hands up, slap both of partner's palms
     S= hold hands up, slap backs of partner's hands
     F= hit right forearm on partner's right forearm
     E= tap partner's r. elbow, cupping it with l. palm
*Note: See diagrams below transcription

# Kye Kye Kule

**An Akan Call-and-Response Exercise Song**

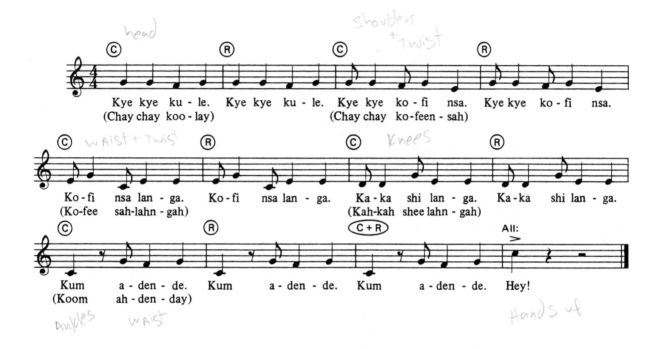

# *Kye Kye Kule*

Leader: KYE KYE KULE
        chay chay koo-lay

Group: KYE KYE KULE

L:     KYE KYE KOFI SA
        chay chay koh-fee sah

G:     KYE KYE KOFI SA

L:     KOFI SA LANGA
        koh-fee sah lahn-gah

G:     KOFI SA LANGA

L:     KAKA SHILANGA
        kah-kah shee lahn-gah

G:     KAKA SHILANGA

L:     KUM ADEN NDE
        koom ah-dehn day

G:     KUM ADEN NDE

L+G:   KUM ADEN NDE, HEY!

## TRANSLATION

This is a very popular motion game played by young children in Ghana. It is even found in other parts of Africa with very similar words which may come from a mixture of dialects, but have not been pinpointed as part of a particular language and do not convey any specific meaning.

Edna Smith Edet includes a Nigerian version of "Kye Kye Kule" in **The Griot Sings**: Songs from the Black World. The words are: **Che che kule; Oku salala; Ela silala; He malila, ho.** She notes, "On 'Ho' the leader chooses a successor." (1978:p.28)

## EXPLANATION

As every Akan children's game song reflects a specific movement, you would see that the motions in "Kye Kye Kule" have not changed over many years. The emphasis is always on mastering what is traditional, and on following what your ancestors have already achieved. Therefore modern children are still using the same head, shoulders, and hips movement and will not change the gestures.

NOTES ON USE

"Kye Kye Kule" is suitable for use with preschool or older children. The leader sings the first phrase, simultaneously patting his or her head four times on the beat. The group responds by repeating the phrase and the motion. Next, the leader sings the second phrase while tapping his or her shoulders four times and twisting the upper torso from side to side as well. Again the group repeats the phrase and the motion. Next hands go to waist, the twisting continues in an animated way, and the group follows. Next the leader taps the knees and the group copies. Lastly the leader bends over to touch ankles on "kum" and touch waist on "adende". The group responds and then leader and group touch ankles and waist in unison, then all throw hands over their head and shout "Hey!"

Students take turns being the leader. Add a little spice by creating a small percussion ensemble to accompany the group, using rhythm patterns found below. (See "Sample Percussion Ensembles" in appendix.)

*Ghanaian youths taking part in Akwanbo festival ("Retracing the Path" of the ancestors). Fathers who have previously carried the sword and treasures of the chief have given that honor over to their sons. The participants are following in the footsteps of their parents, becoming aware of the transition from childhood to adulthood, honoring their ancestors while gaining recognition in their society.*

# Ɔboɔ Asi Me Nsa

## An Akan Stone-Passing Game

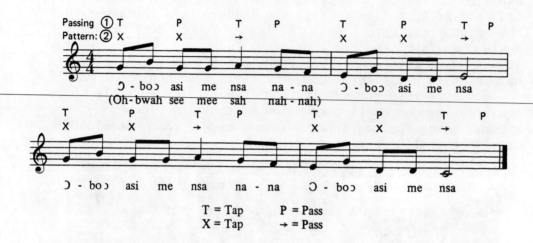

T = Tap      P = Pass

X = Tap      → = Pass

ƆBOƆ ASI ME NSA, NANA, ƆBOƆ ASI ME NSA
oh-bwah see mee sah, nah-nah, oh-bwah see mee sah

ƆBOƆ ASI ME NSA, NANA, ƆBOƆ ASI ME NSA

TRANSLATION

"The rock crushed my hand, grandma" (or other relative)

EXPANDED TRANSLATION

A child singing "Ɔboɔ Asi Me Nsa" is repeately receiving a message of security and comfort, even in the context of a phrase and game which tell of an injury. The injured child can take comfort in the fact that he or she can turn to "Nana" for sympathy and assistance--the ever-present circle of relatives supports Ghanaian children and adults during times of misfortune and celebration both.

EXPLANATION

Like "Sansa Kroma," "Pɛtɛ Pɛtɛ," and "Bantama Kra Kro," this is an Akan song commonly used to accompany a rock passing game. The children sit in a circle and pass a stone counterclockwise in a particular rhythmic pattern. Such games are not as common today in Ghana as they were thirty or forty years ago. However, in 1962, several years after Ghana became independent (1957), the School of Music, Dance and Drama of the Institute of African Studies (University of Ghana) opened. There musicians could receive formal training in the traditions of the many ethnic groups in Ghana. After completing the program of studies, these individuals began to teach in the far-flung villages and schools, and even at the college level, helping old and sometimes neglected traditions re-emerge to meet the challenge of modern lifestyles. In this way, the younger generation is encouraged to understand and appreciate the revered customs which are the foundation of contemporary Ghanaian society.

"Ɔboɔ Asi Me Nsa" reveals the importance the Akan place on cooperation. It can be used as a game of elimination: as the chant is gradually speeded up to increase the level of coordination and skill required, any child who passes or receives the rock incorrectly is out of the game. It most often is played so that if a child places the rock carelessly and his or her neighbor messes up the pattern, the passer is out **as well as or instead of** the receiver. It then is to everyone's advantage to place the rocks carefully in front of the next person in the circle, and to maintain a steady beat. This is not a game of "hot potato" but rather a game of precision and accuracy in rhythm and motion.

## NOTES ON USE

"Ɔboɔ Asi Me Nsa" is played by a group sitting in a circle passing one rock along the ground from child to child, or there can be one rock for each child. In the latter case, the rocks would be passed continuously around the circle in the chosen pattern. If the group is large enough, break into two sections and use both patterns simultaneously. Older children who create additional patterns might break into even more small groups so that the rhythmic variations pop out dramatically.

Even the youngest (pre-kindergarten) child can master this game if a rock-passing phrase is repeated several times before the singing begins. This phrase might be: "Grab, Pass, Grab, Pass, Grab, Pass, Grab, Pass;" "Tap, Tap, Pass, Up, Tap, Tap, Pass, Up," "Grab, Tap, Pass it," "Grab, Tap, Pass it to the right" or something similar.

Begin with this practice chant and the hand motion of tapping on the ground and then moving the hand to the right **without any rocks**. While the children continue in this manner, the leader should sing the song.

Next, all may sing and gesture. Emphasize use of the right hand and the pass to the right.

Finally, add the rocks. If many rocks are to be used they may be fed out one by one from a pile in front of the leader, or placed on the ground in front of each individual participant. Begin with right hands held up in the air so the first gesture is the grab, not the pass.

Warn the students that **throwing** the rock to the right, even in the excitement of the game, is an automatic "out" and that adhering closely to the rhythm will minimize the possibility of smashed fingers, especially when the tempo is picked up.

*Maraire children singing and dancing*

# Sansa Kroma

### An Akan Playground or Mmoguo Song

Key: X = Grab, → = Pass, T = Tap, P = Pass, — = Clap

# Sansa Kroma

SANSA KROMA NE NA WU O ƆKYEKYER NKOKƆ MBA
sah sah kroh-mah nee-nay woo aw-chay chay koh-koh mah

SANSA KROMA NE NA WU O ƆKYEKYER NKOKƆ MBA

SANSA KROMA NE NA WU O -- NKOKƆ MBA

SANSA KROMA NE NA WU O ƆKYEKYER NKOKƆ MBA

## TRANSLATION

"Sansa, the hawk. You are an orphan, and so you snatch up chicks."

## EXPLANATION

In nature, an orphaned animal must fend for itself in order to survive. For a hawk, this means wandering across the sky looking for little chicks to snatch up and carry off. Akan children singing this song are reminded that if anything happened to their parents and they became orphans, they would not have to wander alone, frantically trying to provide for their own needs. They would be taken in by a relative or a family in their village.

A longer version of this song contains two more lines which translate, "You fly and roam about, an orphan." Children in Ghana frequently observe young hawks flying overhead in an apparent search for chicks to kill. Some who saw this sight might have interpreted it to mean the hawks have no one to find food for them, and then added the words to describe the scene.

Kwasi Aduonum includes a variant of "Sansa Kroma" called "Sansa Akroma" in his dissertation, a wonderful collection of Ghanaian folktale songs. He classifies the song as a **mmoguo** song that is a "song interlude" to be used by the audience or narrator at any point during the telling of a story which seems related in some way to the idea of this song. (This is discussed in more detail in the introduction to Chapter II.)

In his version, a baby male eagle chases fowl instead of attending his own mother's funeral, because he thought he had to eat before going to the funeral, if he hoped to eat at all. Aduonum writes "this is a teasing song referring to those who are truant and who do not give proper attention to events or duties which need to be given a priority." (1980:p.340)

## NOTES ON USE

This may be easily adapted for use with a group of very young children by breaking each line into a call-and-response format.  (See transcription.) Two stone-passing patterns  are possible as well; both have been indicated.

Body  motions to enhance the sung rhythm may be a  simple swaying  to the left and right on beats one and three  or  on all  four beats; or an added clapping pattern of  "clap-clap-paw-paw" corresponding to beats one, two, three and four (the "paw"  is  a commonly used motion of first one arm  and  hand reaching out to paw the air in front of the singer,  then the other doing likewise).  Additional claps might be as follows:

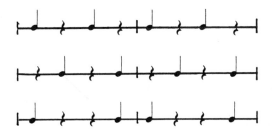

An exciting percussion and dance ensemble is easy to cre-ate by assigning a different type of percussion instrument to each  clapping  pattern,  as noted (or switch  them  around), while at the same time several students step counterclockwise in a circle. The right foot steps out and then in place, then the  left foot comes up to meet the right and stamps again in place,  back bent slightly,  knees loose. (Right-right, left-left,  right-right,  left-left,  in a one-two-three-four rhy-thm). Meanwhile, the right and left arms are bent like wings, and jut out rhythmically in opposite directions, exaggerating the right "wing" by poking the elbow out farther and  leaning the right shoulder into the circle more with each step of the right foot.

"Sansa Kroma"  may be performed vocally in several ways:

*call-and-response as noted;
*in unison;
*primarily in unison except for the third measure in each line,  when  half  the singers hold "wu-o" and half  continue singing "ɔkyekyer;"
*in two part harmony, as noted (Group I and II).

# Bantama Kra Kro

**An Akan Call-and-Response Stick-Game Song**

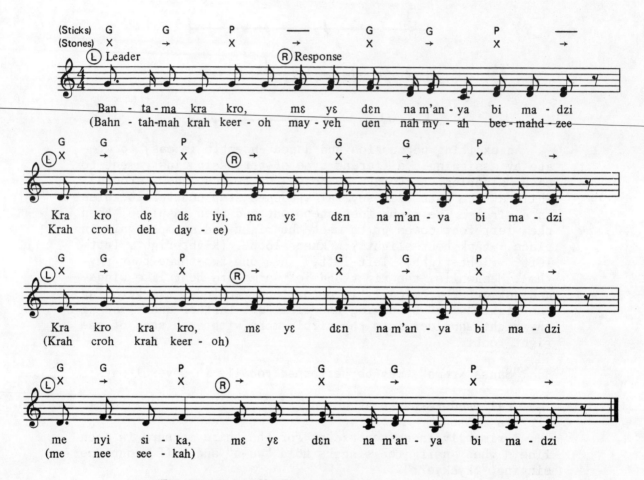

(For stone passing: X = Tap, → = Pass)

To use as a stick game: partners sit facing each other (with short sticks) or stand facing each other (with long sticks).
*G* = hit the ground, *P* = hit partner's stick. Sticks are held in right hand.

Bell
*(optional)*

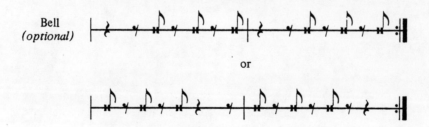

or

# Bantama Kra Kro

Leader: **BANTAMA KRA KRO!**
      bahn-tah-mah krah kroh (may be pronounced keer-oh
                        as variation)

Group: **MƐ YƐ DƐN NA M'A NYA BI M'ADZI?**
      may yeh dehn nah my-ah bee mahd-zee

L:     **KRA KRO DƐ DƐ IYI!**
       krah kroh deh day-ee

G:     **MƐ YƐ DƐN NA M'A NYA BI M'ADZI?**

L:     **KRA KRO KRA KRO**
       krah kroh krah kroh

G:     **MƐ YƐ DƐN NA M'A NYA BI M'ADZI?**

L:     **ME NYI SIKA**
       mee nee see-kah

G:     **MƐ YƐ DƐN NA M'A NYA BI M'ADZI?**

## TRANSLATION

"Bantama pastries!"
"How can I get some to try?"
"How delicious are the pastries!"
"How can I get some to try?"
"Pastries, pastries"
"How can I get some to try?"
"If you don't have any money"
"How can I get some to try?"

## EXPANDED TRANSLATION

"I've heard about those wonderful pastries they make in the
town of Bantama. How can I get some to try or taste if I
don't have any money?"
    Pastries from the town of Bantama are so well known that
a traveler in the region will make a special side trip to buy
one of these delights.

## EXPLANATION

    Songs like "Bantama Kra Kro" and "Sansa Kroma" are used
for a variety of activities by children, even into their teen
years. Many boys in Ghana take part in an organization very
much like the Boy Scouts. They dress in uniform for their

activities, and learn various skills drawn from ancient and modern times. One activity of such a group requires each boy to take a tall staff (about his own height) to bang on the floor in time while singing, or, with a partner, alternately pound the staff on the ground and then raise and cross the sticks with a sharp smacking sound. A variation of this pattern is to toss the stick across to the partner after pounding it on the ground. These sticks are seen as representations of ancient shields or swords; the thrusting motions and skills developed by practicing with them give the boys an insight into protective battle maneuvers.

## NOTES ON USE

Begin with a descriptive chant ("Pound, Pound," "Pound, Cross," "Pound, Throw," etc.) recited by the students while the leader sings the song. Follow with students making the appropriate arm gestures, first without then with singing. Finally add the sticks.

Rhythm sticks, walking sticks, heavy dowels cut to a suitable length, or lummi sticks will work fine. Participants may suggest and demonstrate alternate patterns.

This may also be used as a stone-passing game with a simple grab-pass pattern on the beat.

*Bamboo ensemble in Gomoa Aboso, Ghana. A group of six- to eight-year-old boys try out rhythms they have learned through game songs and by watching their elders at festivals and social events. Different sizes of bamboo stamping tubes give varying pitches as the boys pound them rhythmically on rocks.*

# Vamuroyi Woye

## A Shona Name-Game Song

# Vamuroyi Woye

Leader: VAMUROYI WOYE
vah-moo-roh-ee woy-ay

G:      MANINJI!
mah-neen-jee

L:      TSENZI KUTAMBA NEMBGWA!
sehn-zee koo-tahm-bah nehmb-gah

G:      MANINJI!

L:      HERE (person's name) WOYE!
hehr-ay (          ) woy-ay

G:      MANINJI!

L:      TSENZI KUTAMBA NEMBGWA!

G:      MANINJI!

L:      KUTIGA, KUTIGA, KUTIGA-GA! (spoken)
koo-tee-gah, koo-tee-gah, koo-tee-gah-gah

G:      MANINJI!

L:      TSENZI KUTAMBA NEMBGWA!

G:      MANINJI!:

## TRANSLATION

"Oh, Mr. Witch!"
"A miracle!" ( or, "incredible," "amazing")
"The **tsenzi** is playing with a dog!"
"Amazing!"
"Oh, wow, (name)!"
"Incredible!"
"The tsenzi is playing with a dog!"
"A miracle!"
"This way, that way, like this, like that!"
"Amazing!"
"The tsenzi is playing with a dog!"
"A miracle!"

## EXPANDED TRANSLATION

It is incredible that the tsenzi is playing with the dog which would normally be hunting it. The only person who could make such a miracle happen is a witch. If you want to ask him what is happening, be sure to speak with respect and call him

"Mr. Witch" so nothing will happen to you. They play this way
and that way! Hey, wow! (Judith), it's really amazing what
this Mr. Witch has done!

## EXPLANATION

The tsenzi is an African animal which looks something
like a large rabbit with short legs, usually lives in water
but can survive on land. It is hunted and eaten by the Shona,
who sometimes use dogs in the hunt.

The game is a circle game, often used by Shona children
as a way to learn and remember names. It is an example of the
type of call-and-response song structure in which the response enters either at the end of the leader's phrase only,
or may also join in on the leader's second statement, "Tsenzi
kutamba nembgwa," in unison, with a harmony part, or with
vocables (such as "heya") which overlap a portion of the
words.
The clapping pattern indicated in the transcription is
one that is typically used with this song. It is the sole accompaniment, as this is only a game song and not a dance song
which might also use various drums and rattles.
The melody for the "Here..." section changes according to
the tonality of the Shona name inserted. Only short names
require the use of the word "here" as a filler. Longer names
are sung to the same melody, followed by "woye";e.g.,
"Alexander, woye," but "Here Judy, woye!"

## NOTES ON USE

The participants stand in a circle. The leader (the
person who is "it") sings the first lines with appropriate
group response, then points to someone in the circle and
sings their name, looking at them at the same time. The person whose name is sung, even if it is not the person the
leader pointed to, responds, "Maninji." If the person who is
"it" says the wrong name for the person pointed to, that person simply remains quiet as the correct person sings. The
person actually named then changes places with the former
leader, and the cycle begins again.

# Pɛtɛ Pɛtɛ

## An Akan Playground or Mmoguo Song

## Pεtε Pεtε

*Repeat* C *for verses 5 and 6, then go on to* D

# Pɛtɛ Pɛtɛ

Leader: PƐTƐ, PƐTƐ
     peh-teh, peh-teh

Group: SEE NUA DEDE NDE E SEE NUA
     seh noo-ah day dehn-day seh noo-ah

L:    WO MAME FRƐ WO O
     woh mah-mee fur-eh woh

G:    SEE NUA DEDE NDE E SEE NUA

L:    ƆSE MEBƐYƐ DƐN?
     aw-seem beh-yeh dehn

G:    SEE NUA DEDE NDE E SEE NUA

L:    ƆSE BE DZI DZI O!
     aw-see buh dzee dzee-oh

G:    SEE NUA DEDE NDE E SEE NUA

L:    EBƐN EDZIBAN A?
     ay-behn eh-dzee-bahn ah

G:    SEE NUA DEDE NDE E SEE NUA

L:    FUFU NA ABƐ NKWAN!
     foo-foo nah behn kwahn

G:    SEE NUA DEDE NDE E SEE NUA

L:    M OFRA NKYƐ NDZI O!
     moh-frahn chen dzoh

G:    SEE NUA DEDE NDE E SEE NUA

L:    ƆBƆ, ƆBƆ, ƆBƆ ! (improvise rhythmic variations
     aw-buh aw-buh aw-buh          using "ƆBƆ")

ALL:  SEE NUA DEDE NDE E (3 times)

      SEE NUA

## TRANSLATION

"Vulture, vulture"
(expression of joy)
"Your mom is calling you"
"What does she want me to do?"

"She said food is ready!"
"What kind of food is it?"
"Pounded yam and palm-nut soup"
"Share it, children!"
"How, how, now!"


## EXPLANATION

This version of an extremely popular Akan children's song depicts a scenario where a child may have spent too much time in playing with friends instead of helping with the meal preparations around the home.  When the meal is ready the mother calls to the child using the nickname "Pɛtɛ" or "Vulture" because of the great size of the child's appetite.  The child might want to pretend it is not important to listen to the elders unless the information is especially enticing,  so the conversation develops as a way of finding out just how important the call to come home is.  When it turns out a favorite meal is being served (delicious **fufu**, which is a special kind of cooked and pounded yam or cassava, and palm-nut soup), the child sings and jumps for joy and races home with a pack of friends close behind hoping for a taste.

Nowadays,  children  do not help out at meal  preparation time  as much as they used to,  but even so,  if an elder requests  a chore of a child,  he or she is expected to  comply without delay.

## NOTES ON USE

"Pɛtɛ Pɛtɛ"  may be used in several ways:

\*As a stone-passing game, start the first pass on <u>nua</u> and  continue with a grab-pass pattern as described in " ɔbɔɔ Asi  Me Nsa" or "Sansa Kroma." In other words,  on the  first beat of that measure,  and grabbing or passing on each subsequent beat.

\*To use it as a movement activity, the group forms a circle  facing  inward and takes steps moving  counterclockwise, clapping with each step. Begin moving with the first response on <u>nua</u>:  the right foot moves a step to the right,  then  the left foot is brought next to it. Continue for the duration of the  song until the last line,  then clap three times as  the final "see nua" is sung in an accented manner.

(words)**SEE NUA DEDE NDE SEE NUA**

(step)     R    L    R    L    R    L

(clap)       \*    \*    \*    \*     \*    \*

# Nsa Ni O

## An Akan Handgame Song

N - sa    ni o    min - nya    ko - ra - o.    N - sa    ni o    min - nya    ko - ra
(Ehn - sahn    yoh    meen - yah    koh - rah - oh)

o.    Ma - yɛ    ak wadaa kɔ - nom nsa    n - sa    bo - ko me.    Ma - yɛ
(My - eh    kwah - dah haw - noom sah    en - sah    buh - koo mee)

ak wadaa kɔ - nom nsa    n - sa    bo - ku - me.    N - sa    ni o    min - nya    ko - ra - o.    N - sa

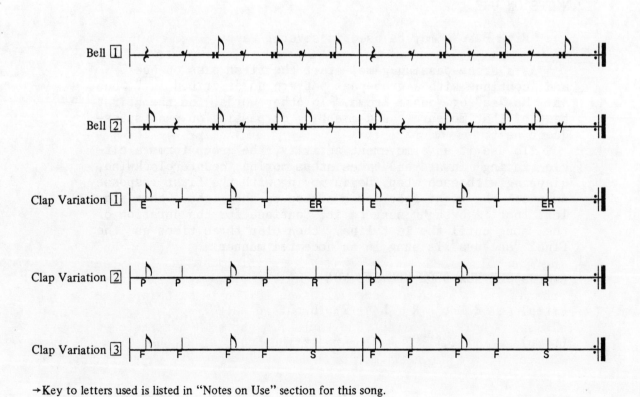

→Key to letters used is listed in "Notes on Use" section for this song.

# *Nsa Ni O*

NSA NI O MINNYA KORA O
ehn-sahn yoh meen-yah koh-rah oh

NSA NI O MINNYA KORA O

MAYƐ AKWADAA KƆNOM NSA, NSA BOKU ME
my-eh kwah-dah kaw-noom-sah, ehn-sah buh-koo mee

MAYƐ AKWADAA KƆNOM NSA, NSA BOKU ME

NSA NI O MINNYA KORA O

TRANSLATION

"Here is some drink (liquor), I do not have a calabash"
"Here is some drink, I do not have a calabash"

"I have turned into a drunk, I will die of too much drinking"

EXPLANATION

"Nsa Ni O" is an example of an Akan handgame song that teaches cultural values to the young people who are singing it for fun. This particular song relays the warning that a young person who begins drinking heavily might find his or her life destroyed by illness, by the actions drunkenness might bring on which go counter to the expectations of the society, by possible abandonment of the drinker by friends or family, and possibly even by death. "Nsa Ni O" therefore encourages young people to find alternatives to drinking, to find more appropriate ways to deal with problems, enabling the youth to live a more worthwhile life within society. As the game progresses the participants might reflect on the lot of the drinker, and also on the fact that others in their community are asking them to be cautious in their actions.

NOTES ON USE

The clapping pattern should start slowly and simply and increase in speed and complexity as participants master the moves. You may include variations which, by **omitting** motions, enhance the syncopated feel. Silently count omissions as rests. Partners may take turns creating patterns, or try to mislead their opposite. One partner might hold outstretched hands in a palms-up position while the other slaps them rhythmically in a downward motion. Many variations are possible.

## KEY TO LETTERS USED IN DIAGRAMS FOR HAND MOTIONS
(Partners sit or stand, facing each other, hands extended)

P=   partners  hold left hands low,  palms  up;  right  hands
     raised, palms down, hovering over left hands
     In this position, slap partner's hands in rhythm shown

R=   reverse above to oppposite position of hands, slap

T=   clap own hands together

E=   partners bend right arms at elbow,  hold left  hands out
     with palms up, ready to tap partner's elbow with cupped,
     outstretched palm

ER=  reverse this position by bending left elbows,  tap  with
     right outstretched palms

F=   partners  hold  palms  up  ("high-five"),  palms  facing
     partner's palms, clap palms

S=   switch so that partners clap backs of raised hands

------------------------------

*NOTE

Freeman Kwadzo Donkor,  a gifted Ewe musician, singer and
dancer  from Ghana who teaches traditional dance and drumming
privately  and as a visiting artist at Brown University  (RI)
and Wesleyan University (CT), taught "Nsa Ni O" to me while I
was doing the research for my master's thesis.  In demonstrating this handgame,  he moved quickly through several  variations of the initial pattern, guiding me primarily by the use
of  "body English" as he anticipated his next move with exag-
gerated preparatory motions. Using the same technique, he was
equally successful at tricking me into making mistakes!  (J C
Tucker)

*Freeman Kwadzo Donkor*

# Chapter II:

# Story Songs

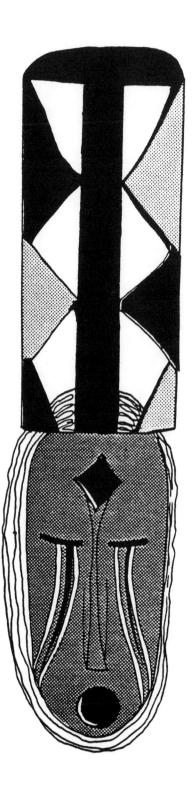

# Story Songs

Throughout Africa, storytelling is a vital, living art which has much to offer both young and old. Before they are old enough to attend school, African children receive an informal yet extensive education when they participate in traditional group storytelling. A bright, full moon is reason enough for a large group of all ages to eagerly gather in the courtyard of the chief, under a spreading tree, in a large workshed, or in the village square. They wait impatiently for the first narrator to begin, certain in the knowledge that all present are essential components in the dramatic production about to take place—partners in the wonderful process of re-stating, reaffirming and strengthening the values and beliefs of their community. Dramatic improvisation, songs, dances, jokes, proverbs and the narrative flow together in ever-changing combinations propelled by the creative energy of the storytellers and sustained by the intense involvement of the audience. The narrators are guides to the land where natural and supernatural coexist, and all present work together to create a multidimensional drama.

The most appreciated storytellers enhance a story by adding sound effects with their voices, mbira, and percussion instruments, make dramatic dance movements, and frequently draw the audience into the telling through the use of songs which require a set response and leave room for little improvisation. Most commonly, the narrator initiates these songs which incorporate a part of the story and thus move the story forward. However, members of the audience might become inspired to interrupt the narrator with one or several songs which relate in some way to the characters or theme of the tale. Inasmuch as these songs are also call-and-response, they provide an opportunity for the entire group to sing, move, and clap their hands. Being less structured, song interludes also offer more chances for improvisation.

Categories of folktale songs are known by different names in different parts of Africa. In Ghana songs which are associated with folktale parties, either as narratives or as song interludes, are **mmoguo**. ("Sansa Kroma" and "Pɛtɛ Pɛtɛ" are sometimes used as song interludes in Ghana.) Some mmoguo contain morals which point out appropriate behavior in certain situations, or which explain why specific actions are considered essential and others are taboo. Some indicate the relationship of tribes, families, and individual histories. In Zimbabwe **nyaya** are true stories about people, and **ngano** are stories which did not and most likely could not happen. Although ngano stories depict events which did not really happen, they do focus on themes intended to teach about life. Robert Kauffman notes that in Zimbabwe,

Folk tales and the songs that are frequently sung with
them are mainly recreational. A good storyteller will
also transmit cultural values by weaving the entertaining
exploits of men and animals around such themes as
the victory of cunning over force and the relationships
between supernatural and natural. The stories are
usually humorous and sometimes very fanciful. The
impact of the stories depends largely upon the
creative skill of the storyteller....The complete
story is really an art form with the boundaries
between music and non-music not clearly
drawn. (1970:p.139)

In Zimbabwe, most story songs are accompanied by one or
two handclapping patterns, occasionally by mbira or hosho and
multiple voice parts, but not drums. As previously mentioned,
the most common form of story song is call-and-response. The
type of call and the type of response can take several forms,
varying in length, repetitive or not, thematically related
to the story in whole or part, and employing single or
multiple parts. The type of entry by the leader or the group
can also vary. (For a more detailed look at call-and-response
structures, see Appendix C: Voices Fitting Together.)

The story songs in this section are all from Zimbabwe. As
is common throughout Africa, themes related to growing,
gathering, protecting or hunting food predominate. And the
concept of the power of music to bewitch and transfix the
listener--as a weapon used by humans and animals alike--also
appears frequently. "Zangaiwa Chakatanga Pano" is the story
of a boy who is sent off on his own to find food after a crop
failure leaves the family starving. He fills his basket with
fruit from a tree which the animals of the forest claim as
their own. The song he teaches them enables him to escape
their wrath. "Chatigo Chinyi" tells of a jealous hunter who
feels his younger brother gets more than his fair share of
food. After being tricked into falling into a hidden pit, the
young man sings his story in response to the sound of an
unseen axe, and is then saved by a passing hunter. "Chawe
Chidyo Chem'chero" tells of the age-old problem of hungry
animals devouring crops. The farm family in this story is
powerless against the magical song of the animals.

As you learn these stories and songs, feel free to embellish the tales, to adapt them in ways that will make a better
fit between them and the needs of your classes. Change the
gender of the protagonist, increase the number of animals,
add additional motions. As you create scripts for dramatic
re-enactments encourage your students to brainstorm. Let them
volunteer even seemingly wild ideas for plot twists and turns
as they carry the theme to its conclusion. In short, make
these your own.

# Zangaiwa Chakatanga Pano

**A Shona Ngano Story Song: "The Boy and the Tree of the Animals"**

# Zangaiwa Chakatanga Pano

Leader: **TSVO TSVO TSVO TSVORIYOTO** (2 times)
choh choh choh choh-ree-yoh-toh

**CHAKATANGA PANO TSVORIYOTO** (2 times)
chah-kah-tahn-gah pah-noh choh-ree-yoh-toh

Group: **ZANGAIWA CHAKATANGA PANO** (2 times)
zahn-gah-ee-wah chah-kah-tahn-gah pah-noh

## TRANSLATION

(Leader): (the sound of the whistle)
"That which came here first (whistle sound)"

(Group): "Round and round to that which came here first"

## EXPLANATION

This **ngano** story is typical of the genre, in that it is about imagined events which most likely could not happen. Quite often such stories involve animals with special powers, but they can be about people as well. "Zangaiwa Chakatanga Pano" is about a boy whose family is suffering from hunger due to crop failure, and who is sent out to look for food in the forest. He finds a tree covered with deliciously ripe fruit and picks some, only to be told by a lizard that the tree belongs to the animals of the forest, who decide to eat him up on the spot. He requests a moment to sing one last song, teaches the second part to the animals who become bewitched by it, and thus saves himself. The theme is the power of cunning over force. In this instance, the power of music is the weapon the human has over the animal world, whereas in other ngano stories (for example "Chawe Chidyo Chem'chero") the animals wield the magic over the humans.

"Zangaiwa Chakatanga Pano" is an example of a story song with a fixed response of medium length. The group complements the leader's part. Because of the length of the response, the leader can cut in and overlap, joining the same words of the response with a harmony part for a time, then continuing on with an independent part.

If the leader wishes to add more texture, he or she may use the **kukaha** technique, which is a way of varying the design of the song rhythmically. Kauffman observes,

> It literally means "to invert, place out of order, variegate, or diversify." In musical practice it can mean to delay, imitate, or rhythmically change a pattern. (1970:p.148)

The third stanza of the transcription shows a kukaha pattern as it is used with a group part continuing unchanged. This is only one example of a kukaha part, but others could be tried and used as alternatives by the leader or by the group during their response. The kukaha variations would not be used by the leader and group simultaneously, however.

## NOTES ON USE

The stories in this book were selected because they lend themselves to dramatic retelling by a group. Students can take the part of the boy/girl, the animals, and the villagers to whom the child returns.

Make masks to represent each animal, and improvise a dance to go along with the song.

Work with the students to develop a script from the story, but encourage them to improvise as they act it out, rather than merely reciting memorized lines.

*Ghanaian women wearing the traditional hairpiece popular particularly among the Fantis of the central coastal area. They are attending a festival but do not have an official role in it, and therefore may wear Western-style dresses rather than ntama.*

*A Ghanaian girl of about seven years old, dressed for a special occasion in the style of older women whose clothing and behavior serve as a model for her own. She wears the traditional **ntama** made of painstakingly woven **kente** cloth, folded and wrapped around her body, and the same hairpiece as the women pictured here.*

# The Narrative:
# "The Boy and the Tree of the Animals"

Long time ago, there was a drought in a nearby country. There was a family in this country who had a young boy about twelve years of age. The parents had tried to find something to eat but had found nothing. So one day they sent all the family members out on their own to find food. This twelve-year-old boy went all alone into the forest. He walked for many miles and he walked alone for many days until one day he found a tree with wonderful fruit all over it. He was very happy, and he began to pick the fruit, putting some in his basket and eating some -- some in the basket, some in his mouth -- until the basket was full and he felt wonderful. As soon as the basket was full, he turned to bring it back home. What he didn't know was that the tree belonged to the animals of the forest. As he was going, a lizard came along, walking with him, and said, "What are you doing? What are you carrying there?"

"I'm carrying fruit," the boy said.

"Well," said the lizard, "What you don't know is that this is not your fruit. It is the fruit of the animals of the forest. It is the tree of the animals of the forest."

"I didn't know, I didn't know," said the boy.

"You just wait here and see what happens to you," said the lizard.

All the animals came, one by one, and asked him the same question and gave him the same information. Finally they were all there, including the Lion, who is the king of the forest. They were trying to decide what to do with the boy.

Some said, "Let him go home!"

Some said, "Let's eat him straight away!"

Others said, "Let's have a judgement -- a jury to decide."

They finally decided to kill and eat him!

He begged, "Please may I sing once before you kill me?"

They agreed to let him sing once. This is the song he sang for the animals: (Tsvo tsvo tsvo tsvoriyoto etc.), and this is the response he taught to the animals: (Zangaiwa chakatanga pano).

Oh, the animals loved the song, and they sang it over and over again. And while all the animals were caught up in singing "Zangaiwa chakatanga pano," they forgot all about the boy. Seeing this, he picked up his basket and ran as fast as he could down the forest path. When the animals finally realized he had gone, the Hyena, who likes to eat people, led them in a chase. They caught up with him and said, "You tricked us into singing a song and now there is no excuse for you. We are straight away going to kill you and eat you up!"

Now some of the animals had followed Hyena so they could hear the song again. These animals begged and begged until the others agreed he could sing his song again, but this time he would be carefully watched so there could be no escape. He started to sing faster and faster, louder and louder. (**Interject song here.**)

After a while the boy's voice faded away, but the animals continued their response loud and long. Before they knew it, the boy was already all the way back to his village with the basket of fruit.

They started to run after him, to eat him up, but they saw they would have to go through villages to catch him, and the people would kill them if they got too close. So they turned around and went back into the forest.

The boy, in the meantime, had arrived safely home to the excited shouts, singing and dancing of his friends and family. He taught them all the song, and they raised their voices in happy celebration.

(Sing entire song several times.)

*Narrative (re-told), song text and taped version from:**African Story-Songs**:Told and Sung by Dumisani Maraire. Copyright © 1969 University of Washington Press, Seattle, WA. Used by permission.

# Chatigo Chinyi

**A Shona Narrative Ngano Song: "The Hunters And The Axe"**

# Chatigo Chinyi

Group:   GO! GO! GO! GO! (at end of certain phrases)

Leader:  CHATIGO CHINYI, CHATIGO CHINYI?
      chah-tee-goh cheen-yee, chah-tee-goh cheen-yee

      CHINONGA MUKOMA VANGU
      chee-nohn-gah moo-koh-mah vahn-goo

      VAKANDI PFIGIRE MUBAKO
      vah-kahn-dee fee-geer-ay mmbah-koh

      NEMBGWA YANGU MACHENA
      nehmb-gah yahn-goo mah-chay-nah

      IMWENI YACHO MASUIPE
      eem-way-nee  yah-choh  mah-shee-pay  (whistle **shee**
                                        slightly)

      MAI VANGU VANO FARA?
      my vahn-goo vah-noh-fahr-ah

      BABA VANGU VANO FARA?
      bah-bah vahn-goo vah-noh fahr-ah

      MUKADZI WANGU UNO FARA?
      mmkahdz wahn-goo oo-noh fahr-ah

      VANA VANGU VANO FARA?
      vah-nah vahn-goo vah-noh fahr-ah

      NGOMBE DZANGU DZINO FURA?
      gohm-bay dzahn-goo dzee-noh foor-ah

## TRANSLATION

(Group): (the sound of the axe chopping)

(Leader):
"What is that chopping sound?"
"It sounds like it is being done by my brother."
"Who buried me in a pit"
"With my dog called 'Whitey'"
"And the other one called 'Blackie'"
"Is my mother all right?"
"Is my father all right?"
"Is my wife all right?"
"Are my children all right?"
"Are my cattle grazing?"

## EXPLANATION

This is an example of a **ngano** story featuring people rather than animals. The response throughout is "Go!," which is sung repeatedly to underline the subject of the story -- the sound of the axe which first spelled the protagonist's doom but later became his salvation when the return of the chopping sound caused him to call out to the unseen hunter who rescued him. The theme is the victory of good over evil.

## NOTES ON USE

As with the other stories presented in this section, "Chatigo Chinyi" can easily be turned into a dramatic piece with individual students taking the parts of the two brothers, the rescuer, the family and villagers, and perhaps even the two dogs! Lines can be extracted from the narrative or improvised as the storytellers become familiar with the tale.

The first line of the song ("Chatigo chinyi? Go!") can be sung and answered whenever the story calls for the chopping sound. The entire song can be sung at appropriate places; for example, while the rescuer is building camp, during the rescuer's search, and after the young hunter relates his tale to the rescuer. The listeners also participate by acting out vigorous chopping motions, clapping and stamping in rhythm, while the leader might use hosho (gourd rattles) to accompany the song and actions.

The leader (who could be the student playing the role of the brother, or a narrator who is independent of the action) is encouraged to memorize the Shona words for the song. The chorus or audience interject "Go!" in the indicated spots. Below is an English translation adapted so that it can be sung using the same melody and phrasing:

> What is go - ing on? Is there some - one here?
> It sounds like it is my brother
> Who buried me in this deep pit!
> With my old dog called "Whitey"
> And also my dog named "Blackie."
> Say, is my mother all right?
> And how is my father feeling?
> And is my dear wife in good health?
> And are my small children happy?
> Are my cattle grazing freely?

# The Narrative: "The Hunters and the Axe"

Long time ago, there was a man who was a very successfull hunter. His older brother was deeply jealous of his hunting ability. The jealous brother came up with a scheme to get rid of the good hunter. He went out and dug a deep pit in the woods, then covered it with thin layers of sticks and leaves to make a trap. The next day he suggested a hunting trip -- just the two of them. The younger brother quickly agreed and they set off. As they were walking together, the jealous brother suddenly suggested they scout in different directions. He took one path, and sent his brother toward the trap. Unsuspecting of any plot, the young hunter walked along and fell into the trap. The jealous brother came running, and quickly started to chop some big logs ("GO! GO! GO!") and laid them across the pit, then some grass, some dirt, some branches on top, and left the young hunter buried with his two dogs, one black and one white.

A day passed, and the young man in the pit heard sounds above his head and nearby. He began to sing his song. (**Sing whole song here.**) There was no response, and he sadly sat down again, leaned against his dogs, and rested.

Another day passed, and again he heard sounds nearby. Trying to attract the attention of whoever might be there, he sang even louder. (**Song.**) But still no one answered.

Three days later, another hunter arrived at the spot and decided it would be a good camp site for the night. He pulled out his axe and began cutting down some branches to make a shelter for himself. He built his camp and lay down to rest. Suddenly, he thought he heard voices coming from the ground! At first, of course, he couldn't believe it so he started to search around for someone in the bushes, looking and listening carefully to the noises of the night. Finally, he realized there must really be someone buried under the ground. He could hear a voice calling. (**Interject song here.**) He located the carefully concealed pit, opened it up, and found the hunter and his dogs, unharmed.

After he helped the young hunter get out of the pit and heard his story, the two went back to the village. There was such excitement, cries of joy, and greetings as if he had been brought back from the dead. The people of the village killed a cow and brought fresh local beer and gave him a welcoming feast. After everybody had eaten, they took all of the leftovers and made the jealous brother eat everything, for he had often said he wished he could kill the younger brother because he ate too much. The older brother had his fill that day -- he ate so much he burst. And that is the end of the story.

*Note to teachers: If desired, the story may end, "...he ate so much he was very sick. After that the villagers sent him away to live in the forest alone. And that is all there is."

# Chawe Chidyo Chem'chero

**A Shona Ngano Song: "The Story of the Kudu"**

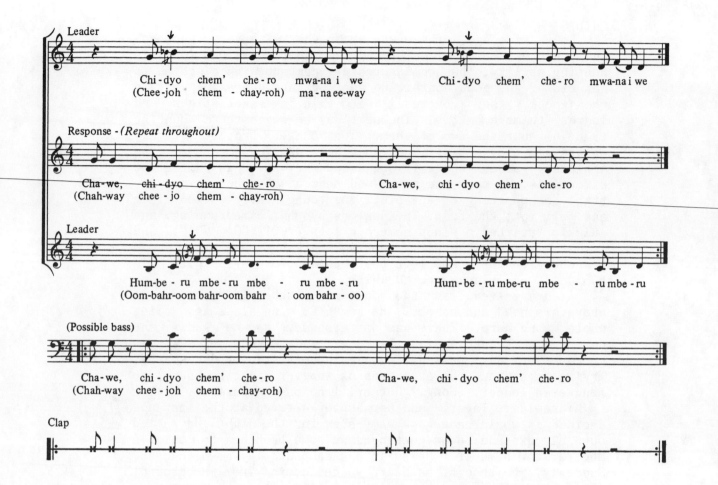

# Chawe Chidyo Chem'Chero

Leader:

CHIDYO CHEM'CHERO, MWANA IWE, CHIDYO CHEM'CHERO MWANA IWE
chee-joh chem-chay-roh mwah-nah ee-way (repeat)

HUMBERU MBERU MBERU MBERU, HUMBERU MBERU MBERU MBERU
oom-bahr (or: -behr) oom-bahr oom-bahr oom-bahr-oo (repeat)

Group:

CHAWE CHIDYO CHEM'CHERO, CHAWE CHIDYO CHEM'CHERO
chah-way chee-joh chem-chay-roh (repeat)

TRANSLATION

Leader: "It is now only the fruit of the forest, kid"(repeat)
        (the sound of eating - munching)

Group:  "It is now just like eating the fruit of the forest"

EXPLANATION

In an agricultural economy, which has been and still is traditional in many parts of Africa, the subject of protection of crops from natural or supernatural forces is a common theme. There is a preoccupation with seen and unseen predators, and many folktales combine stories of families struggling to grow and protect crops with teachings about moral or cultural values.

This story focuses on the power of cunning over force as well as on the magical powers possible in music. A **kudu**, an antelope with grayish fur and spiral horns, sneaks in to eat the crops of a farm family, destroying their hard work and putting them in danger of being without food. Each member of the family tries to chase the animal away by banging pots, throwing things, and threatening it with spears and arrows. The kudu, being clever, magical, and hungry, sings to them. It knows the power music has over humans and succeeds in proving that the force of his song is far greater than the force of their attacks. In turn each guard becomes transfixed by the song and the kudu enjoys the "fruits" of their labors.

NOTES ON USE

Teach the song to the group first, allowing a few repetitions before adding handclapping. Then at appropriate places in the story (told in its entirety below), cue the group by singing the lead part in the persona of kudu, then say, "And this is the response they sang as the power of the song bewitched them." The leader may sing the response once solo,

then as the group joins in, the leader switches to the overlapping call. This will then create spots of harmony as the
set response repeats.

The story may be expanded to include other animals, such
as birds or hyeenas, and more than one kudu, to enable more
students to participate. If this is done, the various "eat-
ers" should divide into groups to sing the leader's part, and
the sound of eating. Increase the size of the family, and divide those singers as well by adding the suggested bass part
to the traditional response. The result is quite simple but
very effective four-part singing.

# The Narrative: "The Story of the Kudu"

Long time ago there was a family. They had a big field and in this field they could grow maize, wheat, yams, millet, beans, or anything they wanted. One thing they were having trouble with was wild animals - especially kudu. They would come into the field and eat the grain. The family decided to send their young boy to go and look after the crops so the kudu could not come into the field and eat.

There was this one kudu who would come very early in the morning all by itself. When it got to the field it found the boy there. The boy banged metal pots "clang, bang, gang gong" that frightened the kudu, and it ran away. This went on for some time until the kudu decided it could not stand to stay away. It said to itself, "Oh, I know what humans like: they like music very much. So I will sing and see what will happen."

So the next time when it got into the field it started to sing.(**Interject song here with response.**) Now this boy was so interested he forgot everything and just listened to the kudu's song, and sang and danced the response the kudu taught him. Meanwhile, the kudu was just going on, eating and singing, eating, singing, until it was full and it left the field.

When the parents came they said, "What have you been doing here? The animals came and ate everything!"

The boy said, "The thing is, the animal came here and it sang so beautifully!"

His mother said, "Next time, I am going to take care of it myself."

So she came very early in the morning, being very careful to see no animal could come and eat. She had sticks to wave about and smack together. This same kudu came sniffing around and was scared by her motions and noises, but it sang the song again. (**Interject song.**) Of course, the mother could not do anything because the music was so powerful she was transfixed by it, and as the mother sang and danced, the kudu ate and sang and ate and sang until it was full and left the field.

Now the father came and said, "You told me you were going to take care of this and now the animals ate something again today! What have you been doing here?"

His wife told him about the kudu's music. "Aha! I will take my spear, my bow and arrows," he said. "I will just kill the first animal I see that even just begins to approach our crops."

The same kudu came very early in the morning again. (Song.) The father heard the song and just threw away his spear, bow, and arrows and stood, singing and swaying as the animal ate its fill. Afterward, the kudu went away.

Then the boy and the mother came and said, "You were blaming us and now look at you!"

And the father said, "This animal had such very, very nice music...."

So the animal found something to eat by entertaining people with music. That is the end of the story.

*Narrative (re-told), song text and taped version from: **African Story-Songs**: Told and Sung by Dumisani Maraire. Copyright © 1969 University of Washington Press, Seattle, WA. Used by permission.

# Chapter III:

# Recreational Songs

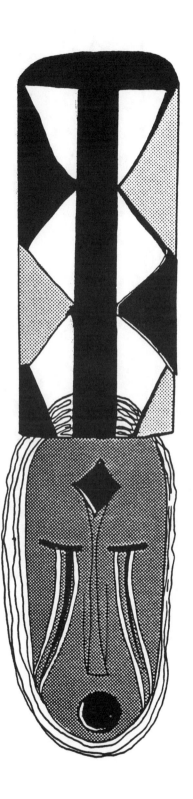

*"I came to play my drum for the dancing, not to deliver a slave into bondage."*

# Recreational Songs:
# Layers of Meaning, Layers of Sound

Although many Westerners think of drumming and percussion ensembles as the most important African musical expression, Africans would most likely identify vocal music as the most pervasive and characteristic form. Africa, notes David Reck, is "a singer's continent." (1977:p.261) According to Nketia, "A great deal of stress is laid on vocal music, for singing provides the greatest scope for participation in group musical activities, as well as an avenue for verbal communication."(1974:p.244) And Kauffman states, "If quantity of output is any guide to assessing the significance of a musical genre, then indeed vocal music is a very important means of expression in Shona culture." (1970:p.135) It stands to reason that in a society whose history, litigation, celebration, and education are carried on in the oral tradition, the verbal aspects of music would supersede all others. The oral literature that has developed over the generations -- proverbs, axioms, family and tribal histories and religious teachings -- finds its way into song directly (through entire narratives or complete sayings set to melodies), or indirectly (through the use of "snippets," references, code words, titles, totems, etc.). In both Ghana and Zimbabwe there are many songs that convey several levels or layers of meaning, just as they employ several layers of simultaneous melodic lines.

Recreational music, according to Nketia, includes "all forms of music not ritually or ceremonially bound." (1963:p.10) In most cases, such music is performed by mixed bands of men and women, not only for entertainment in the evenings but also on other occasions of a festive or social nature. Recreational songs such as "Wɔnfa Nyɛm," "Kyerɛm," "Ɔkwan Tsen Tsen," and even "Meda Wawa Ase" from Ghana and "Cho Kurima" and "Vamudara" from Zimbabwe can be seen as paradigms of African song types which serve purposes complementary to their entertainment value. Such songs inform or remind the community of traditionally accepted beliefs and mores, recount personal or tribal history, and strengthen the ties of individuals to the community through group participation. Although some songs of this type would more often be encountered at a **pito** or palm wine bar in Ghana, a beer park in Zimbabwe, or an evening pot luck supper with casual singing in both countries, most would also be used at funerals, religious ceremonies and festivals. In these instances they would be an important adjunct to music which is part of the set ritual.

The Ghanaian songs in this section are old songs and old sayings given new life in contemporary settings. The settings for "Wɔnfa Nyɛm" and "Kyerɛm" were created by the director of the Akrofor Singing Group, who was the head teacher of the elementary school in Gomoa Aboso. With his group of thirteento twenty-five-year-old volunteers, he put the desired bits of proverbs to a new melody and worked up the arrangements of solos and harmonies cooperatively. The group is typical of many choirs which appear at festivals and other occasions by invitation. "Ɔkwan Tsen Tsen" is a Highlife, or pop song in an arrangement by another, similar, youth group. "Meda Wawa Ase" is an old, widely sung folksong.

The Shona songs range from a teasing wedding song, "Chiro Chacho", polished and recorded by "Dumi and the Minanzi Marimba Ensemble," to "Cho Kurima Woye", a traditional multipart song of a genre sometimes referred to as "ancestor songs" --songs handed down by previous generations, sometimes with spiritual references, often used as ceremonial songs in honor of a chief. "Vamudara" is a Shangara dance song in a setting by Maraire, and "Wai Bamba" is a wedding song with a few basic parts suggested as a point of departure for group improvisation, Shona-style.

## Multiple meanings

All of the songs in this section deal with philosophical subjects, and share the characteristic of incorporating important ideas in a kind of verbal shorthand. Simeon D. Asiama, in his dissertation **Abɔfoɔ: A Study of Akan Hunters' Music**, (Wesleyan Univ., 1977) lists the qualities found in these songs: (It is interesting that the Shona songs share these qualities.)

> The language of the songs differs, to some extent from that of ordinary discourse, employing in some cases, old expressions and preserving forgotten ones....Extensive use is made of imagery which is largely meaningful to those who belong to the community and its continuity.
> There is, on the whole, economy of expression with the language of songs....Some phrases are compressed forms of longer expressions...some words are "sentence words," single words without verbs which convey complete sentence meanings. This device by no means clouds their meaning and message....This use of (fragments of proverbs) is a convenient shorthand which eliminates the need for a more formal development of an incident or idea. The cliches of the language evoke the necessary response of the audience to whom they are presented. (1977:p.160)

As Asiama implies, a prerequisite for full understanding of this type of verbal shorthand is a traditional upbringing. "Traditional" in this context includes a child being spoken to in proverbs by parents and relatives for praise or criticism, attending public functions, and taking part in story-telling parties which include a wealth of societal information. Only after this degree of extensive exposure will bits of proverbs and allusions to animals and events become keys to the storehouse of collective knowledge.

In Zimbabwe, especially in the traditional Shona songs which are passed from generation to generation intact except for a new setting, there can be found literal meaning, and "deep meaning." There are several Shona words that relate to this phenomenon. **Madimikira** or **mufanalidzo** expresses the concept of "proverbs." The Shona people view proverbs with the same mental concept as pictures. If one looks at a picture with understanding, the viewer will perceive something besides what his or her eyes physically see. There will be the literal meaning and behind it another, very important, level. As a matter of fact, one word in Shona means both picture and proverb.

There is also **chisana,** a concept that can make non-Shonas uncomfortable once they become aware of it. It involves rearrangements of words so that a second meaning can be present which might not be expressed overtly, and would generally be perceived and understood only by those within the society.

And finally, there is **kusandirika,** which is often used by musicians who might not want to sing about themselves directly in a composition. They will clothe their innermost thoughts and feelings in an image that can be taken at face value by someone not close enough to them to know the full meaning. Such songs offer the performers and listeners much more than an entertaining musical event. They are an exciting blend of rich musical textures and complex multiple meanings. Non-Africans will find them a particularly enjoyable opportunity to hear and experience fresh approaches to harmony through the medium of multipart form. (Appendix C: Voices Fitting Together takes an in-depth look at harmony, polyphony and structures of vocal music in Ghana and Zimbabwe.) The songs that follow are presented with notes about their traditional context and deep meanings. Enjoy these arrangements as steps along the path to appreciation of these "singing cultures."

*Shona women accompanying their singing and dancing with hosho.*

# Wai Bamba

## A Shona Wedding Song

# Wai Bamba

WAI BAMBA WAI, BAMBA WAI
why bahm-bah why, bahm-bah why (do not aspirate "h")

WI WI WI WI
wee wee wee wee

TRANSLATION

"You have caught him/her, you've got him/her"
("Bamba" is Ndebele, Xosa or Zulu for the Shona word "bata" meaning to hold or catch something.)

(vocable - no meaning)

EXPLANATION

"Wai Bamba" is a wedding celebration song, sung as part
of the festivities in either the bride's or the groom's
village. It is derived from the very old dance form **jangwa**. A
more recent and similar form is **garariya,** which grew from a
combination of hymns, school choral music influenced by
missionaries, and the **tsaba** which is a rhythm, a dance, and a
beat. The group is arranged in a circle with a conductor or
leader who commonly uses a whistle to cue various parts of
the dance and song. Drums might be used to accompany the
singing and dancing, and, in that case, the drums indicate
the dance steps with their specific patterns.

The foundation of the song is melodically quite simple,
but complexity develops with variations and combinations of
melodic and rhythmic improvisation. If four Shona people,
singers who knew the principles of traditional improvisation
and used them freely, were to sing this song, all of the possible variations might take an hour to sing through.

The basic structure of the piece is AA BB AA. Improvisation on the structure can be melodic, or rhythmic to the
point where the words are severely truncated, and whistles,
"unh unh" and "hup hup," or claps and stamps might be all
that remains in a highly syncopated interplay.

NOTES ON USE

Do not adhere rigidly to the melodic or rhythmic notation
once the basic structure has been learned by the group. Begin
with an introduction of the basic part sung in the alto range
to identify "home base." Meanderings may be prearranged or
allowed to happen spontaneously. As noted elsewhere, no two
performances of a Shona song like "Wai Bamba" would be exactly alike, and there is no reason to expect uniformity or in-
flexible duplication from American singers who might savor
the freedom of improvisation during a performance.

# Meda Wawa Ase

An Akan Folksong

# Meda Wawa Ase

MEDA WAWA ASE, MEDA WAWA ASE, MEDA WAWA ASE
mee-dah  wah-wah say,  mee-dah wah-wah say,
                               mee-dah  wah-wah say

ABRANTSƐBA A ƆTSE DƐ M'ARA  MEDA WAWA ASE
 ahb-rahnt-seh-bah tsee-deh mah-rah  mee-dah wah-wah say

MEDA WAWA ASE, MEDA WAWA ASE, MEDA WAWA ASE

AKATAASIABA A ƆTSE DƐ M'ARA ME DA WAWA ASE
 ah-kaht-ah-see-ah-ba tsee-deh mah-rah mee-dah wah-wah say

ATAMFO ENYA ME O, MENYƐ DƐN NYE 'I?
 ah-tahm-foh nyah may, meen-yeh dehn nyee

MEDA WAWA ASE

ABRANTSƐBA A ƆTSE DƐ M'ARA MEDA WAWA ASE
 ahb-rahnt-seh-bah tsee-deh mar-rah mee-dah wah-wah say

MEDA WAWA ASE, MEDA WAWA ASE, MEDA WAWA ASE

ABRANTSƐBA A ƆTSE DƐ M'ARA MEDA WAWA ASE

TRANSLATION

"I am lying under the **wawa** tree" (3 times)

"A young man such as I, I am lying under the **wawa** tree"
or, "A young woman such as I" (**akataasiaba**)
"I am in the hands of my enemies, what should I do?"
"I am lying under the **wawa** tree"
"A  young  man (or, "a young woman") such as I,  I am  lying
    under the **wawa** tree"

EXPLANATION

    This very beautiful,  unadorned Akan song is about a per-
son who feels he has not lived up to the expectations of others in his society,  and finds himself surrounded by his enemies -- those who would lead him astray,  and those who would
observe his actions and judge him critically.  A song of this
type  might  be sung by a group who use it as  a  warning  to
young  people that if they are not observant of the mores  of
their  society  they will create a situation  for  themselves
that could lead to ostracism and shame,  isolation and unhap-
piness.
    "Meda  Wawa Ase" allows the singer to reflect on the  lot
he has created for himself, and also to comfort and encourage

himself. If the singer begins living in harmony with the traditional values and moral teachings of his society, the gossips who take account of his actions will be shamed and the enemies who would push him into inappropriate behavior will be turned away. In the end, as the Akan proverb states, "success will crown his endeavors." Since this is a folksong and therefore not part of any ritual, it can be used in a variety of settings where its message will be seen as relevant and valuable.

## NOTES ON USE

This old folksong sounds best sung simply by a small group, and has been used in the past as part of a drama about young people. A largely parallel harmony line is suggested in the transcription, but voices in octaves or in unison are also appropriate.

The version below, arranged by John Tekyi Essuman from Kumasi, Ghana, is taken from his book **Thirty Popular Akan Songs** (Accra-Tema: Ghana Publishing Corp., 1974). It is an excellent example of the many books of songs published in Ghana and Zimbabwe over the last ten or fifteen years, frequently presented in Western and/or sol-fa notation. (Even in songbooks offering "full parts" it is common to find an introductory note from the compiler/arranger to the effect that the set arrangement is a starting point only.)

**MEDA WAWA ASE**

Arranged by J. T. Essuman
Key E Flat
2 Beats

-60-

# Chiro Chacho

### A Teasing Shona Wedding Song

# *Chiro Chacho*

Leader, introduction:

**MAININI WOYE KANI, MAININI WOYE KANI, MAININI WOYE**
my-nee-nee woy-ay kah-nee (repeat) my-nee-nee woy-yay

Response:

**CHIRO CHACHO CHINE MAKUMBO MANA**
chee-roh chah-choh chee-nay mah-koom-boh mah-nah

Basses:

**BABA HA HAHO, BABA HA HAHO** (repeat throughout)
bah-bah hah hah-hoh (repeat)

Women's voices:

1. **CHATORA YAYA, CHATORA YAYA, CHATORA YAYA**
   chah-toh-rah yah-yah (repeat)

2. **CHATODZE RORI, CHATODZE RORI, CHICHINGE BAZI**
   chah-toh-dzee roh-ree (repeat), chee-cheen-gay bah-zee

3. **MUKOMA WOYE, MUKOMA WOYE, MUKOMA WOYE**
   moo-koh-mah woy-yay (repeat)

## TRANSLATION

Leader, intro.:"Oh, aunty; oh, aunty; oh aunty"

Response: "The thing has four legs"

Basses: "Father, ha haho" or "Father, oh man!"

Women: 1."That took our elder sister" (repeat 3 times)
2."It looks like a lorry, and yet it looks like a bus"
   (a **lorry** is an open-sided truck; a British term)
3."Oh, elder brother," (repeat 3 times)

## EXPLANATION

Weddings in Zimbabwe are traditionally a time for hours of singing. Spontaneous group singing is such a strong tradition at weddings that even if a wedding band of some sort has been hired to provide music, invariably clusters of guests will begin singing while the band is playing, and may continue well into the night!

"Chiro Chacho" is commonly sung in the eastern part of Zimbabwe, Manicaland Province. At all traditional African weddings in Zimbabwe there are usually two choirs, one representing the bride and the other one the bridegroom. Any other people at the wedding who might not otherwise be related to either member of the couple that is getting married and would like to sing will have to take sides. This song is always sung by the bride's side when the bride is being driven to the groom's home. By Shona tradition, there are always two wedding receptions, one at the bride's, which is the first one and is known as "the taking of the bride," and the second, which will be the real celebration, for bringing the bride to her new home, which will be the groom's.

In this song the younger brothers and younger sisters are sad their elder sister is being driven away by this thing that looks like a lorry and yet like a bus. The thing has four legs, meaning wheels, and looks quite peculiar. This can also be seen as a teasing reference to the groom himself! There is usually more than just one vehicle to take the bride away, and these can be buses, lorries and/or cars.

## NOTES ON USE

This particular version was recorded by the Minanzi Marimba Ensemble in 1977 for Minanzi Records. The song was arranged in a traditional manner and included accompaniment by several **marimbas** (wooden xylophones of varying pitch and timbre with large resonators beneath each wood slab), hosho, and drums. For the purposes of this collection, only the vocal parts and one drum pattern have been extracted, but even in this pared-down version, "Chiro Chacho" is a tremendously exciting piece to sing. It can be used with junior or senior high school students. If there are students with a background in xylophone, vibraphone or marimba technique, improvisation on the recorded marimba parts may be easily accomplished.

Gradual layering of parts, using the instruments as the final stage, adds to the intensity of the piece.

# Wɔnfa Nyɛm

## A Contemporary Akan Song of Mourning

# Wɔnfa Nyɛm

# Wɔnfa Nyɛm

nyɛm ... Wɔn-fa nyɛm ɔn-yɛ bir-bi o wɔn-fa nyɛm

nyɛm ... Wɔn-fa nyɛm ɔn-yɛ bir-bi o wɔn-fa nyɛm

nyɛm ... Wɔn-fa nyɛm ɔn-yɛ bir-bi o wɔn-fa nyɛm

Solo: (Da-bi na wod-ze bɛ-ba)
(Dah-bee nah wohd-zee bay-bah)

nyɛm ... Wɔn-fa nyɛm ɔn-yɛ bir-bi o wɔn-fa nyɛm

Solo: (Na-hɔ na wo nso
(Nah-haw nah woh-soh

**1, 2.** **D.S. al Fine** **3. Fine**

Wɔn-fa Wɔn-fa nyɛm ɔn-yɛ bir-bi o wɔn-fa nyɛm

Wɔn-fa Wɔn-fa nyɛm ɔn-yɛ bir-bi o wɔn-fa nyɛm

Wɔn-fa Wɔn-fa nyɛm ɔn-yɛ bir-bi o wɔn-fa nyɛm

Wɔn-fa Wɔn-fa nyɛm ɔn-yɛ bir-bi o wɔn-fa nyɛm

wobe-hu)
bay-hoo)

## PERCUSSION

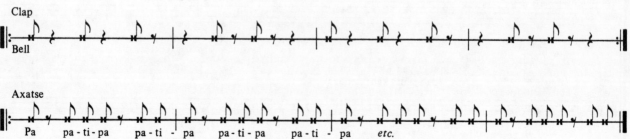

Clap

Bell

Axatse

Pa pa-ti-pa pa-ti-pa pa-ti-pa pa-ti-pa etc.

# Wɔnfa Nyɛm

All:      BUEE, BUEE, BUEE; BUEE, BUEE, HMMM
           bway, bway, bway; bway.; bway, hmmmm

Men:      AWERƐHOW SƐM, AWERƐHOW SƐM
           ah-wayr hoh sehm, ah-wayr hoh sehm

All:      BUEE, BUEE, BUEE; BUEE, BUEE, HMMMM

Cantor (spoken): WƆNFA NYƐM

All:      WƆNFA NYƐM ƆNYƐ BIRBI O  WƆNFA NYƐM (**repeat 2 or 4x**)
           won-fah nyehm awn-yay beer-byoh won-fah nyehm

Cantor: ABOA AKYEKYER E
           ahb-wah chay-chay ray

Chorus: WƆNFA NYƐM ƆNYƐ BIRBI O  WƆNFA NYƐM

Cantor: AGYANKA BA E
           ah-jahn-kah bay

Chorus: WƆNFA NYƐM ƆNYƐ BIRBI O WƆNFA NYƐM

Basses: DABI NA WODZE BƐBA
           dah-bee nah wohd-zee bay-bah

Chorus: WƆNFA NYƐM  ƆNYƐ BIRBI O WƆNFA NYƐM

Basses: NA HƆ NA CH NA WO NSO WOBEHU
           nah-haw nah woo-soh bay-hoo

Chorus: WƆNFA NYƐM ONYƐ BIRBI O WƆNFA NYƐM

TRANSLATION

"Buee" is a wail of mourning, a sign of grief
Men: "A sad situation"
All: wail
Cantor, spoken: "Do it to me"
All:    "Do it to me, it doesn't matter, do it to me"
Cantor: "The animal the tortoise"
Chorus: "Do it to me, it doesn't matter, do it to me"
Cantor: "An orphan"
Chorus: "Do it to me, it doesn't matter, do it to me"
Basses: "Tomorrow it will be your turn"
Chorus: "Do it to me, it doesn't matter, do it to me"
Basses: "Then you will see" (how sweet or sour)
Chorus: "Do it to me, it doesn't matter, do it to me"

## EXPANDED TRANSLATION

(A wail of disbelief or shock at a tragedy)
This  is a sad occasion for me.  Why has this happened to me,
why am I always in this trouble alone and in so much  sorrow.
It  doesn't really matter anymore,  you can no longer hurt me
because the worst has already happened.
He  claimed to be sober and humble like the  tortoise,  self-
sufficient,  and now he is an orphan--alone without  parents,
isolated and alone in society.
Now it is my turn to experience these hardships,  tomorrow it
will be your turn.
Then you will see how it feels to be in sorrow, whether it is
sweet or it is sour.

## EXPLANATION

Although "Wɔnfa Nyɛm" is primarily associated with mourning,  it can be sung both at funerals and festivals as a philosophical statement and reminder to the participants  of the
importance of fulfilling one's  obligations  within  the community  lest you find yourself without help when  orphaned by
death or isolated by other events in life.

"Wɔnfa Nyɛm" presents a fascinating example of the verbal
shorthand Simeon Asiama discusses in his dissertation (see
introduction to this section). It is worthwhile and interesting  to explore the deeper levels of meaning which  would  be
understood by a member of a  traditional  Ghanaian community.

"Buee,  buee,  buee"  is an ancient wailed expression  of
grief  or  mourning,  often a sign of shock and disbelief  on
hearing of the sudden or accidental death of a loved one.  It
is  commonly  accompanied  by gestures  such  as  shaking  a
raised hand rapidly back and forth,  or putting both hands on
the  head and twisting the torso from side to side.  It is  a
powerful word, reaching deep inside the individual to express
overwhelming feelings.

The  reference to the tortoise is an important  one.  All
Akan belong to one of nine **abusua,** or clans. Each clan has an
animal  totem (**akyeneboa**) whose qualities members admire  and
seek to emulate. The clan symbols are displayed on ceremonial
staves  and  mark off the particular lineages from others  in
the same community during ritual gatherings such as funerals.
The  tortoise is not a totem and is therefore seen  as  being
alone during difficult times.  He moves through the world independently,  prepared to get himself through all  eventuali-
ties,  even  taking  his coffin with him (thus saving  others
from the task of making one).  An Akan proverb  states:  "The

tortoise  has no clan and so he carries his casket with him."
The individual in the song claimed to be a self-contained
unit, like a tortoise, and neglected to fulfill his obligations and responsibilities to his clan and his community by
participating in all levels of his society. Consequently, he
faces life's trials as a solitary figure.

Another level of interpretation understood by an Akan
evaluating the reference to the tortoise is the animal's personality. The tortoise is one of the most respected animals
in the Akan oral literature. There are numerous stories and
proverbs that relate to the attributes tortoises embody,
such as the great patience they exhibit in all they
undertake, and the slow deliberate planning of actions. These
qualities joined with the nonaggressive nature of the tortoise can serve as a model for human behavior.

An Akan proverb that illustrates valuable personality
traits attributed to tortoises are: "If it were a tortoise
and a snail in the bushes, there would be no gun fired;" (Sɛ
ɔka akyekyerɛ nna nwaba a ankyɛ itur nkɔtow wɔ wirom).

The term **agyanka ba** (an orphan) can be taken literally
to mean one who has lost his parents through death, or
figuratively as one who lives a solitary life. When one
becomes an orphan, one can tell by the outpouring of support
or the lack of it how fully a person has participated in Akan
society. Prior reluctance to reach out to others in their
times of need may cause individuals to become outcasts in
their own worst hour.

The last phrases of the song relate to the cycles of
life, and the fact that all humans will experience sorrow and
hardship in time. The person who keeps his distance from a
sufferer will, no doubt, find the shoe on the other foot one
day, and will then know personally how misfortune feels.

## NOTES ON USE

The introductory "Buee" section is sung very slowly, with
a nasal wailing quality to the voice. The rhythm of this
section is quite free - the given note values are simply a
starting point. Pause between each "Buee" and let the phrases
swell, fading on "Hmmm."

Once the body of the song gets underway, the rhythm and
attitude change to an up-tempo positive mood. Sustain this
throughout repeats of the bass and cantor's solos, and end
percussively by sharply punching the last three words. Repeat
main body of song as many times as desired. Percussion and
clapping enter as noted at section "B."

# Kyerɛm

## A Contemporary Akan Recreational Song

# Kyerεm

All:    KYERεM NYIMPA A ODZI W'ADZE O
        cheer-ehm neem-pah oh-dzee wahd-zoh

        NA ɔKɔM DZEM A NA MAFA NO O
        nah kawm-ah dzee-mah nah mah-fah noh

        KYERεM NYIMPA A ODZI W'ADZE O

        NA ɔKɔM DZEM A NA MAFA NO O

Women:  MENA SAMAN E
        mee-nah sah-mahn ay

Men:    NYIMPA A ODZI W'ADZE O

Women:  MEGYA SAMAN E
        meh-jah sah-mahn ay

Men:    NYIMPA A ODZI W'ADZE O

Women:  MENA SAMAN E

Men:    NYIMPA A ODZI W'ADZE O

Women:  M'AYε MMɔBɔR O
        my-yeh maw-bohr oh

All:    NYIMPA A ODZI W'ADZE O

## TRANSLATION

"Show me your successor" or "Show me who will guide me"
"When I am hungry I go to him" or "When I am in need I turn
    to him"

(Women): "My mother's ghost (or spirit)"

(Men): "Who will guide me?"

(Women): "My father's ghost (or spirit)"

(Men): "Who will guide me?"

(Women): "My mother's ghost (or spirit)"

(Men): "Who will guide me?"

(Women): "I am in sorrow" or "I have been left alone"

(All): "Who will guide me?"

## EXPANDED TRANSLATION

Who will guide me now that my parents are dead? Who should I turn to when I am hungry or in need? I ask the spirits of those who watched over me to show me their successor now that I have been left alone in sorrow. Who will take their place when I need help?

## EXPLANATION

"Kyerɛm" is a contemporary arrangement of very old Akan sayings set to a new melody by the leader of the Akrofor Choir, in Gomoa Aboso. It is a recreational song which would most appropriately be sung at a funeral, directed to the departed soul of the deceased, or in a less ritualized setting such as a festival where it would be used as additional music for the occasion, as a reminder of important cultural values.

Songs of this type are derived from the old sayings or proverbs which served in the past as teachings by which to live within the society. Bits of the ancient wisdom teachings are used today in everyday language and are sometimes worked together in a new way, as in this piece, to reflect the changing needs of the culture.

"Kyerɛm" serves to caution people to be sure that as the elderly die there will be someone who will take their place as spiritual and moral guides for any children who might be left orphaned. It is important the successor be loyal to the lifestyle and values of the departed ones, and able to bear the responsibility given them.

## NOTES ON USE

Sing unaccompanied, or with a small percussion ensemble as presented below including hand drum, bell, shakers and/or clapping.

*Ghanaian youth choir of eighteen- to twentyfive-year olds who combine traditional and missionary influences in their singing.*

# Ɔkwan Tsen Tsen

## An Akan Highlife Bosoɛ Song

-73-

# Ɔkwan Tsen Tsen

[Cantor A:

Ɔk-wan tsen tsen a-war e - meren-kɔ - o Ɔk-wan tsen tsen a-war e-
(Ohk-wahn sehn sehn ah-wahr ay - mehn-koh - oh)

] [Cantor B:

meren-kɔ - o (meren-kɔ-o) Sɛ 'min-ya me-kɔ n'a-sem bi si m'a-kyir a mɛ-
(Say mee-yah meh-koh nah-sehm bee see mah-cheer ah meh-

]

yɛ dɛn Sɛ min-ya me-kɔ n'a-sem bi si m'a-kyir a mɛ-yɛ dɛn
yeh dehn)

[Cantor A:

Ɔk-wan tsen tsen a-war e - meren-kɔ - o a-sɛm bi si m'a-kyir a mɛ-yɛ dɛn m'at-se
(ah-sɛm bee see mah-cheer ah meh-yeh dehn maht-see)

Chorus:

Ɔk-wan tsen tsen a-war e - meren-kɔ - o Ɔk-wan tsen tsen a-war e-

- meren-kɔ - o Sɛ min-ya me-kɔ n'a-sem bi si m'a-kyir a mɛ-yɛ dɛn

Sɛ min-ya me-kɔ n'a-sem bi si m'a-kyir a mɛ-yɛ dɛn Ɔk-wan tsen

*D.C. al Fine*
*Fine*

tsen a-war e - meren-kɔ - o a-sem bi si m'a-kyir a mɛ-yɛ dɛn m'at-se

-74-

# Ɔkwan Tsen Tsen

Cantor, in a teasing exchange with the chorus: SOO,SOO

Group: YƐƐ,YƐ
      yay, yeh

C: SOO, SOO

G: YƐƐ, YƐ

C: SOO—OO

G: LƐGƐƐ
   leh-geh

C: LƐGƐƐ

G: SOO—OO

C: ASHEWO               G: KƆWUA
   ah-shoo                   kaw-oo-ay

Cantor 1: ƆKWAN TSEN TSEN AWAR E, MERENKƆ—O (repeat)
         oh-kwahn sehn sehn ah-wahr ay meh-rehn-koh

Cantor 2: SƐ MIYA MEKO N'ASƐM BI SI M'AKYIR A MƐYƐ DƐN (2x)
         say   mee-yah meh-koh nah-sehm bee see mah-cheer  ah
                                    may-yeh dehn

Cantor 1: ƆKWAN TSEN TSEN AWAR E, MERENKƆ—O
         ASƐM BI SI M'AKYIR A MƐYƐ DƐN M'ATSE
         ah-sehm bee see mah-cheer ah may-yeh dehn maht-see

Group:   ƆKWAN TSEN TSEN AWAR E, MERENKƆ—O (2x)
         SƐ MIYA MEKO N'ASƐM BI SI M'AKYIR A MƐYƐ DƐN (2x)
         ƆKWAN TSEN TSEN AWAR E, MERENKƆ—O
         ASƐM BI SI M'AKYIR A, MƐYƐ DƐN M'ATSE

## TRANSLATION

Cantor: "Ready?"
Group: "Yeah!"
C: "Ready?"
G: "Yeah!"
C: "Ready?"
G: "Ready!"
C: "Ready!"
G: "Ready!"
C: "Paining you" (jealous) ("You're just showing off to make
                            us jealous")
G: ("If it hurts so much, go hang yourself!")

Cantor 1: "A long distance marriage, I wouldn't dare to go."

Cantor 2: "Should I go and something were to happen, what
          would I do?"

Cantor 1: "A long distance marriage, I wouldn't dare to go.
          If something happened, how could I hear about it?"

Group: "A long distance marriage, I wouldn't dare to go.(2x)
       Should I go and something were to happen, what would
       I do?" (2x)

## EXPANDED TRANSLATION

I wouldn't dare to marry someone from a distant place. If I
married and moved to another area and something terrible happened to someone in my family - a death or some serious trouble - how would I find out about it in time to fulfill my obligations? By the time I heard any news it would be too late
to do the right thing.

## EXPLANATION

"Ɔkwan Tsen Tsen" is an example of a very old Akan song
about the importance of resisting cultural change. Due in
part to inter-tribal disputes, families did not approve of
someone marrying an individual from another region or state,
sadly viewing this infrequent event as "marriage to a stran-
ger." And prior to the advent of improved roads and
transportation, marriage between parties from villages even
as close as thirty miles from each other was discouraged
because of the hardships involved in maintaining contact
between members of the same family. This contact is crucial
for those who are seasonal farmers and expect younger relatives to help prepare, plant, watch over and harvest the
crops. It is also of the utmost importance to be present when
family members are ill, during celebrations and funerals, and
anytime there is an occasion to maintain traditional values
and customs which keep the community strong.

The content of this song arises from the Akan saying,
**"Nyimdzee wo fa no fie"** (Charity begins at home). The child's
social, spiritual, moral and practical education typically
takes place in and around the home and the village. The father, with the help of the mother, is responsible for pro-
viding opportunities for his children to witness and learn
appropriate behavior in observance of the taboos (**akyiwadze**)
of their society. He takes them to state meetings such as the
installation of a chief, festivals, and other public functions such as funeral rites where they will dress like and

model their behavior after that of their elders. They learn
that respect for elders is shown by greeting and speaking
with them politely, by not sitting on the stool of an adult,
by offering and receiving things with the right hand only,
and by refraining from coarse actions such as spitting or
crossing legs in their presence.

A marriage (particularly at an early age) to someone not
fully versed in these and other customs, and who lives far
enough away so that proper observance becomes impossible to
learn or fulfill, may adversely affect the young person's
health, disposition, and community standing.

## The Highlife Tradition and Bosoɛ

The contemporary setting for "Ɔkwan Tsen Tsen" included
here is known as "highlife," specifically the ensemble called
bosoɛ , dance music popular especially among the Fantis of
Ghana. Performances of bosoɛ selections are given by bosoɛ
bands--groups of young people who are members of a social
club. Many songs dealing with everyday life--love, work, sorrow, joy and change--are placed in the context of the bosoɛ
rhythm and instrumentation, which includes the following
basic bell pattern, a variety of traditional drums and shakers and frequently, electric bass guitar.

Basic Bell Pattern for "Bosoɛ":

Highlife, according to David Coplan in his article "Go to
My Town, Cape Coast! The Social History of Ghanaian Highlife"
is

> ...a musical hybrid resulting from the acculturative
> impact of Europe on West Africa during the colonial
> period....(It is) a creative, incorporative response
> to the political and economic impact and cultural
> challenge of the West....(1978:p.97)

The original instrumentation for songs like "Ɔkwan Tsen
Tsen" included only drums, bells and shakers of various
sorts. However the growing familiarity with European and
American popular music styles was reflected in experiments by
West African musicians who added electric guitar and bass
guitar, and then brass instruments to the traditional
ensembles.

Highlife bands are found primarily in the cities where
the style of music and the topics dealt with in the songs are
most relevant. The songs incorporate phrases or proverbs common to the Akan-speaking Fanti community, and although the
ensemble is played for the enjoyment of the spectators (who
are not merely an audience but active participants in

singing, dancing and handclapping), it is expected that they will listen to and carefully consider the message of the words. Highlife music can be seen, therefore, as continuing the "time-honored tradition of music as a means of social commentary, communication, and control," as David Coplan observes. (1978:p.109) He adds:

> Song lyrics have dealt with the typical contemporary social problems of individuals in painfully familiar situations; and they represented an attempt to conceptualize and formulate moral positions on the urban situation in terms of the value system of traditional Ghanaian culture. Amid a social environment radically more complex than the traditional tribal milieus, urban Ghanaian workers clung noticeably to the values and symbols that had guided them or their forebears through life in rural society. (1978:p.109)

Even though disputes and transportation are not such critical issues in modern times, traditional values, bonds to the community and careful consideration of the consequences of cultural change remain important. "Ɔkwan Tsen Tsen" warns the listener to reflect on how his or her actions might affect their family and themselves in a changing society.

NOTES ON USE

Begin with the call-and-response chant led by one of the cantors (lead singer). After the chant, the bells, rattles and claps enter, then the hand-drum patterns (done alternately by one drummer or simultaneously by two), and finally the bass motif. Consider the essential accompaniment to be the claps, bells, and rattles. The energy of the piece intensifies with the drums and bass added.

The cantors are free to improvise on the rhythms of their melodies, and may also enter in an overlapping manner.

The initial chant may be repeated after the chorus has sung in alternation with the cantors once or twice through the entire song.

*Ghanaian youth choir accompanied by a small ensemble of musicians playing (1. to r.)* patsi, oprenten *and* donno.

# Cho Kurima Woye

A Shona Multipart Song from the Time of Starvation (before 1900)

# *Cho Kurima Woye*

(Mazembera = Bass):
NJANGA NJANGA NGE DZE VATONGA (repeat throughout)
 jahn-gah jahn-gah ged-zay vah-tong-ah (repeat)

(Proper kudaira = tenor):
NDI MAMBO, NDI MAMBO  (repeat throughout)
 dee mahm-boh (repeat)

(Kudaira = alto):
TISU NEMADIRANDO, TISU NEMADIRANDO (repeat throughout)
 tee-soo nay-mah deer-ahn-doh (repeat)

---

(Kutema = soprano)
CHO KURIMA WOYE, CHO KURIMA (repeat throughout)
 choh koo-ree-mah woh-ay, choh koo-ree-mah

## TRANSLATION

njanga = the sound of the **mbira** or **magavu** (leg rattles)
"The sound (of the mbira or magavu) is from the Vatonga"
"He (or it) is the greatest, he (or it) is the chief"
"We are the people who are in need"
"That we grow crops"

## EXPANDED TRANSLATION

Where  are  the  crops  we grew?  We who are the people  in
need will depend on the chief. We can get crops from him, for
he is the greatest.  We do not have to beg with the sound  of
mbira  playing  or dancing with leg rattles like the  Vatonga
from the north, who end up humiliating themselves. Begging is
for the Vatonga, not for us.

## EXPLANATION

This  is  a song of the old generation who most  likely
lived  through  the "Time of Starvation" in  Zimbabwe  before
1900.  Zimbabwe  has had relatively few times of severe hardship  from  drought or other natural phenomena  causing  crop
failure.  During  the  drought before 1900,  food  became  so
scarce  that  people lived on roasted animal skins and  were
forced to dip into the seed stored for the next planting season. The people from the north, the Vatonga, experienced crop
failure  as well,  and came repeatedly to Zimbabwe (Southern
Rhodesia at the time) to beg for food.  Incorporated in their
begging  was entertainment such as playing the mbira or dancing  with magavu (leg rattles) in front of a house until  the
occupants would give them something to eat.

Begging was unnecessary in the Shona system, due primarily to the custom of bringing a portion of each harvest to the chief and retaining a portion for planting the next season. The chief had large store rooms for grains and other foods which could then be used like a food bank in time of crop failure or lack of food for any other reason. If a family ran out of food, they could go to the chief and remove a portion of what they had deposited over time. There was no stigma attached to this. Animals and meat could also be given during times of plenty, and traded for grains or returned if necessary. This system was set up to guard against a community being doomed by agricultural misfortune, and eliminated the possibility of having to beg to survive.

## NOTES ON USE

This is an example of a song that has melodic lines derived from mbira playing principles, if not from actual mbira lines. Many vocal pieces are rooted in the repertoire of the mbira and have been lifted from that context and altered as necessary for purely vocal performance. The melodies and structures associated with the mbira are the foundation of all Shona musical expression.

The line employed as the basic melody is **kutema**, and is typically the part of a piece handed down from generation to generation. The bass part is the **mazembera** and may also be known to all who would recognize the kutema. It varies little throughout a song, and is often characterized by short syllables such as "hiya Baba," "ha ha ho," "haiwa Baba o-e," and other similar phrases which may have meaning in some contexts but serve as vocables in the mazembera framework. The middle or very high range parts may or may not be improvised. Often a simple harmonizing part is added to the kutema which is accepted as fixed (rather than improvisatory), called the **proper kudaira**. After that has been sung, a slightly more embellished part may be used to weave through the other singers voices. This is also a **kudaira** part, but not as skeletal or fundamental as the proper kudaira. If syllables rather than words are sung for the kudaira parts, they will be "wo," "i," "ye," "iye," "wo iye ye," "yo we," and others.

Teach each part separately until the entire group is familiar with all of the lines, then introduce each in correct order of entry (see transcription). Allow time for parts to jell before adding the next. After the song is fully under way, individuals may switch from one part to another, being sensitive to the overall balance of parts. Another option is to sing a part an octave higher or lower. Men may use falsetto to sing a high vocal line. The group may, if preferred, be assigned fixed parts as indicated. The clapping pattern (see transcription) is an important accompaniment to the singing.

# Vamudara

## A Shona Shangara Dance Song

## Vamudara

# Vamudara

te - we - ra mam - bo - o    Ndi -no ku - te - we - ra Tu - re - si

le - le    Hai - wa ndom pa - wo zuin -hu zue -se mu - no - da ku -te - te -

Hai - wa ba - ba-o we    Hai - wa ba - ba-o    we    Hai - wa ba - ba-o    we

*D.S.*

hi - ya - a - a Ndi -no ku - te - we - ra mam - bo - o    Va - mu -

re - ka te - te - re -kai che - che - le - le    Hai - wa ndom pa - wo zuin -hu

Hai - wa ba - ba-o    we    Hai - wa ba - ba-o    we    Hai - wa ba - ba-o    we

Percussion

Clap

Hosho
(rattles)
L  L R L   L  L R L

Drum

-84-

**"VAMUDARA"**     Illustration: Saki Mafundikwa ©1986

# *Vamudara*

(Mazembera = basses)
HAIWA BABA O-WE, HAIWA BABA O-WE,(repeat throughout)
hi-wah bah-bah oh-way, hi-wah bah-bah oh-way

(Proper Kudaira = sopranos)
O-WE, O-WE (continue throughout introduction)
oh-way, oh-way

(Kutema = sopranos)
VAMUDARA MWAPFEKE MARENGENA
vah-moo-dah-rah mwahp-feh-kay mah-rehn-gay-nah

MAHUZWEPI SEKUNGE MUNE MARI
mah-hooz-way-pee say-kuhn-gay moo-nay mah-ree

NDINO MUTEWERA MAMBO-O, NDINO MUTEWERA MAMBO-O
dee-noh moo-tay-way-rah mahm-boh-oh

NDINO KUTEWERA TURESI, HIYA-A-A
dee-noh koo-tay-way-rah too-reh-see, hi-yah-ah-ah

NDINO KUTEWERA MAMBO-O
dee-noh koo-tay-way-rah mahm-boh-oh

(Kudaira lines = altos and tenors)
HAIWA NDOM PAWO ZUINHU ZUESE, MUNODA KUTETEREKA
hi-wahn  dohm pah-woh zhwin-oo zhway-say moo-noh-dah
                                        koo-tay-teh-ray-kah

TETEREKAI CHECHELELE
tay-teh-ray-kai chay-chay-lay-lay

TRANSLATION

Mazembera: "Oh, father, oh" or vocables, exclamation

Proper Kudaira: vocables

Kutema: "Mr. Old Man, you are wearing tatters!"
        "Where  did you hear people are drinking,  as if  you
          had money?"
        "I will follow you, chief. I will follow you, chief."
        "I will follow you, Mr. Turesi." (vocables)
        "I will follow you, chief."

Kudaira lines:  "If drinking means that much to you,  we will
                give you everything to get your drink"
                "You can stagger and be happy"

## EXPANDED TRANSLATION

People in the beer hall call out, "Geez, you old man, you are always going out dressed in rags, looking for beer but the problem is you don't have any money."

He answers them saying, "I always follow beer wherever it is, and beer is my chief. For some men a woman is the highest influence and authority, for some women it's a man. Beer is all the authority and woman I need, all rolled into one, so leave me alone - there is nothing else."

"Well," they say to him. "If that is how you feel, we will give you some money to buy beer so you can get drunk and stagger, forget your troubles and be happy. We will not lecture you about drinking."

## EXPLANATION

"Vamudara" is a drinking song which takes the form of a sort of drama. The scene involves an old man who likes to drink so much, he does not even care about dressing well or buying new clothes. He wears **marengena** and **manyatera** -- ragged clothes in tatters and cheap sandals made of cut-up car tires. The other men in the beer hall or beer park who have gathered after work to sing, dance, and drink the fresh local beer are concerned about his welfare, but do not attempt to confront him directly about his habits. Instead, Shona people will discipline each other indirectly through song. A song of this type would not be sung to shame an individual or label him an alcoholic, or even to stop him from drinking further, but simply to give him something to think about. The tone of the song is somewhat sarcastic, but is not meant to be cutting.

## NOTES ON USE

The actual song which passed intact through generations of singers is the kutema part. The mazembera is a typical bass part which would most likely be sung with this kutema. This arrangement by Maraire was created by taking the two basic parts of this common drinking song and arranging it with additional set parts for a group to sing. This version of "Vamudara" presents the song fixed in its structure and parts at one point in time. Although most Shona people would know the kutema and would sing the same or similar mazembera and proper kudaira parts, they would never have heard it arranged with these particular additional kudaira lines. If a group of Shona singers were to learn "Vamudara" with these parts, within a short time the singers would begin to improvise and parts would be added, dropped or changed. The Western custom of assigning specific parts for each vocal range is not commonly found within African performance practice. Aduonum notes:

> In traditional African music practice, the formal structure of each particular piece of music is left to the mercy of the performers. As such, the form of the music may be predicted only when the music is at a complete stop. African music is...alive.(1980:p.104)

"Vamudara" is an example of a **shangara** dance song, based on the shangara dance rhythm noted below:

L  R  L  R  L  R  L  R  R  L  R  R

It is considered a recreational song which would employ hand-claps to define the beat, and drums and hosho to complement it. If the song accompanied a shangara dance (which is from the Karanga area of Zimbabwe) the dancers, both men and women, would be arranged in a circle. As the excitement of the dance grew, pairs of women and men would move to the center of the circle and move to the beat with complex twisting, stomping, or shuffling steps.

Begin with the mazembera or bass part, and gradually layer each part as indicated in the transcription. The kudaira lines enter last. Bear in mind this is not the definitive, fossilized version. In Zimbabwe, "Vamudara" might be sung in just this way once and then, perhaps, never again!

*Shona dancers wearing* **magavu** *(leg rattles) to intensify the sounds of dancing and enhance the overall* **chaka** *(buzz) in the performance. Size varies from small gourds to some as big as hosho!*

# Conclusion

This book is not intended to be a definitive compilation of game songs, story songs or multipart songs of Ghana and Zimbabwe. It is simply an introduction to a body of music which is so closely tied to the cultures which spawned it that each song is a mirror of those cultures in some way. The authors believe that a living human being is a musical human being. Taking part in group music-making reaffirms and strengthens the bonds between individuals, and by extension, the bonds to family, community, country and planet. The process of practicing and performing music in an environment which welcomes every individual's contributions opens the channels for creative energy to flow freely. As this energy moves it nurtures, it heals, it uplifts the participants.

The themes in African songs and dances reveal the importance of being an active, aware, and responsible part of society. We present these songs to help you and your students become better acquainted with the African orientation to music and life and hope that at the same time you personally experience the satisfaction that comes from taking part in the process of cooperative music making. Black, white, yellow red or brown--our bonds grow stronger when we let our voices be heard.

*Drums begin to throb and the dancers leap into action in the hastily formed circle of men and women—not forgetting the children.*

# Appendix A:

# What Is A Master Musician?

Master musicians in Africa are highly motivated, extensively trained and gifted performers. They are also, and perhaps more importantly, living archives of the traditions of their societies – of the history, religious ceremonies, festivals, moral and ethical teachings, proverbs, wise sayings, and praise-poems – and are respected for their character as much as for their musical expertise. Quite commonly, a master musician is an individual who is born into a musical family and who shows interest and promise at an early age. A family with a number of knowledgeable musicians in its ranks is called an **akyerɛma** family in Ghana. Such a family provides a child with unusual access to situations that will enable the aspiring musician to observe and absorb performance techniques and cultural traditions in formal and informal settings on a daily basis over a period of many years.

It is expected that a master musician will have wide knowledge of the varied instruments in his culture and be acquainted with current and past repertoire, although he may be particularly skilled in one instrument or group of instruments. Added to these areas of expertise and knowledge is a role that has become increasingly more significant – acting as a catalyst for ceremonial, religious, or recreational occasions which incorporate both fixed and flexible musical activities, occasions which will renew the bonds that bind the community on many levels. In this way, a master musician is an archive for what is most valued in his culture, and a leader and channel for reintegrating those values into a changing society.

Chernoff photo:*African Rhythm and African Sensibility*, *Univ. of Chicago Press*, c 1979.

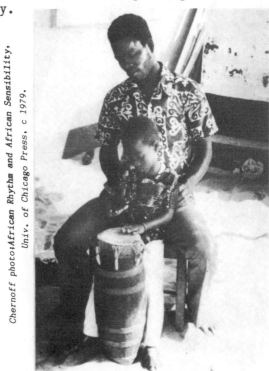

*Ewe boy learning to play the* **kagan**, *small barrel-shaped drum.*

# Appendix B: Percussion Techniques
# Timekeepers: Bells, Gongs, Sticks

Percussion instruments such as bells, rattles, sticks and handclaps are used in African music to provide a sort of substructure to a piece, a point of reference which other instruments, singers and dancers relate to. Members of an ensemble are able to tie individual parts to a particular pulse in the short, repeating bell pattern which helps them maintain a steady rhythm and also their correct relationship to the many layers of rhythmic activity around them. The fundamental pulse of a piece may be easy to identify when it is heard in isolation at the beginning of an ensemble, but it is not necessarily a part which keeps to regular metronomic beats. The timekeepers have a role to play as an integral part of the overall sound texture and therefore the pattern they maintain might be in groups of six or even nine notes, and in duple or triple patterns, not only groups of three or four notes in a simple reinforcement of the beat.

**Gankogui** parts take advantage of the high and low tones on the gong, as well as the timbre variations which result with muffling the mouth of the bell by holding it to the body momentarily. A gankogui part which marks off the first or important beats in a pattern by calling for the player to hit the low bell can be a tremendous aid to neophyte percussionists feeling lost in the conversation created by many drums talking. Each drummer can cue their repeating phrases to a particular part of the bell pattern, and mentally keep track of their cue as it relates to the low bell tone ringing out periodically.

The absence of a conductor in front of the group makes it even more imperative that there be some technique for bringing each player into the piece at the correct point, and for helping all players stay on target. A player who can maintain the time line without dragging or speeding up, and who does not tire of playing the same short pattern for the duration of a piece is a valuable player indeed.

The bell, rattle, stick and handclapping patterns found throughout this book are quite basic yet authentic and are typical of time lines heard in the music of Ghana and Zimbabwe.

*Double gong and **gankogui** with high and low bells,*
*firikyiwa, metal castanet struck with ring, in front.*

# Rattles: Hosho and Axatse

Hosho is the Shona word for a rattle made from a dried gourd that has been hollowed out and filled with several seeds or small pebbles. The special type of gourd used for this purpose is unusual in appearance -- often quite knobby and gnarled, golden brown, with a natural handle from the curved neck of the gourd. The particular sound quality and pitch varies with size, which can range from that of an orange to a grapefruit or melon. Some ensembles will incorporate several players using hosho of different sizes to produce mixed pitch as well as timbre and several rhythms. The sound of a hosho is called **chaka,** which means "splashing." The word "chaka" also describes the sound made by leg rattles on a dancer, shell or bottlecap buzzers on the resonator or body of an mbira, or the swishing of grains or seeds shaken in a metal pan.

In the hands of an expert, the hosho is shaken in a combination of rhythms (called the "beat" of the piece) which sometmes produce alternating swishing and snapping sounds. When well articulated (if the seeds all hit the wall of the gourd in a tight clump), the hosho patterns add excitement and drive to a piece. The hosho player can choose to emphasize the rhythm, timbre, or words of a piece.

The importance of the hosho player in an ensemble should not be underestimated. Many Shona mbira pieces, with or without singing, will seem rhythmically adrift to the listener. The first phrases are often haltingly laid out as the player establishes the skeletal framework of the piece. It is almost impossible to tell what sort of rhythmic pattern serves as the foundation until the hosho enters. Suddenly the rhythm snaps into focus. The precision of the seeds swishing and snapping sharply greatly increases the energy and excitement for the performers and audience alike. A hosho player who can maintain a strict rhythm and clean sound for several hours without tiring or lagging behind the other performers is highly valued in an ensemble. Such a player lends added tension through creative use of cross-rhythms.

Throughout Africa rattle-players use local variants of the gourd rattle, or might even throw several seeds or pebbles into a can, crimp the top, and attach a stick for a different sound. Pop-top cans partly filled with mung beans make an excellent rattle for the classroom.

The rattle most commonly used in Ghana is quite different from the Shona hosho. Called **axatse,** it may also be a dried, hollowed round gourd of widely varying size, but rather than being filled with seeds the gourd is typically surrounded by a netting of small shells, or strung beads or round dried seeds. This netting can be manipulated to produce a range of sounds from sharply percussive clicks (by tapping the fingers on the seeds), to a smooth swishing (made by turning the gourd as the netting hangs loose or is held in place), to a thud (produced by thumping the bottom of the gourd; a large axatse the size of a huge melon or pumpkin will have a deep booming voice). The axatse can also be played by holding the handle of the gourd in one hand and pulling rhythmically on the netting to tighten and release it with the free hand, or by alternating taps on the player's body (with the axatse) with taps on the axatse itself in patterns which often combine the downbeat with cross-rhythms. Spoken syllables sometimes accompany an axatse pattern until the player has mastered the rhythm: **pa** is used for a tap on the body (such as on the lap of a sitting player), **ti** is used for a tap with the hand. (Thus, alternating between tapping one's lap and tapping with the hand might produce the phrase, "pa-ti-pa, pa-ti-pa.")

An adept axatse player is a tremendous asset to an ensemble, just as an expert hosho player is. Carefully maintained axatse patterns help drummers and singers stay on the beat and complement drumming patterns and timbre. In addition, a vocal emsemble can be considered complete even if accompanied only by one bell and an axatse. Fine axatse players also add movement and visual interest to an ensemble as they move the rattle smoothly and gracefully with a fluid body motion, or energetically and dramatically hit it with an elbow or forearm or throw it into the air for effect.

Other idiophones (self-sounding instruments) commonly used include stick clappers, and clapperless bells (large and small double cow bells welded together and hit with a stick, single cow bell hit with a stick, and a boat or banana shaped bell hit with a metal striker--see section on **Timekeepers**), made of iron. Stamping tubes of cut bamboo sections or cut gourds are also common. The bamboo tubes are used by hitting the closed end on a stone slab or the hard ground. They are used in groups of different sizes to produce different pitches, and although the women's choruses of the Ga people of Ghana use these tubes most typically others may use them also. The Ashanti women often use gourds with long necks (or simply long gourds) to make a stamping tube known as **adenkum**. The gourd is cut in two places - at the tip and at the base. The player slaps the bowl of the gourd with her fingers or hits it with her arm or elbow, hits the bowl against the thigh, or hits it with a cupped palm. Each style of attack produces a different sound. (Some women's bands specialize in performing music accompanied by adenkum patterns and are known as adenkum bands.)

# PRACTICE PATTERNS FOR HOSHO AND AXATSE

HOSHO (use two, one for each hand)

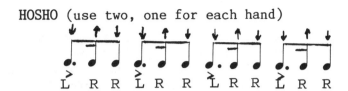

L R R L R R L R R L R R

AXATSE

pa pa ti pa pa ti pa pa ti pa pa ti

pa pa ti pa ti pa ti

pa pa ti pa ti pa ti pa pa pa ti pa ti pa ti pa

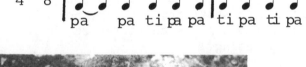

pa pa pa ti pa pa ti pa ti pa ti pa

*Hosho made of dried, hollowed*
*gourds with seeds inside.*

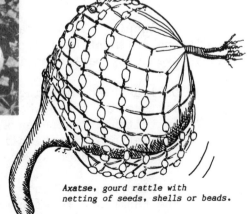

*Axatse, gourd rattle with*
*netting of seeds, shells or beads.*

# Handclapping – A Complex Instrument

Handclapping in Africa is an art. There are many sounds two hands can make, depending on how they are cupped and how they strike each other. An accompaniment of handclaps can be as complex and exciting a sound as a drumming ensemble. In both Ghana and Zimbabwe, children often learn rhythm patterns by clapping certain phrases that incorporate the patterns or by playing games with actions involving clapping. The rhythms learned in these ways will later be transferred with ease to drums, bells, or rattles. If a large group of people are gathered to sing, dance, and drum, those who are able to clap a variety of percussion patterns are thus able to participate more fully.

An informal but highly effective "lesson" takes place when an adult holds a child on their lap during musical events, grasps the child's hands and claps various rhythms with them. Or a child might enthusiastically cling to the adult's hands as he or she claps. Both will enjoy the experience, and the rhythms (and the idea of participation being fun, acceptable and expected) will become second nature to the child.

Among the Shona people, complex handclapping is called **makwa**. Paul Berliner discusses the characteristics of makwa in **The Soul of Mbira**. He writes:

> At their most complex, the makwa patterns are a virtuoso form of drumming. Such parts range from a rapid-fire three-pulse figure that synchronizes with the complete hosho pattern, to long, powerful, improvised rhythmic lines characterized by complex off-beat phrasing.
> Makwa patterns combine in many ways and usually participants perform at least two contrasting patterns simultaneously....They continually change with respect to one another, producing a steady flow of varied rhythmic patterns in the background....(1981:p.115)

Handclapping in African musical settings is seen as an additional element of improvisation and creativity, and also as an avenue of participation and fun. Nketia points out:

> Dull as hand clapping or the beats of an iron bell may seem to those whose cultures treat percussion as "kitchen instruments," they have not only organizational function in African music but also provide an added source of pleasure. (1961:p.590)

> Clapping the hands, stamping the feet, clicking the thumb and forefinger provide ready extra-vocal

sounds that may be used in any situation...by the ordinary performer....Further, sound producing instruments that can be readily improvised are the percussive type. One may resort to a packing case, a stool or chair or anything that comes to hand in an improvisatory situation. (1961:p.587)

Of course, we can see that if what is most easily accessible and most easily used is also valued as part of the total sound, a high degree of participation will result.

Experiment with the percussion ensembles found below.

# Sample Percussion Ensembles

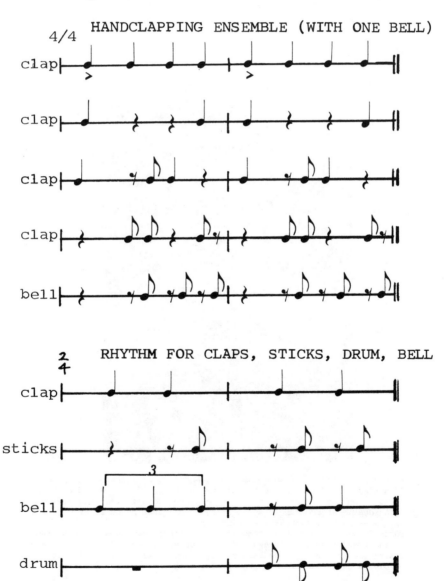

12/8 Based on Ghanaian dance "Agbekor" (slow section)

*A seven year old boy from Gomoa Aboso, Ghana, practicing on the **atumpan** ("talking drums"). After participating in children's games and folktale parties he is ready to move on to more complicated rhythms and techniques. At the same time he learns drum patterns he is also taught to show respect for the traditions of his society and for the drums themselves by approaching them in a prescribed way, wearing the **ntama** cloth wrapped so as to leave the chest bare. Unless he abides by and honors the customs that pertain to the drums he will not be allowed to go behind them, much less learn to play them.*

# Appendix C: Voices Fitting Together

Harmony in most African vocal music arises from the interplay of melodic lines for different voices, and is not seen as a vertical structuring of chordal tones. In Ghana and Zimbabwe, traditional singing is a spontaneous, creative expression utilizing a vast range of vocal techniques and ingenious use of flexible multipart structures. The fluid whole which results when many parts are woven together in a performance is called **kutengezana** in Shona -- the sum of all the parts.

Melodies and harmonies arise partly from the scale system used in a particular tradition (pentatonic, heptatonic, diatonic) and partly from the fact that tonal languages like Akan and Shona impose certain shapes on a sung line. You will hear members of an Akan chorus sing the same melody as the cantor but move it to intervals of a third, fifth or sixth apart. In addition, the cantor might become inspired to suddenly vary the text of a song in response to the particular context of the performance, causing both melody and rhythm to change (because of the different speech tones), while the chorus continues with the original parts. One result will be harmonization, another might be a rhythmic variation. Keep in mind also that most African songs integrate movement as well, and the aural and visual rhythms set up by dancers bodies, sometimes with legs encircled by special bells or rattles, the swaying, clapping crowd and the instrumental players affect and enrich the whole.

## Structures of Vocal Music

There are many ways songs can be structured so as to enable voices to bump into each other harmoniously. **Call-and-response** styles cause parts to alternate between one cantor and a chorus, or between two cantors or choruses (antiphony). The exact relationship between the leader and the responding chorus takes one or more of several forms:

a. The response may be one short note, with all voices in unison, entering after the leader's phrase as a complement to its meaning or simply as a way to focus the audience's attention and provide an avenue of participation (e.g.,"Chatigo Chinyi").

b. The response may echo the leader's part exactly (e.g.,"Kye Kye Kule").

   c. The response may be a sentence or phrase which
completes what the leader sings. If the leader's part
reenters in an overlapping way, a short harmony section
results (e.g., "Zangaiwa Chakatanga Pano", "Pɛtɛ Pɛtɛ").

   The cantor is not bound to only one phrase or melodic
line in overlapping call-and-response. He or she may improvise new words, melody, rhythmic surprises, or employ unusual
vocal techniques to embellish the cantor's part. The chorus,
however, continues as a group in a predetermined pattern.

   d. The response may be more complex than either of
the above types, consisting of an independent part of
fairly long sentences and more complex melodic lines.
Parallel harmony is sometimes used in this response.

   The Akan use the heptatonic scale, and most commonly sing
in parallel thirds or sixths (above or below the melody) or
occasionally a fifth apart.

   e. Some songs may have more than one type of re-
sponsorial structure in evidence.

   In his book **Music of the Whole Earth**, David Reck discusses polyphonic techniques in detail. He writes:

   The peaceful coexistence of simultaneous melodies
   can come about...when there may be anticipations by
   some voices of where the melody is going, as well as
   lagging behind, or a holding of previous notes...(which
   can) be noticed, enjoyed and used intentionally as part
   of the musical texture.
   ...Related to the overlapping call-and-response idea
   is the canon or round. Here each part works through the
   same melodic material but begins at a different time...
   ...Another technique...is the use of intricate melodic/
   rhythmic interlocking patterns, each segment fitting
   into the next like a wonderful invisible...jigsaw puz-
   zle....
   ...There also may be a superimposition of melodic osti-
   natos, which work together to build an active, complex
   and kaleidoscopically changing musical texture.
   (Finally)...music may...be stacked in polyphonic
   layers moving against or independently of each other.
   Each layer in itself may be a complex texture made up
   of many elements....(1977:pp.304-307)

Solo performers might accompany themselves on an instrument such as mbira or a stringed instrument, or by using a bell, rattle, or handclapping. They might go so far as to have musicians, another singer or even a chorus to embellish their performance, but the emphasis will be on the soloist.

**Lead singers or cantors** work within a chorus-- important members of the total ensemble, with the emphasis on the group sound.

There are certain qualities appreciated in a cantor or lead singer. Perhaps most important is a strong voice that can carry over the noise of an outdoor performance and be heard by the chorus and crowd both. Being able to create and maintain a part amid the swirl of melodies, rhythms and movement without faltering is also valued. In Ghana a singer who cannot accomplish this is said to have **nsɔɔdɛ** or "sweet ears."

An important aspect of **multipart** singing in the African tradition is that the parts are neither composed nor assigned, with the infrequent exception of recently composed choral works. Traditionally, harmony parts arise spontaneously and are not inflexibly assigned. Each singer is free to choose the part he or she will sing and may jump from one part to another if they become so inspired. Parts may cross, men and women may sing in octaves, men may join the lower women's voices or create a high part using their falsetto voice. As the excitement of singing grows, participants may add higher and higher parts, dropping quite low to renew their upward climb when the notes exceed their vocal range. Although in some singing situations the possibilities for harmony and improvisation are as varied as the singers' imaginations, in others there is an abundant, already established pool of appropriate embellishments from which to choose. These conventions may be harmonic, rhythmic, or even verbal, and are learned by careful listening during the myriad of musical events occurring each day, or are pointed out by cantors and master musicians and absorbed by their family members as they practice together.

While call-and-response and multipart structures provide ample room for group participation, soloists also have generous latitude to use their specialized skills in creating free melodic, rhythmic, and verbal variations. Nketia observes:

> The creative performer must be guided by a
> knowledge of tradition, a knowledge of how to
> construct a phrase, how and where to add a second
> part, how to build up new material and place it
> against something that is already going on; how
> to increase the animation of the piece....He has

a body of <u>usages</u> to guide him. He learns these
through social experience....(1961:p.591)

In Ghana if a group of singers wants to create an
arrangement of a piece, to practice or polish it, the leader
might start them off by singing a few notes to indicate
suggested vocal ranges or starting tones for different voice
parts. The entire group must determine what parts will be
sung, parts which will be created by the individual singers.
If the leader desires more parts, he or she will call for
some "seasoning to spice up the stew" but will rarely dictate
exactly what to add. On occasion a Ghanaian singer experi-
menting with a part will hit sour notes or use their voice in
an unnacceptable style for a particular song, causing other
singers to be thrown off, or spoiling the arrangement. The
leader will quickly call out that this is an **abokyi** part - a
part that is sour or **wafire akyire** ("out of step"), and
spoils the song. He or she will then guide the singer to
polish and make changes until the part adds to rather than
detracts from the whole. (Singers who chronically use abokyi
parts tend to come from families that are not deeply involved
in musical performance, and so have not had the daily
exposure to accepted options of harmony and improvisation.)

Multipart songs in Africa are reflections of social in-
teractions, relationships, conversations, opinions and moods.
Just as people in a gathering may all agree about a certain
issue and yet discuss it from varying perspectives, so
the variety of melodies, rhythms and verbal/vocal innovations
in part songs reveal individual responses to the stated theme
and events of the moment.

In Zimbabwe, musical "discussions" or dialogues are
facilitated by the presence of some basic structures in both
instrumental (particularly the mbira and marimba repertoire)
and vocal music. First and foremost is the **kutema**. Kutema is
a Shona word which means literally "to cut" (as in "to cut
down a tree") or to chop wood. In its musical sense, it means
"to cut the way" to establish the theme, the melody, the
musical phrase that will identify which song is being sung.
It is sung usually at the beginning of a song, and is often
in the middle voice range. After the piece gets underway, the
kutema might not be heard, but it is the underlying and most
important part and will be continued internally, mentally,
without change. The **kushaura** or second singing part takes off
from the kutema and varies it or develops it.

The **mazembera** is a bass line. There is always a mazembera
part to a song, and if there are several singers with low
voices it would be possible to have several mazembera lines.
They would be very similar, however, and over the course of
the song the part would not vary much. Vocables such as "ha,"
"ho," "haiwa," "baba," and "oh wey" are used in these bass

parts. Although you might find one line sung always with a particular piece (e.g. "Haiwa baba oh-wey" in Vamudara) that same part could also be sung to twenty other songs. It is often an arpeggiated part and frequently starts the ball rolling, with the kutema, kushaura and **kudaira** parts entering as bright strands in a complex and colorful tapestry.

The "kudaira" ("to be in harmony" or "to respond") is the most flexible of the various structural lines, and can change (and usually does change) with each performance. Kudaira lines may be parallel to other parts, interlocking or strophic, and are the parts that function as harmonies. What is sung in the kudaira, and how it is sung relates to the overall relationship of the leaders and other singers and the effect of the many elements noted above. There may be as many kudaira lines as there are people responding. The words may be vocables or phrases, depending on how the speech tones fit a chosen melody. Kudaira lines may be percussive, rhythmic, verbally abbreviated or descriptive at great length. It is common to hear syllables such as "iye iye," "wo iye" and "ah iye" in kudaira parts, sung fairly high in the vocal range.

Pitches in Shona singing do occur simultaneously, of course, as discrete lines build layer upon layer.(The intervals will most likely be fourths, fifths and octaves, and sometimes thirds, sixths and seconds. Western influences are most obvious in church and school music, where there are compositions using chordal harmonies, and at times those harmonies crop up in multipart singing as well -- just more spice for the stew.) The word **kutsinhira** is used to describe the organic growth of such a tangled and exciting musical fabric. It means "to cover with a second layer of sod" but musically means to add a second (or additional) part. If fifty Shona people are singing you might hear fifty parts -- one person singing kutema, and the rest responding individually with great gusto and creativity.

*Mbira made at Kwanongoma College*

# Appendix D: Teaching Methods

The reader might find it interesting to know that I was not taught any of the songs in this collection from musical transcriptions. African musicians are traditionally taught by oral/aural methods, which is primarily how I learned this material as well as West African drumming and Shona mbira techniques. I studied West African singing and drumming at Wesleyan University (CT) (where I earned the MALS degree as an Interfield major with a concentration in Ethnomusicology and World Music for the Classroom) in classes taught by Freeman Kwadzo Donkor and Abraham Kobina Adzinyah as a team or singly, and also learned Ghanaian songs in a tutorial with Adzinyah during the same two-year period. They taught strictly by rote, and only worked with me on the spelling and meaning of the words to the songs when I needed that information written down for my thesis research. They suggested harmony parts by singing examples in each vocal range, but also encouraged the class participants to develop their own. Many of the sessions became in-depth lessons in the nuances of pronunciation of Ghanaian dialects, multiple levels of meaning in the poetry of the songs, historical and cultural information, and performance practice. This approach would be much the same in Ghana. As their students learned melody, words, rhythm, and drumming patterns sufficiently well to maintain a part without assistance, Adzinyah and Donkor switched to more complex or additional parts -- indirectly teaching us what would be considered appropriate harmony or complementary or vocal parts.

I studied mbira and Shona song styles with Dumisani Maraire for several weeks during the summer of 1982. We met for approximately sixty hours of concentrated private lessons. I had intended to focus on singing, but Maraire knew I had begun learning the basic mbira repertoire during the previous summer at Wesleyan with Tom Ross, a former student of his. Maraire was adamant that we begin with mbira, because, he said,

> Mbira is in everything. It is the foundation of all Shona music. The principles which underlie every mbira piece also govern how the voice parts in a song will emerge and interact. I can teach you songs by rote, and you will have a pocket full of songs you will become tired of in five years. Then you will have nothing more to sing. Or I can teach you the principles of mbira, and you will be able to create songs forever. (personal conversation, 1982)

Maraire taught mbira by first discussing the history of Zimbabwe, the tribal and political structure of the nation, the history of the mbira, and the terms he would use in referring to various vocal lines. We then worked through many mbira pieces by having Maraire play them slowly, hands turned so we could each see what the other was doing, moving from simple to more complex phrases and pieces as I followed along on my instrument and with my voice.

As we moved into the vocal repertoire Maraire wrote the words down on a blackboard as he spoke them, then drilled me on pronunciation, melody, and rhythm by saying and then singing each line many times over. As I learned one part of a multipart song satisfactorily he moved on to the next so I could hear how they interlocked. As was the case with Donkor and Adzinyah, Maraire did not resort to musical notation at any time, even though he is adept in Western-style composition as well as the traditional Shona styles.

Learning in this manner requires intense concentration, memory development, and a willingness for the student to take an active role in the learning process. The relationship between voice parts is magnified, and melodic and rhythmic variations in a piece are more easily perceived by a student whose aural acuity is thus gradually refined. The sense of being partners in the creative process often creates strong bonds between teacher and student.

In my own work with students ranging from elementary through adult I have found the most enjoyable learning takes place when I sing and say the words with the group, perhaps play a taped version of the piece, and, on a rare occasison, hand out transcriptions to help in polishing, not learning, a piece. In all cases, I have found the oral/aural method to be effective and a positive and refreshing experience.

*Abraham Kobena Adzinyah with West African Music class; Freeman Donkor is on Adzinyah's right, Maxwell Amoh on his left.*

# Appendix E: Using the Music of Ghana and Zimbabwe in the Classroom – A Sample Unit for Grades Seven Through Twelve

I.    **Collect a classroom library** with selections from the Annotated Bibliography

II.   **Reading requirement for the students**
   A. General books on African history, culture etc.(2)
   B. Books on musical themes (skim a few, read one well)
   C. Several folktales from collections

III.  **Instrument Construction** (One from A, or two from B)
   A. Mbira (directions in Joseph, Hunter, Waring, or Berliner); coconut drums (Hunter); slit log drum (Waring); Kora (Joseph); calabash shaker (Hunter); wooden xylophone (Waring or Hunter); talking drum or hourglass drum (Hunter).

   B. Gourd rattle, coconut rattle, basket rattle (Waring or Hunter); double or single clapperless gongs (gankogui) improvised from tin cans; wooden clappers (Waring, Hunter).

IV.   **Other Arts Projects**
   A. Mask Making: (carved wood, papier mache, plaster on gauze) with designs based on those found in books of African art (as in Glubock, Price, or Marshall).
       1. It is very possible to find a person involved with costume design for children's theater groups to come to a school to lead workshops in mask making.

   B. Carved wooden stools, following designs included in Schuman and Glubock, Price, and Marshall.

   C. Costumes using weaving, tie-dye, batik, and beadwork techniques as described in Schuman, Griswold and Starke, Kerina, and Korty, and using ideas from Glubock, museum catalogs, etc.

V.    **Games**
   A. Mankala (directions in Kerina, and Griswold and Starke) – African board game to make and play

   B. Rock passing, stick pounding and hand games (this book)

   C. Ampe (directions in Nelson)

VI.   **Folktales to use in dramatic renderings,** with a narrator and call-and-response songs, percussion and hand-clapping, and props (including costumes) from this book or
   A. Use tales from collections (Courlander, Fuja, Serwadda) or from individual books (Aardema, Dayrell, McDermott)

VII.  Food
    A.  Select, prepare in school or at home, and have a pot
    luck of typical foods as noted in Ayensu, Wilson, Cooper
    and Ratner, or international cookbooks in the pub. library

VIII.  **Songs and rhythm ensembles**
    A. From this book

    B. Drawn from **Bantu Choral Folksongs** (Folkways FW 6912);
    **African Songs and Rhythms for Children** (Amoaku- Folkways
    FC 78449) **Singing Games from Ghana** (Lowe); **Afro Ensemble**
    and **The Mandinka Balafon** (Jessup); **The Griot Sings** (Edet)

IX.  **Assembly Presentation** during a school-wide Ethnic Aware-
    ness week
    A. Songs to welcome and warm up audience
        1. "Sorida" (with participation)
        2. "Pɛtɛ Pɛtɛ" (audience claps, sings response)
        3. "Sansa Kroma" (audience sings phrase "Sansa
        Kroma", claps)
    B. One story with group participation
        1. e.g. "Zangaiwa Chakatanga Pano" (in this book)
    C. Percussion ensemble and singing with audience partici-
    pation limited to clapping
        1. "Chiro Chacho" or "Ɔkwan Tsen Tsen", etc.

    D. Class leads multipart song with audience participation
        1. "Wai Bamba", etc.

*Homemade instruments including slit box drum, **donno** (hourglass drum),
juice can hosho, dowel staves, tin can gong.*

# Glossary

| | |
|---|---|
| *abokyi* | *Akan--"sour" or out of step vocal part* |
| *adenkum* (ah-den-koom) | *Stamping tube;long hollow gourd with hole at top and bottom typically used by Ashanti women.* |
| *adinkra* | *Cloth stamped with symbols; worn in Ghana.* |
| *Akan* | *Largest ethnic group in Ghana, representing forty percent of the population, found primarily in southern half of country.* |
| *axatse* (ah-hot-say) | *Ghanaian dried gourd rattle with netting of seeds or shells strung around the outside; played by hitting with hand and/or on body.* |
| *beat* | *As used in Shona performance practice, the felt "beat" is not rhythmically regulative and can occur between the sounds of the basic rhythmic pattern or simultaneously with it; often played by* **hosho**. |
| *bosoɛ* (boh-soo-ay) | *Recreational highlife dance developed by Fanti youth in Ghana.* |
| *cantor* | *Lead singer in singing or drumming ensembles with a strong voice and thorough grasp of conventions of improvisation and song structures; functions as soloist, composer, conductor.* |
| *chaka* | *Shona term--"splashing" sound; used to describe buzzing or rattling produced by* **hosho**, *buzzers on* **mbira**, *leg rattles on dancers, etc.* |
| *Fanti* | *One of the ethnic groups of the Akan of Ghana; dialect of Akan language.* |
| *firikyiwa* (free-chee-wah) | *Ghanaian metal castanet played by striking bell portion with heavy metal ring.* |
| *gankogui* | *Clapperless iron double bell; used in Ghana to define time line in drumming ensembles.* |
| *garariya* | *Missionary influenced musical style from Zimbabwe.* |
| *Highlife* | *Contemporary Ghanaian pop music; blend of tradition-al rhythm patterns and singing syle with West-ern styles, and of traditional drums with guitars, bass guitar, trap-set and brasses; most often heard in cities, played by young people who adapt old tunes and sayings, place them in new settings.* |
| *hosho* | *Dried gourd rattle used in Zimbabwe; hollow inside, filled with seeds or pebbles.* |
| *kente* | *Tightly and intricately woven Ghanaian cloth, very ex-pensive, normally worn only on special occasions* |
| *kpanlogo* (pah-loh-goh) | *Highlife dance music played by Ga youth in Ghana.* |
| *kudaira* | *Improvised, embellished melodic lines which complement and weave through other sung parts of a Shona song.* |
| *proper* **kudaira** | *Fixed, fundamental, often skeletal part in Shona song which functions to define as well as complement the melody of the actual song.* |

| | |
|---|---|
| *kudu* | *Grayish animal similar to antelope with spiral horns.* |
| *kukaha* | *Rhythmic improvisation within a vocal part used by cantor or chorus in Shona songs.* |
| *kutema* | *Shona--"to cut"; often a middle range melody representing the core of a song as passed on through the generations.* |
| *kutengezana* | *Shona--"the sum of all the parts"* |
| *kutsinhira* | *Shona--"to cover with a second layer of sod"; to add a second, or additional, vocal part* |
| *makwa* | *Complex handclapping patterns used by Shona* |
| *marimba* | *Wooden xylophones of varying pitch and timbre with large resonators beneath each slab; common in common in southern parts of Africa.* |
| *mbira* | *Sounding board with several tuned tongues of metal or reed attached to top; plucked with thumbs and/or forefingers; important part of religious and recreational events in Zimbabwe; known also as **sansa,kalimba, likembe**.* |
| *mmoguo* | *Ghanaian folktale song* |
| *ngano* | *Shona stories about imagined events* |
| *nsɔɔdɛ* | *Akan--"sweet ears;" a singer who is thrown off by swirl of melodies, rhythms, movement.* |
| *ntama* | *Rectangular cloth worn by Ghanaian men and women who wrap it around their bodies in various ways.* |
| *nyaya* | *Shona stories about real people* |
| *pito* | *Ghanaian beer made from water and millet* |
| *recreational music* | *Not tied to any particular religious or ceremonial ritual.* |
| *Shona* | *Largest tribal group in Zimbabwe; 73% of population; also language group of principal occupants of Zimbabwe and Mozambique.* |
| *shangara* | *Shona dance during which participants stand in a circle and periodically move into the center in pairs, moving feet in complex patterns.* |
| *tsaba* | *Shona, a particular rhythm; also dance, beat* |
| *tsenzi* | *African animal similar to large rabbit with short legs; water and land dwelling; hunted as food.* |
| *vocables* | *Short sung syllables ("iye,""ha,""ho,""woye,"etc.) which have no meaning in present context.* |

# Annotated Bibliography

## GENERAL BACKGROUND AND HISTORY

Bernheim, Marc and Evelyne. **A Week in Aya's World: The Ivory Coast.** New York: Macmillan, 1969. Daily life of a first grade girl in West Africa.

--------. **From Bush to City: A Look at the New Africa.** New York: Harcourt Brace Jovanovich, 1966. Illus. with photos.

--------. **In Africa.** New York: Atheneum Publishers, 1973. The life of African children from the Savanna, forest, desert, coast and city.

--------. **The Drums Speak.** New York: Harcourt Brace Jovanovich, 1971. The story of Kofi, a West African boy. Outstanding color photos showing costumes, customs, daily life, changing traditions.

Coughlan, Robert. **Tropical Africa.** New York: Time Life Books 1970. Excellent photographs.

English, Peter. **South Africa in Pictures.** New York:Sterling Publisher, 1969.

Hopkinson, Tom. **South Africa.** Time Life Books, 1969.

Musgrove, Margaret. **Ashanti to Zulu.** New York: Dial Press, 1976. Illustrated accurately--wonderful drawings of villages, clothing, activities of twenty-six different tribal groups, arranged as an alphabet book. Illus. by Leo and Diane Dillon.

Perkins, Carol Morse and Marlin. **I Saw You from Afar.** New York: Atheneum Publishers, 1972. A photo visit to the Bushmen of the Kalahari Desert. Excellent.

Stein, Mini. **Majola, A Zulu Boy.** New York: Julian Messner, 1969. Good background but somewhat outdated.

Zemba, Lydia Verona. **Ghana in Pictures.** New York: Sterling Publishers, 1966.

## MUSIC, DANCE AND INSTRUMENTS

Amoaku, W.K. **African Songs and Rhythms for Children.** New York: Schott Music Corp., 1971. Orff-Schulwerk in the African Tradition. Transcriptions, percussion ensembles, photographs of instruments, invaluable for the specialist.

Bebey, Francis. **African Music: A People's Art.** Translated by Josephine Bennett. Westport: Lawrence Hill & Co., 1975. A warm, interesting and accessible overview of African music making. Many photos.

Berliner, Paul. **The Soul of Mbira.** Berkeley: University of California Press, 1981. Very readable, interesting, in-depth look at Shona music making, particularly mbira players.

Blacking, John. **Venda Children's Songs: A Study in Ethno-
musicological Analysis.** Johannesburg: Witwatersrand Univ.
Press,1967. Classic study.Tape from Univ. Wash.,Seattle.
-------. **How Musical is Man?** Seattle: Univ. of Wash.
Press,1973.
Chernoff, John Miller.**African Rhythm and African Sensibility.**
Chicago: University of Chicago Press, 1979. Outstanding
account of his relationship with his drumming teachers in
Africa. Many quotes of their conversations capture the
spirit with which an African musician approaches tradi-
tional music and instruments. Difficult in spots for jr.
high students.
Dietz, Betty Warner and Olatunji, Michael Babatunde. **Musical
Instruments of Africa.** New York: John Day Co., 1965. Best
introduction of instruments, musicians and dancers.
Chapt. on body percussion includes ideas to try out.
Edet, Edna Smith. **The Griot Sings.** Songs from the Black
World. New York: Medgar Evers Press,1978.(Dist. Folkways
Records). Children's songs, games, dances from Africa,
Haiti, Puerto Rico, America and the West Indies.
Egblewogbe, E.Y. **Games and Songs as Education Media.** A Case
Study Among the Ewes of Ghana. Accra:Ghana Publishing
Corp., 1975. The integration of music in daily life of
the Ewe people. Inc. song texts but no transcriptions.
Essuman, J.T. **Thirty Popular Akan Songs.** Complete with full
parts and words. Accra: Ghana Publishing Corp., 1974.
Composed or arranged by the author, in solfege, no
translation.
Gwangwa, Jonas and Miller, E. John, Jr. **The World of African
Song: Miriam Makeba.** Chicago: Quadrangle Books,1971.Par-
ticularly good for information on African song and in-
strumentation in general.
Haywood, Charles. **Folk Songs of the World.** NY:John Day Co.
Pages 239-386 contain African songs suitable upper elem+.
Jessup, Lynne. **Afro Ensemble.** Ft. Worth: Harris Music Pub.,
1975. Exc.introduction to drumming patterns in easily
used form.
-------.**The Mandinka Balafon.** An introduction with notation
for teaching. La Mesa, CA: Xylo Publications, 1985.
Clear, interesting, useful introduction, inc. tapes for
learning and listening, and how to adapt Orff inst.
Lowe, Mona. **Singing Games from Ghana.** Cerritos, CA: MM
Publishing, 1970. (Avail. dir.: 19603 Jacob, Cerritos,
CA.) Almost every song and game here can be used!
Mensah, A. A. **Folk Songs for Schools.** Accra: Ghana Publish-
ing Corp., 1971. Songs from Ghana and Tanzania, with
translation, notes, musical notation and some percussion.
Nketia, J.H. Kwabena. **African Music in Ghana.** Evanston:
Northwestern Univ. Press, 1963. In-depth view.

--------.Our Drums and Drummers. Accra:Ghana Publishing House, 1968. Written simply for children, good background.

--------.The Music of Africa. New York: WW Norton & Co,Inc. 1974. A classic. Detailed, scholarly but clearly written in interesting style, many photos and transcribed examples.

Price, Christine. Talking Drums of Africa. New York: Charles Scribner's Sons, 1973. Rhythmic text describes many types of African drums; drawings; how they are made.

--------.Dance on the Dusty Earth. New York: Charles Scribner's Sons, 1979. Comparative look at the traditional dances of many cultures.

Reck, David. Music of the Whole Earth. New York: Scribner's Sons, 1977. Unusual, imaginative, voluminous.

Robinson, Adjai. Singing Tales of Africa. New York: Charles Scribner's Sons, 1974. Seven tales with simple songs.

Seeger, Pete (ed./arranger).Choral Folksongs of the Bantu. For mixed voices. NY: G. Schirmer, Inc. 1960. Fifteen South African multipart songs with notes and English lyrics by Seeger. (See "Williams" entry below.)

Serwadda, Moses W.; transcriptions and intro. by Hewitt Pantaleoni. Songs and Stories from Uganda. New York: Thomas Y. Crowell,1974.(Out of print - now distributed by World Music Press.) Stories, story songs, movement songs from the Baganda tradition; easy to follow transcriptions by ethnomusicologist Hewitt Pantaleoni; companion tape of Serwadda and his daughter available from World Music Press(1986).

Standifer, James and Reeder, Barbara. Source Book of African and Afro-American Materials for Music Education. Reston: Music Educators National Conference, 1972. Inc. biblio. and discog., rhythm activities to try; comprehensive.

Titon, Jeff Todd, gen. editor. Worlds of Music. An Introduction to the Music of the World's Peoples. NY: Schirmer Books, 1984. Includes sections on "The Music-Culture as a World of Music" and "Africa/Ghana" as well as on other cultures. Companion tape available.

Warren, Fred, with Warren, Lee. The Music of Africa. An Introduction. Englewood Cliffs: Prentice-Hall, Inc., 1970. Clear, simply written intro. to various musical concepts as well as the idea of just how fully music is integrated into African life.

Warren, Lee. The Dance of Africa. Englewood Cliffs: Prentice-Hall, Inc.,1972. Exc. background material on integration of dance into African life; inc. dance and game instructions and photographs.

Williams, Rev. H.C.N., and Maselwa, J.N., eds. African Folksongs. Cape Town, So. Africa: St. Mathews College, 1947. Rare collection of South African multipart songs, including songs of the witchdoctor, worksongs, cradle

## INSTRUMENT CONSTRUCTION

Cline, Dallas. **How to Make and Play Nearly Everything.** New York: Oak Publications, 1972.

Hunter, Ilene and Judson, Marilyn. **Simple Folk Instruments to Make and Play.** New York: Simon and Schuster, 1977.

Joseph, Joan. **Folk Toys Around the World.** New York: Parent's Magazine Press, 1972.

Waring, Dennis. **Folk Instruments: Make Them and Play Them.** Winnipeg, Manitoba (Canada): Hyperion Press, Ltd., 1979. Excellent, detailed, the instruments sound good.

## CRAFTS, COOKING, ACTIVITIES, ART

Ayensu, Dinah Ameley. **The Art of West African Cooking.** New York: Doubleday & Co, Inc., 1972. Wonderful recipes, illustrated with informative drawings; author is daughter of Paramount Chief of Ga state (Ghana).

Feelings, Muriel. **Jambo Means Hello.** New York: Dial Press, 1974. Simple Swahili phrases.

--------.**Moja Means One: Swahili Counting Book.** New York: Dial Press, 1971.

Glubock, Shirley. **The Art of Africa.** New York: Harper & Row, Publishers, 1965. Outstanding design, large blow-ups of carefully selected objects; simple, informative text.

Kerina, Jane. **African Crafts.** New York: Lion Press, 1970. Many exciting projects, games, clothing etc.

Korty, Carol. **Plays from Africa.** New York:Charles Scribner's Sons, 1975. Folktales with ideas for acting, dancing, costumes, music.

Marshall, Anthony D. **Africa's Living Arts.** New York: Franklin Watts, 1970. Photos of wide range of functional art objects (clothes, personal ornaments, household goods); excellent writing.

Pine, Tillie S. **The Africans Knew.** New York: McGraw-Hill, 1967. How the people of Africa made and did things in their daily lives; with experiments and things to make.

Price, Christine. **Made in West Africa.** New York: E.P.Dutton & Co.,Inc., 1975. Photos and drawings of wood carvers, weavers, metal workers, sculptors at work; inspiring, fascinating text.

Schuman, Jo Miles. **Art from Many Hands.** Englewood Cliffs: Prentice-Hall, 1981. Excellent multicultural art projects for home and school; cloth, metal work, masks and sculpture in section on Africa.

Thompson, Robert Farris. **African Art in Motion.** Berkeley: University of Calif. Press, 1974.

Wilson, Ellen Gibson. **A West African Cookbook.** New York: M. Evans & Co., Inc., 1971. Customs and recipes.

Zaslavsky, Claudia. **Count on Your Fingers African Style.** New York: Thomas Y. Crowell, 1980. Traditional finger counting methods of the Maasai, Kamba and Taita of Kenya, Zulu of South Africa, the Mende of Sierra Leone. Detailed illus. by Jerry Pinkney.

## RECORDS (by title)

**African Dances and Games.**(S&R 2000) Ladzekpo brothers recording with booklet by Odette Blum. Descriptions, instructions, Labanotation, basic rhythm parts notated.

**African Heritage Dances.** Educational Activities, Inc., Freeport, NY (AR-36). The Ibo, Bela Kawe and Hallecord, in adapted but realistic form; clear directions; good accompaniment.Mary Joyce Strahlendorf, Sue Gwinner.

**African Mbira, The.** (Music of the Shona People of Rhodesia). Nonesuch Records (H-72043). Dumisani Maraire playing the **nyunga nyunga mbira** accompanied by hosho and vocals.

**African Songs and Rhythms for Children.** Folkways (FC7844). Companion to Amoaku book; makes book easier to use.

**African Story Songs.** University of Washington Press, Seattle, WA 98105. Dumisani Maraire tells the stories in English, sings the songs in English with a group of American students; suggestions for use, notes on back.

**Ba-Benzele Pygmies.** An Anthology of African Music. Barenreiter Musicaphone (BM 30L2303). A UNESCO collection of exciting songs, drumming and stories; unusual and wonderful vocal techniques.

**Bantu Choral Folk Songs.** Folkways (FW 6912). Detailed notes and transcriptions of South African songs arranged by Pete Seeger, most quite singable by high school groups.

**Chiro Chacho.** Minanzi Records (MB001). Dumisani Maraire with the Minanzi Marimba Ensemble. 45 rpm.

**Ghana Children at Play: Children's Songs and Games.** Folkways Records (FC 7853).

**Mbira Music of Rhodesia.** University of Washington Press (UWP 1001) (tape and booklet) Dumisani Maraire on mbira/vocals

**Olatunji: Drums of Passion.** Columbia (CS 8210). Michael Babatunde Olatunji and a Nigerian drumming and singing group; exciting music for group movement, percussion practice and call-and-response singing.

**Rhodesia I.** The African Music Society and International Library of African Music. Recorded by Hugh Tracey.

**Singing Games from Ghana.** MM Records (MM103) Mona Lowe, ed. and compiler. Companion to book.

**Soul of Mbira, The.** Traditions of the Shona People of Rhodesia. Nonesuch Records (H-72054). Variety of players.

**Spirit of Mbira.** Dumisani Maraire in live farewell concert, Seattle, WA 1982. (Prod. and dist. by D.Maraire).

**Talking Drums.** (Distributed by World Music Press) The Talking
  Drums West African ensemble, led by Abraham Kobina
  Adzinyah. Highlife and traditional drumming, singing,
  bamboo flutes.

## ARTICLES

Coplan, David. "Go to My Town, Cape Coast! The Social History
  of Ghanaian Highlife." **Eight Urban Music Cultures.** Bruno
  Nettl ed. Urbana: Univ. of Illinois Press, 1978.
  pp. 96–114.
Jones, A.M. "African Rhythm,"**Africa** 24 (No.1, 1954): pp.26–
  47.
Kauffman, Robert Allen. "Some Aspects of Aesthetics in the
  Shona Music of Rhodesia,"**Ethnomusicology** xiii (1969):
  pp. 507–511.
-------. "Multipart Relationships in Shona Vocal Music," in
  **Selected Reports in Ethnomusicology,** Vol. V: Studies in
  African Music (Los Angeles: University of California,
  1984), pp. 145–160.
New, Leon J. "The Person First, or the People First? A Third
  World Dilemma," **International Music Education Yearbook**
  (New York: Schott, ISME VI, 1979), pp. 38–41.
Nketia, J.H.Kwabena. "Drums, Dance and Song," **Atlantic,** April
  1959, pp. 69–72.
-------. "African Music,"AMSAC Newsletter,Vol. III, Supple-
  ment 19, 1961; reprinted in Skinner, Elliot P., ed.
  **Peoples and Cultures of Africa.** New York: Natural
  History Press (a div. of Doubleday & Co.,Inc.), 1973,
  pp.580–599.
-------. "New Perspectives in Music Education,"**International
  Music Education Yearbook** (New York: Schott,ISME V,1978),
  pp. 104–111.
-------. "African Traditions of Folklore," International
  **Music Education Yearbook** (New York: Schott, ISME VII,
  1980), pp. 157–164.
Omibiji, Mosunmola. "Folk Music and Dance in African
  Education,"**International Folk Music Council Yearbook** 4
  (1972), pp. 87–93.
Ringer, Alexander L. "Kodaly and Education: A Musicological
  Note," in Landis, Beth and Carder, Polly, **The Eclectic
  Curriculum in American Music Education: Contributions of
  Dalcroze, Kodaly, and Orff.** Reston: Music Educators
  National Conference, 1972, pp. 145–151.
Twerefoo, Gustav Oware. "Music Education with Mentally
  Retarded Children in Ghana,"**International Music Education
  Yearbook**(New York: Schott, ISME VI, 1979), pp. 65–73.

## DISSERTATIONS, THESES AND PAPERS

Aduonum, Kwasi. "A Compilation, Analysis, and Adaptation of Selected Ghanaian Folktale Songs for Use in the Elementary General Music Class." Ph.D. Dissertation, University of Michigan, 1980.

Adzinyah, Abraham Kobena. "Acquisition of Musical Knowledge by Traditional Musicians of the Akan Society." Master's Thesis, Wesleyan University (CT), 1978.

Asiama, Simeon D. "Abɔfoɔ: A Study of Akan Hunters' Music." Ph.D. Dissertation, Wesleyan University (CT), 1977.

**Becoming Human Through Music.** Reston, Music Educators National Conference, 1984. Papers from joint conference (MENC and Wesleyan Univ.(CT) GLSP) on perspectives of social anthropology in the teaching and learning of music.

Kauffman, Robert Allen. "Multipart Relationships in the Shona Music of Rhodesia." Ph.D. Music, Dissertation, UCLA, 1970.

Maraire, Abraham Dumisani. Untitled ms. on song structures in Shona music, 1967.

Tucker, Judith Cook. "Context and Meaning of 'Buee'--An Akan Recreational Song." Unpub. manuscript, 1981.

## FILMS

"'Dance Like A River:' Odadaa! Drumming and Dancing in the US" - A portrait of Odadaa!, a traditional drumming and dancing ensemble from Ghana in residence in the U.S., under the direction of master drummer Yacub Addy. The film shows the members at home, in rehearsal and in performance, and through interviews reveals why they are in the U.S. and their experiences here. For junior high and older. Well made, interesting. Dir. by Barry Dornfeld and Tom Rankin. Avail. from: Barry Dornfeld, 294 Huron Ave., Cambridge, MA 02138.

"Atumpan" - Documentary of construction and uses of the Atumpan drums. Mantle Hood, producer. UCLA, dist.

"Discovering the Music of Africa" - Bailey-Film Assoc. Made at UCLA. Good introduction for jr. - sr. high. Shows instruments, dancing, ensemble playing etc.

# Index

Adenkum: 92
Aduonum, Kwasi: 1,18,87
Akan: xi,106; map of Akan area of Ghana, xvii;
Akwanbo:13
Animals: in songs, 18,24,27; in stories,35,38,47
Asiama, Simeon: 54,68
Aural/oral teaching and learning: 102
Axatse:description,playing techniques 91-2

Bebey, Francis: 2,8
Berliner, Paul: 94
Bells: 8,90
Blacking, John: 3
Bosoɛ: bell pattern,77; song, 73-78; bands, 76

Call-and-response: in game songs, 8;patterns,97,98; principles of, 98;
    songs using,19,25,44,47
Cantor:2,78,97-99
Chaka: 91
Chants: 7
Chernoff, John Miller: 2,3
Chisana: 55
Clans: 68
Cooperation: in game playing, 15; in music making,3,54
Coordination: facilitated through games,7,8,10,96
Corrective songs: 8
Crafts: Ghanaian, xvi
Crops: Ghanaian, xvi; Zimbabwean, xviii
Crossrhythms: 8

"Deep Meaning:" 55, see "multiple levels of meaning"
Donkor, Freeman Kwadzo: 32
Drums: 36;and time line, 90in percussion ensembles, 95,96

Edet, Edna Smith: 12
Education: traditional education of children, 76-77
Essuman, John Tekyi: 60
Fanti: xvi,39,77,
Food: as topic in songs, 18, 21, 29,36,80; in stories,38,47
Functional integration of music: 2,
Funerals: singing at, 53,67, 68,71,72;participation in, 76

Game songs: 5-32
    introduction to,7;Akan: "Bantama Kra Kro,"20";Kye Kye
    Kule,"11;"Nsa Ni O,"30";Ɔboɔ Asi Me Nsa,"14;"Pɛtɛ Pɛtɛ,"26;
    "Sansa Kroma,"17;Shona:"Sorida,"9;"Vamuroyi Woye,"23;
    importance for African children,5,6,31; function of, 7,31;
    handgames,9,30; stick games,20;exercise/movement,11,17,26;
    stone passing,14,17,20,26; name game,30;
Gankogui: 90,95,96;106
Ghana: background info, xvi;  map of, xvii
Gongs: 90

Handclapping:  as accompaniment,19,25,47;techniques, 94;rhythm exercises,
95-96; patterns, 23
Harmony: 97; songs with,17,20,22;see "call-and-response,""multipart,"
   "improvisation"
Highlife: 77,78
Hosho: description, playing techniques 91-2

Idiophones: 92
Improvisation: 4, 57;instrumental,94; vocal,97,99
Industry: in Ghana, xvi; in Zimbabwe,xviii

Kauffman, Robert: 35,38, 53
Kente cloth: xvi,39,106
Kudaira: 100-101
Kudu: description, 47; story of, 46-50
Kukaha: 38,39
Kusandirika: 55
Kutema: 80,81,85,86,100
Kwanongoma College of Music: xix

Lead drummer: See also Master drummer; Master musician,
Lead singer:38,47,97; see also Cantor

Magavu: 80
Magic: music as, 38,47
Marimba:63, 107
Master Musician: 89
Mazembera: 79,80,81,86,100
Mbira: 81,102, xviii
Mmoguo: 35
Movement: in game songs, 12,19,29
Multicultural education:purpose of, 1,3; materials for, 1
Multipart: singing, 53-55,99,100; songs with layered repeating parts,
    56, 79, 81,82
Multiple levels of meaning: in songs, 54,69;in Shona conversation,55
    in game songs, 15
Musical bow: xix

Name game: "Vamuroyi Woye," 22-25
Narrator:35
Ngano: 35, 36, 38, 44
Nketia, J.Kwabena: 1,3,53,94,99
Nkrumah, Kwame: xvi
Ntama: 39,96
Nyaya: 35

Oral tradition: 7, 18,

Participation:  in African music-making, 2,3,88; in game songs,7; in story
songs, 35,44; in community life, 76
Percussion: ensembles, 66, 95, 96
Pito: xvi,53,
Process: of music making, 3
Proverbs:  in songs,7,54,55,72,77; as teaching tool,2,55;in Akan
    society,60; in Shona society, 55; as verbal shorthand, 68

Rawlings, Flight Lt. Jerry: xvi
Reck, David: 98
Recreational Songs:51-87
    introduction to,53;Akan:"Kyerɛm,"70;"Meda Wawa Ase,"58;
    "Ɔkwan Tsen Tsen,"73;"Wɔnfa Nyɛm,"64;Shona: "Chiro Chacho,"61;
    "Cho Kurima Woye,"79;"Vamudara,"82;"Wai Bamba,"56
Rock passing: see stone passing

Scouts: 21,22
Singing: in Africa, 53
Stick games: 22
Stamping tubes, bamboo: 22
Stone passing: 15,19,23,27
Story songs:33-50
    introduction to,35-36;Shona: "Chatigo Chinyi,"42;"Chawe Chidyo
    Chem'Chero,"46;"Zangaiwa Chakatanga Pano,"37
Storytelling: as education,xi,35; participation in,35;singing during, 38,47
    song interludes,36
Syncopation: ix

Timekeepers: 90;see rattles; hosho; axatse; bells;
Time line: 90
Totems: 68
Transcriptions:  in aural/oral  learning,  102;  difficulties with,ix
Tsenzi: description, 25; in song, 24

University of Ghana (Legon): xvii
Verbal shorthand:54,68
Weddings: music during,56,62,63
Xylophone: 63; see marimba
Zimbabwe: background info, xviii; map of, xix

# Is multicultural music exciting to you?

Copy this coupon to order additional copies of *Let Your Voice Be Heard! Songs from Ghana and Zimbabwe*–or any of these other unique and refreshing World Music Press publications:
*Yes! Please send me:*

Quantity:

_____*Let Your Voice Be Heard! Songs from Ghana and Zimbabwe,* by Abraham Kobena Adzinyah, Dumisani Maraire and Judith Cook Tucker, $14.95

_____*Let Your Voice Be Heard!* companion tape $8.50

_____*Songs and Stories from Uganda,* by W. Moses Serwadda, illustrated by Leo and Diane Dillon, Narrated by Moriah Vecchia, $17.95 Book (two-colors throughout) and tape set.

_____*Teaching Asian Musics in the Elementary and Secondary School,* by William Anderson (An intro. to the music of India and Indonesia), $7.95

_____*Teaching Asian Musics,* companion tape $6

_____*Teaching the Music of Six Different Cultures,* by Luvenia A. George, $14.95

_____*Step It Down,* by Bessie Jones and Bess Lomax Hawes, $10.95 (pbk)

$_____SUB-TOTAL + s/h = $_____TOTAL (Check or PO)

(Please add $1.50 s/h for first book or set; 50¢ for each additional book or set; CT residents add 7 1/2% sales tax.)

Name_____

Address_____

City_____ State    Zip_____

___*Please send me your current catalog!*

Send to: **World Music Press**, PO Box 2565, Danbury CT 06813   (203) 748-1131
**Multicultural Materials for Educators** - *our only focus*
[Or order from your favorite bookstore!]

(*Libraries:*Please order Let Your Voice Be Heard! from Quality Books, Inc)

# ACHIEVE
## COLLEGE SUCCESS

# Learn How in 20 Hours or Less

FOURTH EDITION, BRIEF

**RAYMOND GERSON**
Austin Community College

**UPBEAT** PRESS

ISBN 978-0-9841364-5-2

| | |
|---|---|
| *Revision Editor:* | Vera Steves |
| *Acquisitions Editor:* | Lorna Adams |
| *Cover Design:* | Adie Russell |
| *Cover Illustration:* | Jason Cring |
| *Page Layout and Design:* | Adie Russell |
| *Compositor:* | Cybermedia Services |

**Achieve College Success: Learn How in 20 Hours or Less, 4/e**

Printed in the United States of America

UPBEAT PRESS, LLC
info@upbeatpress.com
Toll Free: 888 583 0044
www.upbeatpress.com

# Table of Contents

# Meet the Author

During junior high and my first two years of high school, I was such a poor student that a counselor told my parents I was not capable of getting a college education. My parents waited until I earned my master's degree in psychology before telling me that a school counselor had said I wasn't college material. Today, I teach students how to succeed in college.

As a teenager, I felt lost, had no goals, did not believe in myself, and was in danger of dropping out of school. An illness in my senior year gave me a wake-up call, and I started getting more serious about my education. I really needed a book like this, but none was available. I wrote this book for you—to give you the gift I needed when I was in school. It is a blueprint for your success.

Helping you to overcome your obstacles, to believe in yourself, and to learn the skills necessary to succeed in college is my passion, because of what I had to overcome.

Eventually, I found out that I had my own special abilities, just as you do. This is my sixth book, and I have had a wonderful career that would not have been possible without a college education. I've been a career counselor, vocational rehabilitation counselor, owner of a job placement business, and training specialist. I came out of retirement to be an adjunct professor of career and college success courses.

Forty-five years of "real world" experience teaching success strategies, several years of classroom experience, and a passion for motivating and inspiring students all came together for me to write *Achieve College Success: Learn How in 20 Hours or Less*. I wrote this book to help you gain the knowledge and skills you will need to become successful in college, in your career, and in your life.

ACHIEVE COLLEGE SUCCESS

achievecollegesuccess.com

# Foreword

I met Raymond Gerson almost twenty years ago when he began teaching as an adjunct professor in the Human Development Department at Austin Community College. I remember being impressed even then by his enthusiasm for teaching and learning and his ability to inspire his students to levels of achievement beyond their expectations. At ACC, he teaches extended orientation courses for entering "at risk" students, learning strategies courses for college-level students, and career exploration and planning courses for students in academic transfer and workforce programs. In all of these courses, Raymond has connected with students in a personable, responsive way that generates very positive feedback, and some remarkable stories of transformative change in students' lives.

This book captures Raymond's energy, insights, and experience from a lifetime of guiding people to success in school, career, and life and makes them available to students in high schools and colleges everywhere. It is particularly powerful in its focus on the attitudes as well as the actions that can transform a student's performance to a new level of effectiveness.

Unfortunately, all too many students in high schools and colleges are never explicitly taught the essential knowledge, skills, attitudes, and behaviors that lead to success in learning. As educators we teach topics and courses in specific departments and disciplines, but not often enough that most important of lessons—how to learn. That is the intent of this book.

*Achieve College Success: Learn How in 20 Hours or Less* can help students clarify what is important to them and what they hope to accomplish in school and in life; give them some insight into their unique learning preferences and patterns and how they can make the most of them; introduce them to the most effective strategies for learning and performing on key educational tasks; and provide students guidance in how to take control of their time and attention so that the effort they put forth brings them the success they seek. The chapter on preparing for career success and making a positive difference connects students to the world beyond college and to the goal of all successful learning—the creation of a successful life.

Raymond's book is a fine contribution to that worthy goal and one that will bring benefits to students and teachers alike. Make the most of it!

—Tobin Quereau
*Professor, Human Development and*
*Assistant Department Chair for Behavioral Sciences*
*Austin Community College*

# Preface

## For the Student

*Achieve College Success…Learn How in 20 Hours or Less* is intended to help you become an excellent student and to prepare you to succeed in college.

Earl Nightingale, a leader in the field of Personal Development, once said that "Success is the progressive realization of a worthy goal or ideal." In other words, success happens when you are making progress toward worthwhile goals. By this definition, success for you, as a student, is to begin making progress in improving your learning and grades, and finding that reaching your academic goals is becoming much more likely.

I have seen first hand, in my courses, that when a student studies, understands, and applies the strategies in this book, grades on tests and papers quickly improve. The student also reports that grades start improving in other courses. Quick improvement does not mean a student gets something for nothing or that motivation and the will to study are not required to succeed in college. The ability to read well and taking the time to study are a must for college success. When you combine willingness to work and learning how to study, you will find success quickly comes your way. As you start getting better and better grades, you will find it fun and will look forward to working harder and smarter.

EARL
NIGHTENGALE
earlnightengale.com

## Write for Success

Self-reflection leads to self-knowledge. Self-knowledge results in better choices and actions, which leads to success. This is why self-knowledge is power.

One of the best ways to self-reflect is to keep and use a journal. Please purchase at least a spiral notebook, or better yet, a hardbound journal to use as you read this book. Keep a record of your thoughts, feelings, dreams, and goals. At the end of each chapter, there will also be a written assignment for your journal and several questions to answer. Writing out your thoughts will help you to know yourself better and be clear about what is important for you. It will provide you with many benefits.

## Features of the Book

❶ Pre-Course and Post-Course Assessment: In the beginning (after this Preface) and end of this book, there is a questionnaire for you to find out how much you know about the topics in this book. You will learn about your strengths and weaknesses as a student. It will allow you to measure your progress when you take it again at the end of this book.

**❷ Each chapter contains:**

↗ An introduction of the topic and the benefits you will gain from learning it

↗ Activities that you can do individually or with others to strengthen the lessons

↗ A journal assignment

↗ Student comments about the benefits of using the strategies in this book

↗ Author's note: this is a personal note from me about each chapter topic

↗ An inspiring article or paper written by one of my former students

↗ Goal for the week: this is a small goal you want to accomplish

↗ A summary of main points

↗ Questions to answer in your journal and/or to discuss with others

**❸ Supplementary website:** I have a website, which provides you with more study, success, and career strategies. It contains lots of free articles and several free gifts, including two of my career e-books. The website address is www.successforcollegestudents.com.

My other website is www.achievecollegesuccess.com. It contains a free online college success quiz for students.

ACHIEVE COLLEGE
SUCCESS

achievecollegesuccess.com

## For the Instructor
### COLLEGE SUCCESS STRATEGY COURSES MAKE A POSITIVE DIFFERENCE FOR STUDENTS

In the fall of 2005, I came out of retirement to begin teaching three part-time courses for the Austin Community College (ACC) in Austin, Texas. One course covers career exploration and planning. The other two courses—a twenty-hour, eight-week class and a forty-hour full semester class—teach students study skills and success strategies to help them succeed in college. Both "at-risk" and regular students take these courses.

Assessment studies by ACC for the two study skill courses indicated positive outcomes for students who successfully complete the courses when compared to similar students who have not taken these courses. Positive outcomes are indicated by fewer course withdrawals and greater retention the following semester. There was a slight improvement in grades in their other courses for the eight-week students and significant improvement for the full semester students when they successfully completed these courses. Students re-enrolled in subsequent semesters at much higher rates as well. The results seem to support the observations of mine and student anecdotes that report that improvement begins in less than eight weeks. Students continue improving when they find more time to learn and use these new skills. I chose the subtitle, *Learn How in 20 Hours or Less,* because students who use these success strategies begin showing progress in the eight-week, twenty-hour course.

When students begin learning more easily and their grades start improving, they experience a growing sense of accomplishment. They begin to build a "success mind-set" and "can-do" attitude, which increases their self-esteem and motivation. I'm often amazed at how quickly students improve when the ideas and strategies contained in this book are learned and applied.

Several professors, including myself, have used this book to teach courses to ninth grade students.

## How is This Book Different

**Twelve Reasons that** Achieve College Success **is unique and useful for everyone:**

1. Professor Gerson uses many inspirational stories from his own life to motivate students and reinforce the lessons.

2. Professor Gerson's conversational style makes students feel he is talking directly to them.

3. All the ideas and strategies in the book have been successfully class-tested with the author's students and with other teaching and counseling professionals.

4. Based on student and professional feedback, Achieve College Success, is updated frequently to ensure the text works well for students, instructors, and counselors, alike.

5. Practical and user-friendly language is used throughout the book to make reading easier for regular college, "at risk", and high school students who want to succeed in high school and college. However, there may be a couple of activities where students may need to use a dictionary.

6. Contains strong career development and exploration components.

7. Offers "writing good papers" tips.

8. Includes psychological and motivational tips on building a healthy, successful self-image, and character.

9. Each chapter features actual former student success stories designed to engage and inspire new students.

10. Professor Gerson pulls from his vast experience to offer easy-to-use techniques that motivate and inspire students to succeed.

11. Many of the general life success principles presented throughout the book are distilled from some of the best self-help books ever written.

12. Professor Gerson has written original articles in the book with a two-fold purpose: 1) as cooperative learning activities to teach students specific skills and, 2) to motivate and inspire students to develop a "success" mind-set from the first page to the end.

## Ways for Instructors and Counselors to Use this Book

This book can be used to teach either an eight-week, twenty-hour or a full semester course. In an eight-week course, the pace will be fast and you will cover one chapter a week. In a full semester course, you will have more time for class discussions and exercises, and will cover a chapter every two weeks. The chapters and the topics within each chapter can stand alone. They can also be used for short workshops. Counselors can use the book, or parts of it, to work individually with students or with small groups.

I designed the assessments and activities so that it would be possible for students who are not in school to do them individually. However, most students who use this book will be in school. All of the activities and assessments are intended to be used by instructors as cooperative learning activities for students in a class room setting.

## CHANGES TO THIS EDITION

1 This book is being used in both colleges and high schools.

2 New unemployment and education charts have been added to the Introduction.

3 The section on health tips has been moved from Chapter 2 to the end of Chapter 3.

4 Mind maps that visually feature key points have been added to the beginning of each chapter.

5 Online resource links have been added to the end of each chapter featuring scannable QR codes.

6 A new Goal Setting paper is now in Appendix A.

7 Chapter 7 now contains a section on using online resources and social media for job searches.

# Acknowledgments

I want to thank Mary Cervantez for helping me type part of the first draft. I would also like to thank Laura Tabor-Huerta for helping me with several of the graphs and charts. Thanks also to my friend Deb McCarthy for her constructive feedback.

My gratitude to Tobin Quereau who hired me to teach college success strategy courses at Austin Community College. Without the opportunity to teach these courses, this book could not have been written.

I owe special thanks to Lynn Skaggs, PhD, college professor of psychology, for making many helpful suggestions to improve the text.

Thank you to my lovely wife, Bonnie, for her support and understanding, while I spent endless hours at the computer writing this book.

Thanks to my former students who gave me permission to use their stories and comments throughout the book.

I deeply appreciate Lorna Adams, President, Upbeat Press, for publishing this book and for all of her assistance.

A big thank you to Vera Steves - for the wonderful work she did on the manuscript.

Thanks to Cheryl Spector, Director of First Year Experience, California State University, Northridge, for her suggestions which improved my annotation example and convinced me to add some longer student comments throughout the book.

I would like to thank Ross Oliver for helping me improve "How to Choose a College Major" and for the list of campus resources.

My appreciation to Christie Carr for creating and contributing information about online education. Her article, "Distance Learning/Distance Education" is a welcome addition to the Appendix of this book. Thank you to Melinda Townsel for her feedback on my information about using college libraries.

# Student Testimonials

**Comments from former students who have benefited from strategies in** Achieve College Success: Learn How in 20 Hours or Less.

"The most valuable part of this course was that it made me a better reader by giving me tips on how to understand a story. It also made me a better test taker and increased my self-esteem and positive thinking."
— JOSH SMITH

"This class helped me in three ways: how to take good notes and write well, setting goals that I achieved, and learning how to improve my memory and test-taking strategies."
— ROSEMARY MARIN

"I had not been to college for several years and was out of the loop. I decided to give this course a try. I have been able to successfully apply these ideas to my other courses. It gave me confidence. I would encourage anyone who is starting college for the first time or in a long time to learn these ideas and strategies."
— JAMES SANDERS

"This course improved my grades because I now look at test questions differently. I also know the best learning skills that fit me."
— JOSE ONTIVEROS

"I learned how to turn my dreams into goals and better time management. I learned that doing activities first because I like them isn't good for me unless the activities are important priorities."
— LYJAE JOHNS

"This course helped me to get a better understanding of my career and my life. I learned more about myself in this course than in any other course I have taken. This course has reassured me that I have a bright future."
— JOSEPH GONZALES

"The most valuable part of this class for me was getting the blueprint for a successful college experience. I wish I could have taken this class when I was younger, but I can honestly say that because of this class I am a better student, mother, wife, and friend."
— BETTY VILLAREAL

"I learned how to manage my time, my writing skills improved, and my study habits are so much better. This course has been an inspiration to me."
— DEVON KERR

# Comments by Educators

"This book captures Raymond's energy, insights and experience from a lifetime of guiding people to success in school, careers and life and makes them available to students in high schools and colleges everywhere."

— TOBIN QUEREAU, Professor of Human Development and Assistant Department Chair
for Behavioral Sciences, *Austin Community College*

"This is an excellent book that will prepare students for the transition from high school to college. Raymond's book will be the key to success for all students planning any type of post-secondary education. Therefore, I would like to see the book in the hands of every student before they graduate from high school because the book shows you how to achieve success in college, in your chosen career and in life. It is one book that students should keep and refer to throughout their lives."

— THOMAS S EVERSDYK, VAC Coordinator/Special Services,
*Oak Ridge High School and College Park High School, Conroe ISD*

"This is the third book I have used in my Transition to College Success courses. The book is a definite upgrade based on student performance and evaluations. It is a complete package for teaching students how to achieve student success."

— ROSS OLIVER, Professor of Human Development, *Austin Community College*

"I really like the book. It is well written, very approachable and packed with great ideas for student development."

— LYNN SKAGGS, PhD, Professor of Psychology, *Central Texas College*

"I loved the Power Points because they lessened my handouts and were easy to follow. Most of my students came to Austin Community College from high school special education classes this semester. They were concerned at first about whether the book and course would be too difficult. They were happy to discover that it was clear, they could do it, and they were successful. My students liked the book's personal style and were encouraged by Raymond Gerson's stories about overcoming his own obstacles."

— GLORIA "GLO' FOLEY, PhD, Counselor and Professor of Human Development,
*Austin Community College*

"I have pilot tested and plan to adopt Professor Gerson's book for my "Transition to College Success" course because of its simplicity and read-ability. It helps students stay focused on reading which is a major event and most important for college achievement. Many of my students are not proficient readers. This book helps to open their minds."

— BILL YOUNG, PhD, Professor of Human Development,
*Austin Community College*

# Pre-course Assessment

This questionnaire is not a test. It is an opportunity for you to find out what you know and don't know about the topics in this book. It will help you to see your strengths as a student and the areas in which you need improvement. At the end of the book, you will have an opportunity to repeat this questionnaire so you can measure your progress. Please be honest where you see yourself now.

Read the statements below and give yourself points for each one. Use the point system below, and then add up your total points for each of the eight topics. Then, add up all of your points for an overall total score.

↗ 5 Points    The statement is mostly or always true

↗ 4 points    The statement is often or frequently true

↗ 3 points    The statement is sometimes true

↗ 2 points    The statement is rarely true

↗ 1 point     The statement is never or almost never true

## PRE-ASSESSMENT

**❶ Goals**

A. __ I have clear goals for what I want to accomplish in life.

B. __ My goals are written down.

C. __ My goals have deadlines or dates for completion.

D. __ I have short, medium, and long-range goals.

E. __ I have goals for all major areas of my life: education/career, physical, mental, spiritual, financial, social, and family.

F. __ I practice visualizing my goals as if I have already achieved them.

Total _____

**❷ Learning Styles and Types of Intelligence**

A. __ I am familiar with different learning styles.

B. __ I know which is my preferred and best learning style.

C. __ I am familiar with theories of different types of intelligence.

**D.** __ I know my strongest types of intelligence and how to use them.

**E.** __ I know how to use my preferred learning style and types of intelligence to overcome my weaknesses.

**F.** __ I take good care of my body and my brain.

Total _____

**❸ Time Management**

**A.** __ I have a clear picture of how I spend my time.

**B.** __ I know several time management strategies and use them regularly.

**C.** __ I know how to prioritize, I make a daily list of my priorities, and do them most of the time.

**D.** __ I am able to get my class assignments done on time.

**E.** __ I use time management tools such as planners and calendars.

**F.** __ I know how to balance my activities so there is enough time for work, fun, school, and family.

Total _____

**❹ Reading and Studying**

**A.** __ I know and use reading and study systems.

**B.** __ I know how to create and use study aids.

**C.** __ I break my study periods into small chunks.

**D.** __ I know and use annotation while reading.

**E.** __ I am skilled in the art of using questions to be engaged with what I am reading.

**F.** __ I know and use strategies before, during, and after reading my textbooks.

Total _____

**❺ Note-Taking and Writing**

**A.** __ I use a note-taking system.

**B.** __ I regularly take notes in my classes and when I read textbooks. I review and study my notes shortly after taking them and before tests.

**C.** __ I use a writing system, and I know how to write good papers.

**D.** __ I know the Cornell Note System and how to use it.

**E.** __ I know what a thesis statement is and how to use it.

**F.** __ I ask and use journalistic questions before I write my essays.

Total _____

❻ Memory Strategies and Test-Taking
   A. __ I know and use several techniques for improving my memory.
   B. __ I create memory aids to prepare for tests.
   C. __ I know how to use my preferred learning style to aid my memory.
   D. __ I know and use several strategies to reduce test anxiety.
   E. __ I know several strategies for taking objective and essay tests.
   F. __ I predict questions that may be on the tests and create practice quizzes to take before the actual exam.

Total _____

❼ Career Development
   A. __ I have identified and know my strongest values, skills, and interests.
   B. __ I know my strongest personal traits.
   C. __ I know how to research occupations.
   D. __ I am familiar with Holland's six personality types and work environments.
   E. __ I have identified needs and problems in the world, which I would like to help with or solve.
   F. __ I know how to pick majors in college or jobs that would be a good match for me.

Total _____

❽ Create the Life You Want
   A. __ I know my purpose and mission in life.
   B. __ I know and use many success principles and strategies.
   C. __ I am improving myself and my character on a regular basis.
   D. __ I understand why my thoughts are powerful and how to use positive self-talk.
   E. __ I know ways to create the life I want and how to make a positive difference.
   F. __ I understand the importance of my self-image and how to improve it.

Total _____

## Overall Total Score _____

# Campus Resources

Use your campus resources, which are usually free and can help you to have a successful college experience. Counselors can also help you to identify appropriate campus resources to meet your needs. (**Instructors—Please go over these and any additional appropriate resources for you campus.**)

Here are a few campus resources:

↗ **Academic advisors.** They are usually found in counseling offices and centers. Advisors can help you in choosing courses for your major. They help you to meet degree requirements and can provide information about which courses will transfer to other colleges and universities.

↗ **Admissions.** This is where you can go to add or drop a course or get a copy of your transcript.

↗ **Career counseling.** Your campus will probably have either a career center or counseling offices where you can go for career guidance. They can help you to: assess your skills and interests, take career tests, find matching careers, and provide assistance in determining your major.

↗ **Computer center or lab.** The campus computer center provides you with computer access. Staff are usually available to help you with computer-related questions or problems. You can use computers to complete: class assignments, email, print documents, access the Internet, and other uses.

↗ **Counseling.** Counselors can provide you with short-term personal counseling and guidance. They can also refer you to appropriate agencies if you or your family members need crisis management.

↗ **Disability services.** You can get accommodations if you need help with learning disabilities or other mental and physical barriers.

↗ **Employment services.** Some colleges offer job placement assistance and help find work on campus.

↗ **Financial aid office.** You can get information about financial aid and scholarships.

↗ **Health center.** You can get services for health problems, medication, and shots. Health centers are usually not available on community college campuses.

↗ **Housing.** On-campus housing is provided for residential colleges. Residential housing is not provided at most community colleges.

↗ **Library.** Your campus library has databases you can trust for writing your research papers. Often the reference librarian can guide you to the many library resources you may need.

↗ **Policy and procedure manual.** Most colleges have these available for free. This helps you to become familiar with campus policies and grading procedures.

↗ **Security.** You can go to campus police if you see a suspicious person on campus, have an on-campus car accident, or lock your keys in your car.

↗ **Student center.** Provides information about clubs and organizations where you can meet other students who have similar interests.

↗ **Testing center.** You can take make-up tests here. Students who are referred by the Office for Students with Disabilities and need extra time on tests can take their tests in the testing center.

↗ **Tutoring services and learning labs.** Tutors can help you with courses in which you face  Tutors are often found in learning centers and computer labs.

# Introduction

❶ Why are you going to school?

❷ What do you want to get from your education?

❸ What dreams do you have that a good education can help you achieve?

Only you can answer these questions. By answering these questions, you will discover a purpose and goal to give you direction in your life. When you find a clear and strong purpose, you will have the motivation and determination to work hard to achieve your goals.

The purpose of a good education is to bring out your best self so you can use your full ability. A good education will give you the knowledge and skills to open doors to a better career so you can make more money. For example, data collected by the U.S. Department of Commerce

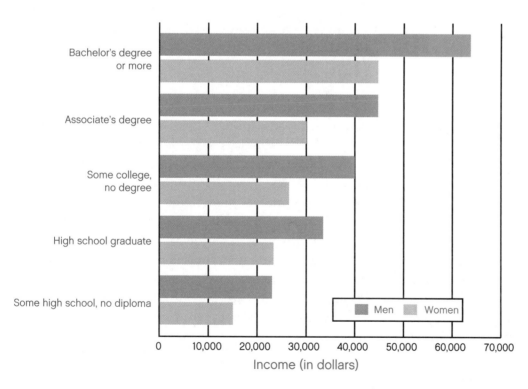

Median annual income of persons with income 25 years old and over, by gender and highest level of education, 2009

**FIGURE 1A**   MORE EDUCATION IS LIKELY TO RESULT IN MORE INCOME

*Source:*  U.S. Census Bureau, from "Income, Poverty, and Health Insurance Coverage in the United States, 2009," *Current Population Reports, Series* pp 60-238, 9/2010.

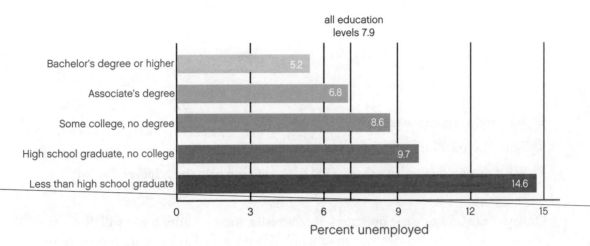

FIGURE 1B    MORE EDUCATION IS LIKELY TO MEAN
MORE CONSISTENT EMPLOYMENT

*Source:* From U.S. Department of Labor, Bureau of Labor Statics, Office of Employment and
Unemployment Statistics, "Current Population Survey," 5/2010.

and the U.S. Department of Labor indicates that more education is likely to result in higher
income and less unemployment. If you are a high school graduate, you will most likely earn more
than a high school dropout. If you are a college graduate, you will likely make more money than
a high school graduate. See Figures 1A and 1B.

## Blueprint For Success

Achieve College Success: Learn How in 20 Hours or Less will help you get more from
your education because it gives you a blueprint for success. You will learn better ways to learn
and study, how to manage your time better, how to discover a great career, how to achieve
your goals, ways to take great notes, how to make better grades on tests, how to memorize, and
other tools for success. Not only will you learn how to succeed in school, but you will learn
new attitudes, work habits, ideas, and strategies for succeeding in your career and life.

Your success in school, career, and life depends less on you having a high IQ and more on
you developing good study habits and the will to succeed. The actions you take today will determine your future. Your habits and actions will determine what kind of student and person you
become and what your life will be like in the years ahead. No matter what your past experience
in school has been, you can start succeeding now! Look at your education as a great opportunity
to learn and grow. Few people in the world get the opportunity for a good education. You can
make it an exciting journey to the life you want.

Before your life is over, make sure to sing your special song (use your special talents and
abilities) and make your mark. Your education can be a path to becoming your best self, to a
rewarding career and life, and to making a positive difference in the world.

Now let's get started making the most of your education so you can begin traveling the
road to your dreams.

## CHAPTER 1

# How to Turn Your Dreams into Goals and Achieve Success

Why is this book starting with a discussion about goals? Because when you have goals and see the relationship between them and your education, you will be motivated to do well in school. A good education will also help you to accomplish many of your goals. Without goals, it will be difficult to see how your education can be applied to your life. Having goals will help you to understand the value of a good education.

## Turning Dreams into Goals Can Make Your Dreams Come True

1. What are your dreams?
2. Do you have dreams for your life?
3. Do you want a college education?
4. Do you want a great marriage someday?
5. Would you like a new home of your own?
6. Do you desire to have a successful and fulfilling life?

Great accomplishments begin with a dream or vision. "Nothing happens but first a dream," said Carl Sandburg. You will experience success when you turn your dreams into measurable goals and back your desire for these goals with the right actions. Henry David Thoreau spoke of this type of success when he said, "If one advances confidently in the direction of his dreams

Goals provide purpose
and direction

⬍

Set a
completion date

⬌

Set Goals
for education, career,
physical, mental,
spiritual, financial,
family, and social

⬌

Identify small
steps to take

⬍

Set short, medium,
and long-term goals

*"Good thoughts are no better than good dreams, unless they be executed."*
— Ralph Waldo Emerson

and endeavors to live the life which he has imagined, he will meet with a success unexpected in common hours."

Keep moving toward your life dreams and they will happen unexpectedly during the most ordinary times. For example, you may be washing your clothes when a phone call comes to offer you a great job that you interviewed for a couple of weeks ago. You might be watching TV when a letter is delivered, letting you know that your magazine article has been accepted for publication only. You have already put in the hard work, but the results often come when you least expect them or in ways you did not think would happen.

## Answer These Questions to Get What You Want

❶ Ask yourself: "What do I really want?"

_____

❷ Then ask yourself: "Do my actions and habits support my goals and values?"

_____

To help you answer the questions above, let's look at the following example:
Let's say you want to become an excellent student.
Do you study enough to support the goal of becoming an excellent student?

One of my students was watching TV forty hours a week, but only studying two to three hours a week. She said her main goal was to do well in college, but her school work was not getting done, so she dropped out. Her actions did not support her desire to succeed in college.

What can you do when you see that your habits are not supporting your goals? You can keep changing your actions until they start getting you what you want, or at least until they are moving you in the right direction. My student, who was watching forty hours of TV a week, could have made a different choice, if she realized what she was doing would not take her where she wanted to go. She could have studied more and watched less TV. It is good for you to have dreams, but they must be turned into goals that are backed up by your actions.

Goals are what you aim to reach or achieve. Having an end date in mind provides you with an added reason to make them more than just dreams.

Later in this chapter, we will work on goal setting—how to set and accomplish your goals. It is okay to change your goals. When you achieve them, you can set new ones. Goals give direction and purpose to your life.

## Benefits of Goal Setting

↗ Gives you a sense of direction and purpose
↗ Helps you stay motivated
↗ Provides a way for you to measure your progress
↗ Builds your self-confidence and sense of self-worth
↗ Increases self-responsibility
↗ Helps you determine actions needed to support your goals
↗ Provides you with a sense of accomplishment
↗ Makes your priorities clear
↗ Provides you with a roadmap for good planning
↗ Guides your decision-making
↗ Increases your ability to get the life you want

## Set Goals for Great Accomplishments

You can set short-term goals for one year or less, intermediate or mid-range goals from over one year up to five years, and long-term goals for over five years. For example, if you are a senior in high school, a short-term educational goal could be to graduate in one year. A short-term goal could also be to make an A on your next test. You might even have a goal to graduate from college in four years with a bachelor's degree, which would be an intermediate goal. A goal to receive your master's degree in six or seven years would be an example of a long-term goal.

Form a habit of breaking all of your goals into small steps or small short-term goals. For example, let's say you need to complete a particular course to reach your goal of graduating from high school or college. You can break this down by having a goal to earn a specific grade on each of the tests and papers that are required in this particular course.

Big goals and tasks may seem scary, but almost anything can be achieved in small steps.

The Japanese word *kaizen* means small steps for continued improvement. Any large goal or project can be broken into small steps, which can lead you to achieving the goal. Slow and steady often wins the race.

According to Robert Mauer, author of *One Small Step Can Change Your Life*, taking small steps helps you to bypass fears that often arise when you are facing big changes. A huge task does not seem too big when you break it down into small steps. Fear and anxiety limit your ability to think clearly and to be creative. When you take small steps to your large goals, you remain relaxed, confident, and think more clearly.

Here is an example from my life of how small steps often lead to big gains. I started weight lifting when I was eighteen years old. In the beginning, I weighed 120 pounds and could only bench press 75 pounds. Two of my weights were a quarter of a pound each. I would tell myself every couple of weeks that I should be able to add these small weights totaling just a half a pound to the barbell. I continued adding them to the barbell a half pound at a time. In a few years, I was able to bench press 300 pounds at a body weight of 145 pounds. This is an example of using small steps, like a ladder, to accomplish a big goal. I kept increasing the weight by a small amount and, in a few years, was lifting 225 pounds more than when I began weight lifting. It is amazing what can be accomplished with little steps. This approach can be used to achieve any type of goal you wish to pursue.

> ## Student Comment
>
> "When I arrived on campus I was lost and afraid of the challenge. I was losing integrity, courage, dependability and self-awareness. This course and book were like a hand being stretched out for me to reach and to guide me. Now I will always keep improving and building the blocks to accomplish my goals."
> —RUBEN RODRIQUEZ

You can decide what you want in life, whether it is a great relationship, education, career, or any other goal. Begin taking small steps toward your goal until you achieve it!

## Building a Successful and Fulfilling Life

There are eight major categories or parts of life in which you should consider setting goals so that your life will be balanced, successful, and rewarding. These categories are: education, career, financial, family, social, physical, mental, and spiritual. If you do not relate to the word "spiritual," you can think of personal development goals to strengthen your character, ethics, and virtues.

## 1. EDUCATIONAL GOALS

Your educational goals can be varied. For example, you might be setting a short-term goal like getting a paper in on time or making a minimum of a "B" in a course. An intermediate goal might be to get an associates degree in two years. Whereas, earning a master's degree in six years would be a long-term goal.

ACTIVITY 1.1 Brainstorm several possibilities (write them down as fast as they come into your mind) and then write three education goals below that you would like to accomplish.

A. _____

_____

_____

B. _____

_____

_____

C. _____

_____

_____

## 2. CAREER GOALS

Your career goals include any goals that prepare you for your professional career. If you are in school now, look at it as your most important job. The education you are getting now is your path to your "dream job."

The average person will spend over eighty thousand hours of his or her life working. Most people spend more time working each day than they do sleeping, socializing, or doing anything else. A big chunk of your life will be spent working. It is important to enjoy the work you do because how you feel about your career will affect every other part of your life. For example, if you are stressed and unhappy at work, it can hurt your physical and mental health, relationships, and overall quality of life. If you enjoy your career, it can have a positive influence on all of the other areas of your life.

Examples of career goals you might consider, while you are in school, could be courses you want to complete, volunteer or internship opportunities, skills you wish to acquire, your college major and specific careers of interest, extra-curricular activities, and leadership development opportunities. These are just a few examples to consider, but you will want to decide on your own goals.

After you begin your professional career, you can continue to set goals for getting additional skills, for promotions, and for other desired career achievements.

A good education can open the doors of opportunity into a career you love and do well.

Now you will brainstorm about your career goals.

ACTIVITY 1.2 Brainstorm several possibilities and then write three career goals below that you would like to accomplish.

A. _____

_____

_____

B. _____

_____

_____

C. _____

_____

_____

## 3. FINANCIAL GOALS

How much money will you need to be happy? This is worth thinking about now because earnings can vary a lot from one career to another. Some people need more money to be happy and others need less.

Certainly you want enough money to meet your needs so that you are not under financial stress. Financial problems can have a negative influence on other areas of life such as your health, relationships, career satisfaction, and quality of life.

Set short-range (1 year or less), mid-range (1-5 years), and long-range (over 5 years) financial goals. For example, you can set a short-term goal to save 10% of your income from each paycheck. Then, you can set a longer-range goal to buy a house or earn a certain amount of income two years after you graduate from college.

Even if you have very little money now, you can start creating good habits such as saving a little money and avoiding credit card debt. These habits will help you build a mind-set for being in control of your finances instead of money controlling you.

ACTIVITY 1.3 Brainstorm several possibilities and then write three financial goals below that you would like to accomplish.

A. _____

_____

_____

B. _____

_____

_____

C. _____

_____

_____

## 4. FAMILY GOALS

For most people, family relationships are important. There are usually only a few people in anyone's life that will be there when the chips are down. If you maintain good relationships with your family members, they will often be some of your best friends for life. Therefore, it is worth investing some time and energy to keep good family relationships.

You can set goals for the type of relationships you want to build and keep with your family and then schedule the time to do it. One of my busiest students set a goal to spend a half day helping her mom do some shopping for clothes to prepare for her mother and father's wedding anniversary. She said she and her mom had a special time together and will have many great memories.

You do not know how long your loved ones will be on this earth, so now is the time to love and appreciate the important people in your life.

ACTIVITY 1.4 Brainstorm several possibilities and then write three family goals below that you would like to accomplish.

A. _____

_____

_____

B. _____

_____

_____

C. _____

_____

_____

## 5. SOCIAL GOALS

You can set goals for the types of social relationships that you want to have. Social goals include friends, recreation, and fun. All of us need time to recharge our batteries and have fun with others. Good friendships are important and can add quality to your life.

Set goals for the type of social relationships you want to build and schedule the time to do it in your calendar.

Research studies have shown that social relationships are important for physical and mental health. The reverse is also true. People who are isolated, cut off, and without friends, usually have more major illnesses and die earlier than people with strong personal relationships.

ACTIVITY 1.5 Brainstorm several possibilities and then write three social goals below that you would like to accomplish.

A. _____

_____

_____

B. _____

_____

_____

C. _____

_____

_____

## 6. PHYSICAL GOALS

You need your physical body to function efficiently in this world. It is worth taking care of because it is the only body you will have in this life.

Once a student of mine told me that she did not take time to exercise or to eat well. She said, since she has only one body, which is temporary, her approach to life was "Eat, drink, and be merry for tomorrow you may die." She thought that taking care of her body was a waste of time. I asked her, "If you knew that you had to keep your car running for life because it could not be replaced, wouldn't you take excellent care of it?" She replied, "Yes, that makes sense." I said, "You only have this one body for the rest of your life, so doesn't it make sense to take good care of it?" She said, "Yes" and began taking better care of herself.

Our habits tend to go on autopilot and follow us for life. They are easier to change when you are young, than in later years. Bad habits can be replaced with good ones. Your day-to-day habits have a growing effect over time. Positive habits bring positive results and negative habits bring negative results.

Small positive habits done on a regular basis can pay off big over enough time. For example, walking a mile a day might seem like a small habit, but in one year you will have walked 365 miles; in ten years, you will have walked 3,650 miles. Imagine the benefits to your heart and lungs after ten years of walking just one mile a day! On the other hand, let's say you drink one can of soda a day. This gives you about ten teaspoons of sugar a day. What effect will this have on your weight and long-term health compared to a healthy habit like walking?

Your habits may seem small, but they can have big effects. Habits can follow you through life and are usually difficult to break. Doesn't it make sense to replace your negative habits with positive habits? You can use small positive habits to maintain excellent health, achieve your dreams, and live a fulfilling life.

You can set short- and long-range physical goals. For example, let's say you want to lose thirty pounds. That's a big goal that will usually take some time. However, you can set short-term goals along the way. For example, you decide to lose an average of two pounds a week. This small, short-range goal supports your big (long-term) goal of losing thirty pounds. Other physical long-term goals can involve exercise or changes you want to make to your diet.

You could set a short-term goal to run, swim, or walk a certain number of miles each week. There are many goals that can be set to have the body and energy that you want.

ACTIVITY 1.6 Brainstorm several possibilities and then write three physical goals below that you would like to accomplish.

A. _____

_____

_____

B. _____

_____

_____

C. _____
_____
_____

## 7. MENTAL GOALS

Each of us has a mind, and you can keep it sharp by using it effectively. Your mental development goals can include improving your mental performance, deciding what you would like to learn, gaining greater psychological or mental health, and more self-control. For example, you might set goals to increase your vocabulary and sharpen your mind by playing crossword puzzles, or increase your power of concentration by using mental exercises.

Many athletes practice visualization exercises to prepare for athletic events. A golfer may picture putting the ball in the hole or a diver might visualize making a perfect dive over and over.

Many years ago Dr. Maxwell Maltz, author of a groundbreaking book called, *Psychocybernetics,* discovered that an imagined experience can greatly improve one's performance. In one study, three groups of people with a basketball shot free throws to determine their baseline scores. One group just practiced shooting free throws, another group pictured themselves shooting free throws, and the third group did nothing. Once again, the three groups shot free throws. The group that did nothing did not improve. The group that shot free throws improved by 24%; the group that practiced visualization improved by 23%. Those who practiced in their minds did about as well as those who actually practiced with the basketball. Today, many athletes use mental imagery to improve their performance in sports. You can also use mental imagery to improve your performance in school and to help you accomplish other goals.

Another way to improve your mental development is to increase your self-awareness and self-knowledge. One way to do this is to keep a journal. Observe your emotional reactions, thoughts, and feelings throughout the day. Jot down your observations in your journal before you go to sleep at night, then review over time. This practice will increase both your awareness of yourself and others and keep your mind sharp.

ACTIVITY 1.7 Brainstorm several possibilities and then write three mental development goals below you would like to accomplish.

A. _____
_____
_____

B. _____
_____
_____

C. _____
_____
_____

KEEP A JOURNAL

wikihow.com/keep-a-journal

## 8. SPIRITUAL GOALS

People will choose different paths for their spiritual growth or for developing their character and virtues, but the result should be more peace of mind and inner strength. Spiritual or character development will help you to maintain your mental balance when you face difficulties, obstacles, and even tragedies.

According to a national study of 112,232 college students by Higher Education Research Institute at U.C.L.A., four out of five first-year students are interested in spirituality. Many students said that they were on a spiritual quest. Goals can be set for doing any spiritual or character-building practice that works for you.

Most of us have heard of people who seem to have everything the world has to offer and yet, they are depressed, suicidal, drug addicts, or alcoholics. They may be famous, physically attractive, wealthy, and super successful, but still they feel empty inside and unhappy. The missing part of them seems to be an inner quality, which can provide a sense of meaning and purpose.

Examples of spiritual or character traits (inner qualities) could be peace of mind, patience, compassion, integrity, more love for others, etc.

> ### Student Comment
> "I can't believe I have accomplished so much in this short period of time. I laughed when I was told to take this class and thought it would teach me nothing. I became more intelligent about myself and now I know how to make my goals come true."
> — SUJIN LEE

ACTIVITY 1.8 Brainstorm several possibilities and then write three spiritual or personal development goals that you would like to accomplish.

A. _____

_____

_____

B. _____

_____

_____

C. _____

_____

_____

All eight major categories that were discussed affect each other. Sometimes one or more of these seven goal areas takes priority and requires extra time and attention. This is natural. However, if you totally ignore any of these major parts of your life, you will probably feel that something is missing or that your life is out of balance. If you need to focus more on a given area of your life at certain times, it is still wise to give some attention to all eight areas.

## Additional Tips for Setting Goals

To accomplish anything important, you will need to know where you are going. A person without goals is like a ship without a destination. The ship may never leave the harbor and if it does, there is no telling where it will end up. Do you want to leave the outcome of your life to chance? If not, it is important to steer the course of your life's direction by setting clearly-defined goals. For a successful program, your goals need to be specific, time-controlled (start and end dates), your own (not goals someone else wants for you), and written down. Writing down your goals helps you to make them clear in your mind; it helps you feel committed to achieving them. Your goals need to be in harmony with your values and with each other. It is also important to consider the following questions:

1. Can I work on these goals on a daily basis?

2. Are my goals morally sound?

3. What obstacles must I overcome?

4. What solutions and plan of action will I use?

5. What knowledge and skills will be needed?

6. Are my goals big enough to create a sense of challenge? (It is helpful to set big goals, if they are realistic).

7. What benefits will I gain by reaching my goals?

8. Did I include some goals which will help others?

9. Can I commit myself to start and complete this project?

10. Are my goals believable and achievable?

## Identify One Goal For Each of the Eight Categories To Start Working on Now

The purpose of the brainstorming and goal setting exercise was to help you come up with several goals, and to begin thinking about what you want. After going over your list of goals, you may find that some are unrealistic or unimportant to you. You may wish to add goals, redo others, and make some of them more specific. You are now ready to set one goal and a plan of action in each category so that you can begin working on them now.

For now, please concentrate on writing down just one goal (short-term, intermediate, or long-term) under each of the following eight categories. These may be chosen from the goals you brainstormed, but they do not have to be. Later, you can continue to add and revise goals. Think of your goal setting program as a work in progress.

By setting goals for the following areas, you will be improving yourself as a person and your life will take on a sense of purpose.

## My Goals

1. Education:                                          Date of completion:

   Plan of action:

2. Career:                                             Date of completion:

   Plan of action:

3. Financial:                                          Date of completion:

   Plan of action:

4. Family:                                             Date of completion:

   Plan of action:

5. Social:                                             Date of completion:

   Plan of action:

6. Physical:                                           Date of completion:

   Plan of action:

7. Mental:                                             Date of completion:

   Plan of action:

8. Spiritual or character:                             Date of completion:

   Plan of action:

You should have at least one goal in each category. Remember the question, "Do my actions support my goals?" Now you will have a way of answering this question and staying on track. Break your goals down into small steps and keep marching forward until you accomplish them.

## Managing Your Money for Success

How well do you manage your money? This will be one of the keys to your success in the future. It will be difficult to feel successful if you are in debt.

The way to successfully manage your money and save is by keeping your expenses less than your income. In other words, don't live beyond your means. You can keep track of your income and expenses by using a monthly budget. A budget is simply an itemized estimate of your monthly income and expenses.

*Student Comment*

"This class benefited me in learning and applying study skills. It also made me look at my goals and my life."
— LYNN CARPENTER

### HERE ARE A FEW TIPS:

↗ Spend less than you earn

↗ Do not carry a credit card balance (pay it off each month)

↗ Pay yourself first. Set aside and save at least 10% of your income

↗ Focus on your most important budget items first

↗ Look at your spending patterns. What would you change?

## FINANCIAL GOAL ACTIVITY

Fill in the monthly budget work sheet, then brainstorm ways you can earn more and/or spend less so that you will be able to save a minimum of 10% of your income.

| MONTHLY BUDGET WORKSHEET | | | |
|---|---|---|---|
| **Monthly Income** | **Amount Earned** | **Monthly Expenses** | **Amount Spent** |
| Your paycheck | $ | Rent or house note | $ |
| Bonuses or tips | $ | Food | $ |
| Student loans | $ | Tuition | $ |
| Grants | $ | Books | $ |
| Scholarships | $ | School supplies | $ |
| Money from family | $ | Transportation | $ |
| Other | $ | Utilities | $ |
| — | — | Personal needs | $ |
| — | — | Credit card payments | $ |
| — | — | Insurance | $ |
| — | — | Health care | $ |
| — | — | Entertainment | $ |
| — | — | Other expenses | $ |
| **Total $** | — | **Total $** | — |

AMOUNT SAVED FOR THE MONTH: $_____

## JOURNAL ASSIGNMENT

Identify a short-term that you can accomplish in one week or less. This can be a complete goal in itself or it can be a step toward a long-term goal. An example of a short-term goal in the career/education category could be to make a specific grade (which you determine) on an upcoming test or, if procrastination is a problem, to turn in a paper on time.

You can also set a short-term goal, which is part of a larger goal. For example, let's say you want to lose thirty-six pounds in twelve months which is a big goal. You would need to lose an average of three pounds a month to achieve your goal. You might set a short-term goal to lose one pound a week.

After you set your short-term goal, identify the obstacles to overcome and the specific steps you will take to accomplish the goal.

At the end of the week, write at least one page in your journal explaining what your goal was, whether you achieved it, the obstacles you overcame, the steps or plan of action you used, and what you learned from this activity that can be applied to school and your life.

## AUTHOR'S NOTE

One of the main reasons that I was not a good student in junior high and my early high school years was that I had no goals. Without goals I did not understand the reason I needed a good education and I lacked motivation. As I began setting goals, I started realizing how education could help me to get what I wanted. My schoolwork took on a new meaning and purpose.

Most students become discouraged at some time or another. The following is an article I wrote to give hope to students who are discouraged now or who may be in the future. It was also written to inspire all students, whether they are discouraged or full of hope.

## Hope for Discouraged Students

Are you a discouraged student?

Do you think that teachers or other students see you as dumb and a failure? What others say or think about you is not as important as how you feel about yourself. Don't let others define or label you. Find your own limits and discover from experience what you are capable of accomplishing. Discover your own abilities.

There are many different types of intelligence. Everyone has their own special talents and types of intelligence. For example, some have a gift for music, teaching, counseling, writing, sports, comedy, etc. These require different types of intelligence. Also, your intelligence is not fixed at birth. You can continue to increase your intelligence throughout your life in spite of obstacles.

Read the biographies of great men and women and you will see that many of them were once labeled by others as unintelligent or mediocre. Winston Churchill failed the sixth grade and his teachers thought he was not smart. Helen Keller was born deaf and blind. She was unable to speak until she was taught to do so by Anne Sullivan. Most people had no faith in her ability to accomplish anything of importance. As an adult, Helen Keller gave inspirational talks to audiences all over the world. It is not the hand that we are dealt that determines whether we win the game, but it is how we play the game that counts. Helen Keller was born with a difficult hand but came out a winner. Some people are born with a good hand and lose the game by wasting their lives.

There are many other examples of intelligent people who were considered unintelligent by others. When Albert Einstein and Thomas Edison were in elementary school, their parents were told their children were not smart. Abraham Lincoln was demoted from being an officer in the military to the rank of private because he was considered incompetent. Even though some people considered Churchill, Keller, Einstein, Edison, and Lincoln to be unintelligent, they proved to be intelligent and made important contributions to others.

It is difficult to predict what others will accomplish in their lives. Who can predict what you are capable of achieving, if you work hard in school and are determined to succeed? Success in school depends more on skill and will than a high IQ. Good study skills, combined with the motivation to succeed, can take you a long way in school and life. Will or motivation must come from within you. Study skills can be developed. Study skill courses are usually offered at high schools, early college programs, community colleges, and universities. Many of these courses contain success strategies, which can be used to achieve your goals not only in school, but in your life. I could have used these types of success courses when I was in school to build my self-confidence and learn how to study.

In middle school and during my early years of high school, I experienced self-doubts, insecurity, and a lack of self-confidence. Like you, I also felt discouraged. When I compared myself to others, they seemed smarter, more popular, and superior in many ways. I had no goals and I did not understand how my classes were relevant to my life and future. Needless to say, my

### Student Comment

"I used to stop short of my goals if I thought I could not get them done. Now I finish everything I do. I did what the book says and learned that when you take small steps you can get anything done. I realize now that I want to become a baseball coach and there is no way anyone can take that from me."
— PABLO PENA

grades were poor to average. IQ tests indicated that I was of average intelligence and this is how I perceived myself.

My parents were concerned about my poor performance in school and they spoke to a high school counselor about me. He told them not to encourage me to go to college. He said that I was not capable of succeeding in college and that I would probably perform at a below average level at anything I did throughout my life. Fortunately, my parents did not tell me this story at that time, which I probably would have used as an excuse to quit school. I did not find out what this counselor said about me until I graduated from college with a master's degree and an A average.

I thought about quitting school many times when I was a teenager. And, I am so thankful that I continued my education in spite of obstacles and periods of discouragement.

Over time and through my life experiences, I discovered that I had talents, and I began to develop my strengths. I discovered that I was capable of making a positive contribution to others through inspirational writing, public speaking, coaching, counseling, and teaching. I love my work. It gives me much joy and a deep sense of purpose.

Do not give up on yourself. You were born for a purpose. Search within yourself. Discover your own special abilities and how you want to use them to make a positive difference.

## A Success Story

The following paper was written by James Sanders, a former student of mine. As a young man, he had goals and a vision of the life he wanted to create for himself. He lost sight of his goals, got in with the wrong crowd, and lost his way. After much suffering, James refocused, created new goals, and returned to college. Here is his inspiring story.

### To the Brink and Back

#### By James Sanders

After graduation from high school, I lost control of myself, forgot what was important, and gave up on my personal goals. I was the kid who thought he knew it all and had all the time in the world to find or complete what was missing somewhere along the way.

During my last year of high school, I got in with several different crowds, but regretfully, I followed the kids who were doing nothing with their lives and I went right into the party scene.

I had been a leader who others respected and followed. It's hard to remember why I chose to follow the party crowd, but I suppose I was on a journey of rebellion. I became party central myself and my accomplishments were few and far between. Living a life of drugs and late nights turned into years and I got swallowed up by darkness.

Exhausted from what seemed to be years of hell, I knew it was time to make a change. It would not be easy because I had no job, no place to live, lost my right to drive, had no money, and had lost touch with my family members.

I decided to set small goals and use what was in front of me. I needed a job and took one tending bar so I could earn some cash fast. My survival depended on it. I supplied free drink tickets to my party friends in exchange for places to stay at night. This allowed me to save money quickly, which was part of my plan. I was taking one small step at a time and in a few months I had saved enough to get my own place.

Still faced with the party crowd and scene, I decided to get an apartment close to restaurants within walking distance. This would get me away from the night clubs.

I took a job as a bar tender in an upscale restaurant. My coworkers started having a positive affect on me because they were not only working, but they were going to college and trying to make something of themselves.

Money was tight, so I got a sober roommate, who was in college, to cut expenses and he was a positive influence. I then cut ties with some of the losers and bad influences. As painful as it was to watch those I loved stay chained to drugs and alcohol, I could not have felt better about looking out for myself.

In the years that followed, I reconnected with my brother, mom, and dad for the first time since high school. I also returned to college and felt really good about myself. I am grateful for the skills and lessons. I learned so much about people, saw the difference between good and evil, and gained self-respect. Today, I feel self-worth, see life through multiple perspectives, and above all else, have a clear path to a great future.

## SUMMARY OF MAIN POINTS IN CHAPTER 1

↗ Goals are dreams with a plan and an end date.

↗ Goals provide a direction for your life, self-motivation, and purpose.

↗ Set short-term and long-term goals in eight major categories: education, career, financial, family, social, physical, mental, and spiritual.

↗ Break goals into small steps.

For examples of a student Pre-Course Assessment and Goal paper see Appendix A, page 132.

## QUESTIONS TO ANSWER IN YOUR JOURNAL AND DISCUSS WITH OTHERS

↗ What is the value of turning my dreams into goals?

↗ Which of the eight major categories of goals needs more of my attention right now and why?

↗ What is an example of one tiny step that I can take in the direction of my most important goal?

↗ What are three examples of goals that I have already achieved in my life and what did I learn from these accomplishments?

In the next chapter, you will be learning about your favorite styles of learning and in what ways you are already smart. By knowing and using your strongest learning styles and types of intelligence, you can become successful. You will also learn a few ways to take excellent care of your body and mind to stay healthy and function at your best.

JOE'S GOALS
Free goal-tracking tool

joesgoals.com

GOAL SETTING
Tips and articles

success77.com

## CHAPTER 2

# How to Use Learning Styles and Types of Intelligences to Perform at Your Best

There is great news regarding learning styles and intelligence. People have different styles of learning, which influences how they learn best. When you identify and understand your preferred learning style(s), you will learn more easily. You will be able to use your favorite learning style to make up for the ones which are not as natural. You will also be able to use your less preferred learning styles when needed. This knowledge will help you, even when one of your instructors teaches in a style that is different from the one you prefer to use.

Not only are there different learning styles, but there are also different types of intelligence. People are smart in different ways. Everyone is not the same. This chapter will help you to identify and more easily use your best types of intelligence. As you will learn in this chapter, an IQ test is not the only measure of intelligence, but instead, it indicates two particular types of intelligence, mathematical and linguistic.

Your intelligences is not fixed at birth. You can actually increase your intelligence throughout your life.

When you become aware of your preferred learning style or styles and your strongest types of intelligence, your self-confidence will grow, and school will become easier and more enjoyable. Now let's take a look at some additional benefits you will gain from this knowledge.

Visual, auditory, and kinesthetic learning styles

Careers to match different intelligences

Study Strategies to match different learning styles and intelligences

Successful Intelligence by Sternberg

Learning Styles and Intelligence

Emotional Intelligence by Goleman

Exercise and eat well for good health

Gardner's Eight Multiple Intelligences

Don't smoke; get enough sleep for good health

*"Having intelligence is not as important as knowing when to use it, just as having a hoe is not as important as knowing when to plant."* —Chinese Proverb

## Benefits of Knowing and Using Your Preferred Learning Style and Types of Intelligences

↗ Allows you to be your best and most natural self

↗ Increases your ability to learn

↗ Increases your self-confidence

↗ Shows you how to overcome your weaknesses

↗ Makes learning easier and more enjoyable

↗ Helps you to not only succeed in school, but also in your career and life

↗ Gives you an edge over your competition

↗ Helps you to learn more easily from instructors who use teaching styles that are different from your preferred learning styles

↗ Improves your self-image

ACTIVITY 2.1 Now you will have an opportunity to take an assessment to determine your preferred learning style or styles.

Your Name _____

## LEARNING STYLE QUESTIONNAIRE

Circle either A, B, or C for each of the 15 statements according to your top choice or preference.

**1** **I learn best when I:**

   A.  Picture the lesson in my mind.

   B.  Listen to the lecture.

   C.  Go on a class field trip.

**2** **I enjoy it most when I:**

   A.  Use charts, maps, and pictures to help me remember a lesson.

   B.  Receive a verbal explanation.

   C.  Move around the room while learning.

**3** **It helps me when an instructor:**

   A.  Shows me a DVD or PowerPoint presentation.

   B.  Explains and discusses the lesson.

   C.  Gives a hands-on demonstration.

**4** **I remember best by:**

   A.  Reading instructions.

   B.  Hearing and discussing instructions.

   C.  Trying out and practicing the instructions.

**5** **I am best at:**

   A.  Turning words into pictures.

   B.  Turning pictures into words.

   C.  Role-playing with words and ideas.

**6** **I am best at:**

   A.  Putting puzzles together.

   B.  Explaining my ideas.

   C.  Working with my hands to make and fix things.

**7** **I learn best when I:**

   A.  Write things down so I can see it.

   B.  Teach a lesson to others.

   C.  Am in a lab where I can learn hands-on.

**8** **When I take a test:**

   A.  I can see answers from the textbook in my mind.

   B.  I hear answers in my mind.

   C.  It helps to trace answers with my finger.

**9**  **I would rather learn a lesson** by:

   A.  Reading the book.

   B.  Listening to the book on tape.

   C.  Participating in a skit.

**10**  **I like teaching others by:**

   A.  Showing them pictures and then explaining the information.

   B.  Explaining and discussing the information.

   C.  Acting out the ideas.

**11**  **I learn to spell best by:**

   A.  Seeing the words over and over in my mind.

   B.  Saying the words over and over in my mind.

   C.  Tracing the words with my fingers and saying the words while moving around.

**12**  **I like to:**

   A.  See the teacher's facial expressions while hearing a lecture.

   B.  Hear stories and examples while learning.

   C.  Fidget while hearing a lecture.

**13**  **When a friend gives me directions, I prefer** to:

   A.  Receive them by e-mail with a map.

   B.  Hear an explanation of the directions over the phone.

   C.  Be taken there and shown the way by my friend ahead of time.

**14**  **I prefer a teacher who uses:**

   A.  Slides.

   B.  Discussions.

   C.  Demonstrations.

**15**  **You purchased a new computer and before setting it up, you prefer to:**

   A.  Look at the pictures in the manual.

   B.  Get verbal instructions from a friend who has the same computer.

   C.  Try to put it together first on your own.

*Source:* Questions developed by Raymond Gerson based on many theories of sensory learning styles.

Scoring: Add up your choices for each letter and write your totals on the lines below:

Total A's circled _____ Visual

Total B's circled _____ Auditory

Total C's circled _____ Kinesthetic

Determine the differences between your highest and other two scores. If the difference is three points or more, your highest score represents your primary or main learning preference. If the differences are two points or less, you probably have more than one dominant learning preference. Some people do not strongly favor one over the others and use two or even all three learning models equally well.

No questionnaire is totally reliable in determining your preferred learning style. If you think this assessment was inaccurate, then use your best judgment to decide which is your preferred dominant learning style—after you read an explanation of three learning models in the next section.

## Sensory Learning Styles

Learning styles are preferred ways of learning. They are how you prefer to take in and process information.

There are many different learning styles. In this section, we will be looking at three learning styles which rely on different senses. The three primary sensory learning models are: visual (eyes or seeing), auditory (ears or hearing), and kinesthetic (hands or touch). Some schools of thought identify four sensory learning styles by dividing the visual learning style into two segments: a preference for pictures and a preference for seeing and writing words.

**Visual learners prefer and learn best by seeing.** They learn best by turning words into pictures and by seeing visual presentations. Visual learners prefer slides, videos, DVDs, movies, charts, maps, graphs, diagrams, and lots of handouts.

**Auditory learners prefer and learn through listening.** They learn best through class discussions, lectures, teaching others, books on tapes or CDs, and from reading lessons from the book out loud.

**Kinesthetic learners prefer and learn best by hands-on opportunities and demonstrations.** For example, a chart or diagram of how to fix something may not make sense or appeal to kinesthetic learners until they first try fixing it with their hands. It is difficult for kinesthetic learners to sit still and listen to lectures because they like to move around.

## All Three Learning Styles Are Important

Even though most people prefer one learning style over the others, it is of great value to be able to use all three when needed. You can also use your strongest learning style to excel and make up for your less developed styles.

Try to find ways to use your preferred style as much as possible. While reading a textbook, if you are a visual learner, you can draw pictures to give meaning to the words. If you're an auditory learner, you can read out loud and discuss the lessons with others. If you're a kinesthetic learner, you can read while moving about or create a skit and act it out to make the lesson come alive and be understood.

The following section will provide you with additional information about the three sensory styles of learning.

## Tips to Effectively Use Visual, Auditory, and Kinesthetic Learning Styles

1. VISUAL

   - ↗ Use images: photos, colors, maps, charts, and graphs
   - ↗ Use DVDs, radios, and films
   - ↗ Create mind or idea maps (these will be explained in Chapter 4) and time-line charts as study aids
   - ↗ Highlight, circle, and underline the text and your notes
   - ↗ Read the text before lectures
   - ↗ Create your own symbols and drawings to illustrate key points
   - ↗ Create study cards to learn terms and definitions
   - ↗ Ask your instructors to use more visuals
   - ↗ Color code to organize notes

2. AUDITORY

   - ↗ Read the text out loud
   - ↗ Tape lectures and listen to audios
   - ↗ Participate in study groups to reinforce lessons
   - ↗ Sit where you can easily hear the lecture
   - ↗ Avoid studying with disturbing noises in background
   - ↗ Talk problems through
   - ↗ Teach yourself lessons in your own words out loud
   - ↗ Use jingles and rhymes to memorize information

3. KINESTHETIC

   - ↗ Read the text and your notes while walking around the room
   - ↗ Trace words with your index finger or with a 3 by 5 card while reading
   - ↗ Study for short periods followed by brief exercise breaks
   - ↗ Take courses which have labs and field trips
   - ↗ Study with others
   - ↗ Get your hands on what you are learning
   - ↗ Participate in role playing exercises
   - ↗ Use study cards while moving around
   - ↗ Use a computer to rewrite your notes
   - ↗ Read and highlight to create movement and hands-on activity

## Discover Your Strongest Types of Intelligences

Our schools value IQ tests, which measure linguistic and logical-mathematical intelligence. Students who are gifted with numerical and reasoning ability and who are good with words and language usually do well in school because much of the learning requires these skills.

"So why are multiple intelligences important?"

**Multiple Intelligences** are eight different ways to demonstrate intellectual ability. The theory of Multiple Intelligences was presented by Howard Gardner in his book, *Frames of Mind: The Theory of Multiple Intelligences.*

Dr. Gardner believes that it is important for schools and teachers to recognize and teach in a way that will benefit you by presenting lessons in a variety of ways, if you are gifted with other forms of intelligence.

A student who might be considered to be an underachiever can shine when teachers use a variety of teaching methods such as music, games, role plays, self-reflection exercises, and creative cooperative group activities. For example, a student might have the potential to become an excellent musician, artist, carpenter, or business owner.

So, it is valuable for you to develop and use many of the eight types of intelligences, but you will usually be strongest in one to three of them.

Here are Dr. Gardner's eight Multiple Intelligences with brief descriptions of each:

1. **Verbal** – Ability to use written and spoken language to express oneself and communicate well. Excellent with words.

2. **Logical-Mathematical** – Ability to detect patterns and think logically. Problem solving and reasoning ability in math and science. Excellent with numbers.

3. **Visual-Spatial** – Ability to create images and understand spatial relationships. This is not limited to visual sight, but is seen within the mind's eye. Excellent with pictures, graphs, and charts.

4. **Bodily-Kinesthetic** – Ability to use the body with skill. Ability to use one's mind to control bodily movements such as with athletes and dancers. Excellent control of one's body.

5. **Interpersonal** – Ability to understand other's feelings and intentions. Ability to relate well to others. Often referred to as "people skills." Excellent with people.

6. **Intrapersonal** – Ability to be self-aware and to understand one's own feelings, thoughts, goals, and actions. Excellent self-knowledge.

7. **Musical** – Ability to understand and create musical sounds and recognize musical patterns. Excellent with music, sound, and rhythm.

8. **Naturalistic** – Attraction to and understanding of nature and the environment. Attuned to and excellent understanding of nature.

### Multiple Intelligences Questionnaire

Rate yourself on the following questionnaire. Check the statements that you strongly agree with. Remember that no questionnaire is totally accurate. You can also get a feel for which Multiple Intelligences are your strongest by reviewing the descriptions and doing some self-reflection.

*Student Comment*

"The main benefit of this chapter for me was understanding that even though you may struggle in classes it doesn't mean you are 'dumb.' Learning other methods of intelligence and learning styles can make anybody a genius."

— DUSTIN HALL

## VERBAL-LINGUISTIC

1. ___ When I share a story from my life, it flows with ease.
2. ___ I love to read.
3. ___ I enjoy writing.
4. ___ It is easy for me to remember poems and quotations.
5. ___ I can easily persuade others or sell them something.
6. ___ I remember a lot of what I read or hear.
7. ___ I express myself well.

___ Total

## LOGICAL-MATHEMATICAL

1. ___ Adding, subtracting, multiplying, and dividing are easy for me.
2. ___ I can add up numbers fast without using a calculator.
3. ___ Puzzles are fun and easy for me.
4. ___ I am good at problem solving and enjoy math and science.
5. ___ It is easy for me to remember telephone numbers.
6. ___ I like to investigate things to understand how they work.
7. ___ I prefer making decisions based on logic instead of feelings.

___ Total

## BODILY-KINESTHETIC

1. ___ Dancing comes easy, and I am good at it.
2. ___ I am good at sports.
3. ___ I am well coordinated.
4. ___ It is difficult for me to sit still in class, and I fidget a lot.
5. ___ I learn best by doing instead of by watching or hearing.
6. ___ When I study, I like to get up often and move around.
7. ___ Scary rides at a carnival and dare devil challenges appeal to me.

___ Total

## VISUAL-SPATIAL

1. ___ I easily understand maps, charts, graphs, and pictures.
2. ___ If I go somewhere once, I can always find my way back.
3. ___ I can easily picture images in my mind.
4. ___ I like drawing and doodling.
5. ___ I prefer a map instead of written directions.
6. ___ I easily turn words into pictures.
7. ___ When I explain something to someone, I like to draw them a picture.

___ Total

## INTERPERSONAL

❶ ___ I am very social and relate easily to people.

❷ ___ I am sensitive to how and what people are feeling.

❸ ___ I like to share and teach others something I just learned.

❹ ___ People feel comfortable telling me their personal troubles.

❺ ___ I can easily make people feel comfortable and at ease.

❻ ___ I really like helping others.

❼ ___ I like listening to other people tell their life story.

___Total

## INTRAPERSONAL

❶ ___ I need time alone to self-reflect.

❷ ___ I am in touch with my feelings.

❸ ___ I like keeping a journal or diary of my thoughts and feelings.

❹ ___ Spending time alone recharges and energizes me.

❺ ___ I have goals and know what I want.

❻ ___ I am a deep thinker and think often about what is important to me.

❼ ___ Self-improvement is very important to me.

___Total

## MUSICAL

❶ ___ I learned to play a musical instrument without difficulty.

❷ ___ I like to sing and often have a song in my mind.

❸ ___ Music is a very important part of my life.

❹ ___ I have excellent rhythm.

❺ ___ If I hear a song once, I remember much of it.

❻ ___ I like to study with music in the background.

❼ ___ I listen to a lot of music each week.

___Total

## NATURALISTIC

❶ ___ The environment is very important to me.

❷ ___ I love being outdoors and in nature.

❸ ___ I have special feelings for plants and animals.

❹ ___ I like being outside as much as possible.

❺ ___ I can recognize different types of plants and trees.

❻ ___ I believe strongly in recycling.

❼ ___ Environmental pollution and issues concern me, and I take an interest in them.

___Total

---

*Source:* Developed by Raymond Gerson. Based on Howard Gardner's *Frames of Mind: The Theory of Multiple Intelligences.* New York. Harper Collins, 1993.

Name your three strongest intelligences in order of preference below.

1. _____

2. _____

3. _____

Using your multiple intelligence results, you can identify your best study strategies.

## Study Strategies for Each Type of Intelligence

Linguistic
1. Read the textbook and write down main points in your own words.
2. Teach what you are learning to others.
3. Rewrite class notes.

Logical-Mathematical
1. Create an outline of the text and organize information into a logical sequence.
2. Create practice quizzes with problems that may be on the test and solve them.
3. View and treat class projects like a scientific experiment.

Visual-Spatial
1. Create graphs, charts, and pictures.
2. Create pictures to show relationships between concepts and ideas.
3. Review your class notes and draw pictures to remember the words and ideas.

Bodily-Kinesthetic
1. Pace and move around when you read.
2. Turn a lesson into a skit.
3. Take short exercise breaks when studying.

Interpersonal
1. Study with and listen to others.
2. Teach the lessons to others.
3. Write papers that contain stories about people.

Intrapersonal
1. Keep a journal reflecting your thoughts.
2. Make some time to study alone.
3. Set many small goals for what you want to achieve in your classes.

Musical
1. Memorize by putting words to jingles and music.
2. Play soft music in the background while you study.
3. Listen to pleasant music to relax before going to take exams.

Naturalistic
1. Study outside when possible.
2. When studying inside, surround yourself with pictures of nature or with natural plants.
3. Take breaks from studying and walk around outside.

## Some Career Examples that Match Types of Intelligence

| | |
|---|---|
| Linguistic | Teachers, writers, and lawyers. |
| Logical-Mathematical | Scientists, engineers, and computer programmers. |
| Visual-Spatial | Artists, architects, and inventors. |
| Bodily-Kinesthetic | Dancers, athletes, and firefighters. |
| Interpersonal | Counselors, salespersons, and nurses. |
| Intrapersonal | Writers, psychologists, and inventors. |
| Musical | Singers, composers, and musicians. |
| Naturalistic | Environmental scientists, gardeners, and geologists. |

## Successful Intelligence to Achieve Your Goals

Robert Sternberg, a psychologist and professor at Yale University uses the term, "Successful Intelligence" to identify the type of intelligence needed to accomplish goals. In his book, *Successful Intelligence: How Practical and Creative Intelligence Determine Success in Life,* Sternberg explains the three parts of successful intelligence. It consists of the following three abilities:

1. **Analytical thinking** is needed to analyze and evaluate information. It plays a big role in school success.

2. **Creative thinking** has to do with the ability to come up with new ideas or different ways to solve problems.

3. **Practical thinking** involves putting the first two into action. It helps you to get from where you are to where you want to go.

Let's say you are trying to decide if a part-time job would be right for you.

Begin by brainstorming and determine several job possibilities that you would enjoy and do well. This process uses your creative thinking skills.

Then, use your analytical thinking ability to evaluate and weigh job options to decide which one is your best choice.

Finally, when you take action by contacting employers and scheduling job interviews, you are using your practical thinking process to get the job you want.

Sternberg was an underachiever in school and did poorly on standardized tests until a fourth grade teacher recognized his ability and potential. He began to believe in himself and became a successful leader in the field of psychology. His work provides further evidence

*Student Comment*

"Now when I study I know and use the learning style that works best for me."
— MONICA ACOSTA

that IQ and standardized tests measure analytical and recall ability, but this ability alone does not necessarily result in success in a career or in relationships.

I have a friend who did not do well in college and dropped out after his first year. He had learning disabilities and ADHD, but only discovered this years later. Unfortunately, he did not get the right type of support because his learning disabilities were not identified at the time. However, he had strong creative and practical intelligence, and today he makes over one million dollars a year with his own Internet business.

Remember to use all three: analytical, creative, and practical thinking, which makes up Successful Intelligence, and this will help you to achieve success in school, career, and life.

> *Student Comment*
> "When you know what kind of learner you are it helps you to pinpoint exactly how to learn in better ways. After taking the self-evaluations I found out that my learning type was kinesthetic. This means I learn more from hands-on activities than I do from listening to a lecture. The stuff I learned from taking this course will help me make better decisions, know myself better, use better learning strategies, and much more."
> — KATE ELLIS

ACTIVITY 2.2 Use your creative thinking to brainstorm five ways (below) that you can use to be more successful in school:

1. _____

2. _____

3. _____

4. _____

5. _____

**Analyze** the five ways you listed and decide on the best choice for you. Use your **practical thinking** to take action and use the method you selected to improve a grade on an upcoming test.

## Emotional Intelligence can Increase Your Success

Daniel Goleman wrote a groundbreaking book called, *Emotional Intelligence: Why It Can Matter More Than IQ*. Goleman discussed a form of intelligence in the book which he referred to as Emotional Intelligence (EI). EI is the ability to know, use, and manage your emotions.

A person with high Emotional Intelligence tends to be more successful in life than someone with low emotional intelligence, even if his or her IQ score is average. There have been people with high IQ scores who did not do well in their careers because of low EI.

## Daniel Goleman's Five Components or Parts of EI

**Self-awareness** – Ability to understand your emotions and their effect on others. It also includes your ability to identify and monitor your emotions.

**Self-regulation** – Ability to control your impulse to act before thinking.

**Motivation** – Ability to pursue your goals and work for reasons that go beyond external rewards such as money and recognition.

**Empathy** – Ability to put yourself in another person's shoes and to understand what they are feeling.

**Social skills** – Ability for you to relate well to others and manage relationships effectively.

---

*Source:* Goleman, Daniel. *Emotional Intelligence: Why It Can Matter More Than IQ*. Bantam, 1997, p. 43–44.

Emotional Intelligence is especially important in today's workforce because of the need for teamwork among different types of people. Many projects are done in teams today, and it is important for you to be able to work well with many different types of people. EI is also very important for you if you want to become a manager or leader.

The good news about EI is that you can develop and increase it. By using many of the strategies in this book, you will automatically increase your Emotional Intelligence. You can purposely develop your self-awareness, ability to manage yourself, awareness of others, and your ability to relate to others.

## JOURNAL ASSIGNMENT

Think about your educational journey up to this time in your life. Recall a time in elementary, middle school, high school, or college in which you used one of the types of intelligence discussed in this chapter. Perhaps you surprised yourself or others by using an ability that you didn't know you had and it resulted in an achievement.

Write at least one page in your journal explaining what type of intelligence you used, how it made you feel, and what was the outcome or achievement.

## AUTHOR'S NOTE

Many students do poorly in school or drop out, even though they are capable of succeeding. A student might think he is "dumb" or "a slow learner" when he is actually smart in his own way. Unfortunately, in some cases, neither the student nor teacher has recognized the student's ability and how to use it in school. I have seen many students begin to excel in school when they discovered their preferred learning styles and strongest types of intelligence. I know you can do the same.

When I first heard about Dr. Gardner's theory of Multiple Intelligences in the early 1980s, a light went on in my mind. I realized that this knowledge of Multiple Intelligences and how to use them was missing when I was in school, and that it would help many students just like you.

## Student Success Story

In the following story, a student talks about how "dumb" he felt for years before finding out about his strongest forms of intelligence. He expresses his anger because no one taught him about multiple intelligences and learning styles until college, and his gratitude at finally getting this knowledge.

## Smart After All
By Rodney Richardson

For many years, I struggled in school and felt stupid. I compared myself to everyone else and they seemed to be smarter than me. I saw myself as a slow learner.

I was always restless in school, got bored easily, and it was hard for me to sit still and pay attention. My role was to be the class clown and make people laugh, which made me popular with the other students, but often in trouble with my teachers. I love talking with people and having fun.

I was diagnosed with ADHD a few years ago, which I guess explains why paying attention to the teachers was so hard for me. Accidentally, I discovered that I learn more when I read a book and dance around the room at the same time. I love music and play the guitar. I'm also a good dancer. So, when I would put on music and read while dancing around, it would help me remember more. Also, if I put anything to a jingle or rap it helps me to learn it better.

I didn't know anything in middle school or high school about learning styles and multiple intelligences. When I took this course, I learned about these things. Now it makes sense why I learned better while dancing around the room. I see now that I have my own kind of intelligence and I am good at a lot of things. I have a gift for music, dancing, and relating to people. I am a kinesthetic learner which explains why I get restless when the teacher only gives lectures. Now I know that I learn best hands-on, during field trips, labs, performing skits, and things like that.

All those years of comparing my weaknesses to other people's strengths was really dumb. I feel kind of angry that nobody taught me these things in school until now. Many kids drop out thinking they aren't smart when they can do a lot of things well.

This information about learning styles and types of intelligence hit me like a bolt of lightening. Now I get how I am smart and somebody worthwhile. Even though I could have really used this information earlier in my life, I'm grateful to have it now. It's already helping me to do better in my other classes.

Many teachers probably never expected me to go anywhere in life. I plan to prove them wrong. I now expect to be successful in college and to do something great with my life.

ACTIVITY 2.3  **Goal for the week**

In Chapter 1, you set a small goal for the week. In Chapters 2–8, you will have an opportunity to continue this process. Setting and achieving at least one small goal each week will increase your number of successes and build your self-confidence. Make the goal specific and measurable. An example follows:

I will achieve the following goal: Make a ninety or above on my math test this Friday.

Three steps I will take to achieve my goal:

❶ Study my class notes and math chapters for three hours this week.

❷ Get one hour of tutoring in math.

❸ Create and take a practice math quiz before the actual test.

Now you try it.

I will achieve the following goal this week: _____

_____

Three steps to achieve my goal:

1. _____

2. _____

3. _____

## SUMMARY OF MAIN POINTS IN CHAPTER 2

↗ There are many different learning styles and types of intelligence.

↗ You can increase your success in school by knowing and using your unique abilities.

↗ Your intelligence is not fixed at birth, and you can increase it throughout your life.

↗ Your IQ score only measures a couple of types of intelligence. A student with an average IQ score can excel in school, career, and life by using her preferred styles of learning and best types of intelligences.

## QUESTIONS TO ANSWER IN YOUR JOURNAL AND DISCUSS WITH OTHERS

↗ What is my preferred learning style and strongest type(s) of intelligence(s)?

↗ What are the three ways I plan to use my type(s) of intelligence(s) to succeed in college?

↗ What were my thoughts and feelings when I learned that there were different types of learners and intelligences?

↗ What are a couple of careers worth exploring and researching that might allow me to use my strongest types of intelligences?

In Chapter 3, you will be learning time management skills and strategies. These skills will help you to make the best use of your time and will provide you with another major key to the success you want.

HOWARD GARDNER
AND MULTIPLE
INTELLIGENCES
For more information

howardgardner.com

## CHAPTER 3

# To Students Who Want To Manage Their Time But Can't Get Started

Time is your most valuable resource. You cannot replace it, and it passes very quickly. Time is life, because as it passes so does your life. Managing your time well is managing your life well.

You can take time from activities of lower importance and priority and spend more time on your highest priorities. Time management begins with thinking about what is really important to you. **What do you really want?** Once you know your priorities, you can decide whether your actions support them. If your actions are not taking you where you want to go, just keep changing what you are doing until you are back on track.

❶ Ask yourself, "What is the best use of my time right now?"

❷ What are you willing to cut out or reduce so that you have time to do what you believe is most important?

Don't sacrifice your most important priorities for things which are of less importance.

## 80/20 Rule

The 80/20 Rule says that 80% of your unfocused effort is usually responsible for only 20% of your results. The remaining 80% of your results are achieved with only 20% of your effort. By applying time management strategies, you will be able to direct more energy into 20% of the activities which bring you the greatest results. Good time management will help you do what is important with focused attention.

```
                    ┌─────────────┐
                    │   Reduce    │
                    │ time wasters│
                    └─────────────┘
  ┌──────────────┐                    ┌──────────────┐
  │   Overcome   │                    │ Use a planner│
  │procrastination│                   │ and calendar │
  └──────────────┘    ┌──────────┐    └──────────────┘
                      │   Time   │
                      │Management│
                      │Strategies│
  ┌──────────────┐    └──────────┘    ┌──────────────┐
  │Spend most time│                   │ Break tasks  │
  │on important, but not│             │ into chunks  │
  │  urgent tasks│                     └──────────────┘
  └──────────────┘
                    ┌─────────────┐
                    │  Use the    │
                    │  80/20 rule │
                    └─────────────┘
```

*"Time is at once the most valuable and the most perishable of all possessions."*
—John Randolph of Roanoke

## Benefits of Effective Time Management Strategies

↗ Reduces your time wasters

↗ Helps you overcome procrastination

↗ Better planning for what you want to accomplish

↗ Keeps you on track to your goals

↗ Helps you accomplish your highest priorities

↗ You get more done with less effort

↗ You gain extra time for fun and recreation

↗ Supports your most important values

↗ Reduces your stress

↗ Helps you to live the life you really want

## Do You Make These Common Time Management Mistakes?

Rate Yourself

| 4 | 3 | 2 | 1 |
|---|---|---|---|
| Very much like me | Somewhat like me | Not much like me | Not at all like me |

❶ ___ I do not plan my actions and study time, but instead go by moods.

❷ ___ My study environment is usually messy and disorganized.

❸ ___ I often study and do school work when I am sleepy, not alert, and not at my best.

❹ ___ I let too many distractions and temptations come between me and what is really important for me to be doing.

❺ ___ I have low energy because of a lack of exercise and poor diet.

❻ ___ I study for long periods of time without taking breaks.

❼ ___ I have too much to do, and I don't cut out time wasters.

❽ ___ I usually do not set deadlines for my school work and other priorities that need to get done on time.

❾ ___ I spend too much time on low priorities.

❿ ___ I usually do what I like first even if these activities are not that important.

⓫ ___ I don't make good use of small pockets of time throughout the day.

⓬ ___ I spend too much time trying to understand difficult material instead of seeking help.

___Total

---

*Score Results:* The higher your score, the more you need to reduce your time management wasters.

## Tips For Managing Your Time

1. **Plan of action.** It would be a mistake for you to only do your school work when you feel like it, instead of planning and scheduling the time. It could cause you to fail, especially in college, because there is so much homework and reading to do.

2. **Studying when you're not at your best.** It is important for you to get enough sleep so that your mind is alert, and you can concentrate on your studies. Lack of sleep will

reduce your ability to remember what you study. Know when you are at your best. Are you a morning or evening person? Schedule your most difficult classes and school work when you will have the most energy and feel your best.

3. **Allowing for many distractions.** It is difficult to focus on school work if your cell phone is ringing, you are receiving text messages, the TV is playing, and friends are dropping by unannounced. Remove these distractions so you can focus your attention on studying. Tell friends and family "no" when they want to socialize during your study time. Make plans to play at a better time.

4. **Disorganized study environment.** Create a study environment that helps you concentrate and do your important work. Have the necessary supplies (pens, pencils, highlighters, notebooks, etc.) so you don't have to get up and down to get them. Make enough space so you can spread out and work.

5. **Poor diet and lack of exercise.** You need energy and good health to do your school work well. Take short exercise breaks between study periods. Eat healthy snacks instead of junk and fast foods.

6. **Studying too long without breaks.** If you study for thirty to forty-five minutes, take a short break. You will understand and remember more of what you read. Break your studying into small steps, so you can stay focused.

7. **Too much to do.** There are times when you may have too much to do. See what you can reduce or cut out so, you have time for your top priorities. Balance is also important. There is a time for study and a time for play. You will benefit from both.

8. **Not setting deadlines.** You can set many small goals with deadlines for completion. If, for example, you have a paper due in two weeks, set a deadline to begin and complete your paper.

9. **Spending too much time on low priorities.** Decide what your most important tasks are. Spend more time, energy, effort, and attention on your top priorities and less on activities which don't support your goals.

10. **Doing activities you like first.** This is fine, if these are your important priorities. Don't do an activity first just because it is pleasant. Do your important activities first, even if they are difficult and unpleasant for you.

11. **Failing to use small pockets of time wisely.** You can study between classes or write part of a paper while sitting in a doctor's office. While waiting in line at a store, you can review flash cards. Use these small pockets of time wisely. They will add up to big results.

12. **Not seeking help.** Beating your head against a concrete wall is not productive. Reading something over and over without understanding it can use up valuable time while accomplishing nothing. Seek out assistance when you need it. Use your school's resources, counselors, tutors, etc.

**Student Comment**
"The time log exercise revealed a lot of weak areas including not prioritizing my time. So my plan of action was to plan my work and work my plan. This helped because I was procrastinating, not planning ahead and was making poor decisions. I learned how to overcome these weaknesses."
—RUBEN RODRIGUEZ

**Student Comment**
"I learned to use my time wisely and now use calendars and planners every day."
—VALERIA RANGEL

Planning ahead is one of the most important time management strategies you can do. There is a saying, "If you are failing to plan, you are planning to fail."

What follows is a brief self-assessment for you to see how well you are planning.

## Planning Self-Assessment

**Circle** the number for each statement that best describes you.

| | | Never | Rarely | Sometimes | Often |
|---|---|---|---|---|---|
| 1 | I plan ahead and block out study time. | 1 | 2 | 3 | 4 |
| 2 | I use a daily planner and/or a "to do" list. | 1 | 2 | 3 | 4 |
| 3 | I enter my academic and social plans on my planner and calendar. | 1 | 2 | 3 | 4 |
| 4 | I allow for the unexpected, so I can be flexible and adapt. | 1 | 2 | 3 | 4 |
| 5 | I accomplish most of my plans. | 1 | 2 | 3 | 4 |
| 6 | I plan well. | 1 | 2 | 3 | 4 |
| 7 | I meet assignment deadlines by planning ahead. | 1 | 2 | 3 | 4 |
| 8 | I estimate how many hours I will need to study each week. | 1 | 2 | 3 | 4 |
| 9 | I start work early on long-term projects. | 1 | 2 | 3 | 4 |
| 10 | I set short-term goals with deadlines. | 1 | 2 | 3 | 4 |

For items you answered with a number 1 or 2, consider trying new habits to improve in these areas.

## Time Management Tips for Making the Best Use of Your Time

↗ **Use a planner and calendar.** Use an electronic or paper planner and calendar for your daily, weekly, monthly, and yearly goals. Write down your important plans including school assignments, work, personal development, and social activities.

↗ **Identify your common time wasters.** Being aware of your time wasters is your first step toward making positive changes. Begin substituting your more important activities and tasks for your time wasters by writing them down in your planner.

↗ **Prioritize.** List five of the most important things you need to get done each day. Arrange the list of activities in order of priority from number one through five. Focus only on your number one item until it's done. Then go to your number two item and on down the list. Make your to-do lists in the evening for the following day.

↗ **Delegate.** You may have some household chores or responsibilities that can be delegated or given to someone else in the household once in a while. For example, you may need to study for a test and you might be able to pay a younger brother or sister to do a few of your chores for you. You might be able to trade chores which you can do at a better time.

↗ **Set time limits and deadlines.** Know how much time you have available to complete assignments. This will allow you to start early, prepare for the unexpected, and to complete your assignments on time.

↗ **Let others know your needs and your schedule of important activites.** Your friends and family need to be aware of your needs, and you should respect and be aware of their needs. There are times for you to say "No, I can't go play at this or that time because I have to study. Let's set a date for another time."

↗ **Schedule your work for the right or best time.** Plan to do your important and difficult tasks when you are at your best and you have enough time to focus on them.

↗ **Review your class notes and readings before class and often.** This saves you last minute cramming for tests and reduces stress. You will retain more and be better prepared for your classes. Study daily and keep up with assignments because this will keep you relaxed and productive.

↗ **Get a good night's sleep and take naps, if helpful.** Most students between fifteen and twenty-two years of age need eight to ten hours of sleep to feel at their best. Sleep deprivation negatively affects your memory and concentration. Studying without focus wastes your valuable time.

↗ **Set small goals and break your large tasks into small chunks.** This keeps you from feeling overwhelmed. It is easier to start and complete small projects, which helps build your self-confidence and create a "success" mind-set. Study in small segments with short breaks in between.

↗ **Work on your important, but unpleasant activities a little each day until completed.**

↗ **Include rewards for yourself when you accomplish your tasks and goals.** Build in consequences or a negative effect when you do not follow through, such as not giving yourself the reward. Examples of rewards are you go to the movies, out for pizza with a friend, etc. Find ways to motivate yourself by using rewards when you get the job done, and use a take away when you fail to come through.

↗ **Exercise and eat well for maximum energy.** You need good health and energy to work hard and to concentrate.

↗ **Concentrate on one thing at a time.** This will be more effective for you than multi-tasking when you need to really concentrate. When you are able to focus on the assignment at hand, it will save you time, and this is a key to success.

↗ **Use resources and seek assistance.** Use your school tutors, counselors, library, and any other help you need.

*Student Comment*

"I learned how to manage my time wisely so I can work to the best of my ability to be more productive and successful."
—STEPHANO ALVAREZ

*Student Comment*

"The assessment we did in class showed me how little I knew about succeeding in college. The result was like a punch in the face. I learned so much and improved in many areas like my study skills, time management and goal setting."
—AARON KWOK

↗ **Be present and enjoy the moment.** Instead of regretting your past and worrying about your future, focus on what you are doing now. Do small things with care and attention because this will give you the best results. This is how you can best use and benefit from your time.

## Time Management Strategy to Accomplish Your Priorities

In his book, *First Things First*, Steven Covey presents a time management strategy which uses the following four quadrants or squares.

|  | Urgent | **Not Urgent** |
|---|---|---|
| **Important** | Quadrant 1 | Quadrant 2 |
| Not Important | Quadrant 3 | Quadrant 4 |

In the **first quadrant**, you list activities that you feel are both important and urgent. These take top priority. In the second quadrant you list activities and things that need doing which you consider to be important, but you don't have to complete them right away. These activities take second priority. The third quadrant contains activities and tasks which are not important to you, but others are trying to make you think they are urgent. Quadrant 4 consists of activities that are not important or urgent for you right now and there is no need to do them.

If something is both important and urgent to you, it needs to be taken care of first. For example, you may have to take someone to the hospital. However, these demands in quadrant 1 are stressful and are not where you want to spend unnecessary time and effort.

**Quadrant 2 is the best place to focus your attention and effort because it will prevent many things from becoming urgent** and ending up in quadrant 1. If you start early on these important tasks, then you will complete most of your assignments on time without creating urgency. Quadrant 2 is the most productive and best place to spend your time.

**Quadrant 3** activities are not important to you, but others try to make you think they must be done now. For example, a friend wants you to return his phone call immediately about something that can wait a couple of days.

**Quadrant 4** consists of activities that you usually consider a waste of time such as sitting and doing nothing. You want to cut out or at least reduce time wasters. However, there may be times where a few minutes of doing nothing is actually useful. For example, you may feel burned out and need some down time to just zone out and relax.

In the exercise that follows, decide which of the four quadrants you would list each of the activities.

## The Four Quadrant Exercise

Assign each activity below to one of the four quadrants, either quadrant 1, 2, 3, or 4. Your answers should show the number of the quadrant you would use for each of the seven activities below.

A. ____ A paper is due in your English class tomorrow and you haven't started working on it.

B. ____ A paper is due in your History class next week and you have half of it done.

C. ____ Your best friend left a message to call back right away about a movie he wants to see with you in a few days.

D. ____ You have a Psychology test in a week and you are prepared, but you want to review your notes before the test.

E. ___ Your friends want you to attend a meeting tomorrow which they say is urgent, but it has nothing to do with your interests and goals.

F. ___ You feel like watching several hours of television today even though you have a test tomorrow.

G. ___ Your favorite charity called and asked you to give them some money.

Keep in mind that the more you say no to Quadrant 3 and 4 activities, the more time you can spend on your top priorities listed in Quadrants 1 and 2.

*Source:* Questions developed by Raymond Gerson. Based on Covey, Stephen, Roger Merrill, and Rebecca Merrill. *First Things First*. Free Press., 1996, p. 37.

## Do You Procrastinate For These Reasons?

Procrastination is when you put off doing something that you need to do. Procrastination can keep you from getting what you want in life. Procrastination is how things that need to be done pile up until you feel stressed.

### SOME OF THE COMMON REASONS THAT PEOPLE PROCRASTINATE

↗ **Going by moods.** If you are not careful, you might avoid important but unpleasant tasks because you do not feel like doing them.

↗ **Fear of failure.** If you avoid doing the task and fail, you can say, "I failed because I didn't try," not because you could not accomplish it.

↗ **Fear of success.** It is important for you to feel worthy of success or you might avoid it. If you fear the demands, expectations, and criticism that might come from being successful, you might hold back from big accomplishments.

↗ **Poor decision-making skills.** If you cannot make a decision, you will not do what you need to get done. First, you must decide; then act.

↗ **Poor organizational skills.** If you have difficulty putting things in the right order and organizing, you may hesitate to begin the task.

↗ **Perfectionism.** If you feel the need to be perfect or to do something perfectly, you may hold back because anything less might seem like failure.

↗ **Not planning ahead.** You cannot do everything at the spur of the moment. You will only accomplish some important things well, if you plan ahead.

↗ **Being unsure of the next step.** If you don't know where to start or what to do first, then it is likely that you will not begin.

### WAYS TO OVERCOME PROCRASTINATION AND ENJOY THE SUCCESS YOU WANT

1. **Know when you are procrastinating.** Be aware of when you are putting off important activities and honestly admit it to yourself.

2. **Procrastinate on low priorities instead of high priorities.** Use the habit of procrastination to put off your time wasters.

3.  **Set up rewards for not procrastinating important tasks.** Deprive yourself of rewards if you put off doing what needs to be done.

4.  **Estimate the monetary cost.** For example, figure out what a semester of your classes will cost you. Now figure how much each class will cost. If you are putting off going to a class, now you will be able to figure out how much money missing class will cost.

5.  **Set small goals and take little steps.** We discussed this as a time management strategy, and it can help you to avoid procrastination.

6.  **Tackle the most important task first.** This time management strategy can also help you to overcome procrastination. Do your unpleasant but important activities first and play later.

7.  **Do it now.** Clement Stone, a successful entrepreneur, used to repeat "do it now" over and over for motivation to do the task right now. You might try this approach.

8.  **Ask for help.** Do not try to do everything by yourself. Use resources and seek assistance from others when you need it.

9.  **Do not expect perfection.** Realize and accept that you are human. Even though you want to do well, don't think you must do things perfectly. The road to success is often paved with failures along the way.

10. **Set deadlines.** Let's say you have a paper due for a class in two weeks. This is the final deadline, but you can also set some of your own deadlines. For example, set a deadline to write a page a day. Set a deadline to have a rough draft completed three days before the final paper is due. You can also set a deadline to complete your paper one day before the final due date.

11. **Use time management tools previously mentioned.** You can use time management tools such as calendars and planners to overcome procrastination.

12. **Prioritize.** This is another important time management strategy we discussed earlier that also helps to overcome procrastination. Make a daily to-do list the night before. Arrange your list in order of importance. Totally focus on your #1 item until it is done; then go to #2 and continue in this manner.

13. **Use positive self-talk.** Explain to your mind the benefits of doing the task now. Reframe or change how you see your unpleasant tasks by recognizing they have value.

14. **Try to make the tasks fun.** See if you can be creative and make the task or assignment into a game.

*Student Comment*

"The one big thing that helped me out was the time management section. It helped out because I got to see where I was spending most of my free time which was mostly in video games and sleeping. So because of that I cut down my gaming time for more school work time. I think that I'm getting better at getting my school work down. Now I do school work first and after that I get into my gaming."
—ROBERT ROBINSON

Remind yourself that you can accomplish great things in small steps. A brick layer starts working on a house by putting one brick in place. The job to be done might seem huge and overwhelming to the brick layer, but brick by brick he gets it done. Thousands of bricks end up in place, but the brick layer accomplished it one brick at a time. In the same way, you can break things into small manageable chunks and go step-by-step to successfully complete your tasks. As Doc Childre and Howard Martin put it, "You're writing the story of your life one moment at a time."

ACTIVITY 3.1

Where does your time go? Guess how much time you spend each week in the activities listed below in the left column. Keep track of how you are actually spending your time for one week and record your results on the Time Log Sheet (which follows on the next couple of pages). At the end of a week, you will be able to fill in the right side below; then compare your guessed and actual times. Now, fill in your estimated time in the left column (which is a guess as to how much time you are spending in each category per week). It should add up to 168 hours, which is a full week.

## Assess Your Time Exercise

| Estimated Time | Actual Time |
|---|---|
| Time in class ____ | ____ |
| Time at work ____ | ____ |
| Study time ____ | ____ |
| Grooming ____ | ____ |
| Commuting ____ | ____ |
| Sleeping ____ | ____ |
| Cooking/eating ____ | ____ |
| Time with family ____ | ____ |
| Time with friends ____ | ____ |
| Shopping ____ | ____ |
| Exercise ____ | ____ |
| TV ____ | ____ |
| Computer fun ____ | ____ |
| Hobbies ____ | ____ |
| Other ____ | ____ |

Total hours per week: <u>168</u>        Actual total: _____

## Time Log Sheet

Use the **Time Log Sheet** below to track your activities for seven days. Then, go back to the **Assess Your Time Exercise** and fill out the actual time in the right column and total the hours.

| | Monday | Tuesday | Wednesday | Thursday | Friday | Saturday | Sunday |
|---|---|---|---|---|---|---|---|
| 6–7 a.m. | | | | | | | |
| 7–8 | | | | | | | |
| 8–9 | | | | | | | |
| 9–10 | | | | | | | |
| 10–11 | | | | | | | |
| 11–12 | | | | | | | |
| 12–1 p.m. | | | | | | | |
| 1–2 | | | | | | | |
| 2–3 | | | | | | | |
| 3–4 | | | | | | | |
| 4–5 | | | | | | | |
| 5–6 | | | | | | | |
| 6–7 | | | | | | | |
| 7–8 | | | | | | | |
| 8–9 | | | | | | | |
| 9–10 | | | | | | | |
| 10–11 | | | | | | | |
| 11–12 | | | | | | | |
| 12–1 a.m. | | | | | | | |
| 1–2 | | | | | | | |
| 2–3 | | | | | | | |
| 3–4 | | | | | | | |
| 4–5 | | | | | | | |
| 5–6 | | | | | | | |

## JOURNAL ASSIGNMENT

Compare your estimated and actual times once they are recorded in the **Assess Your Time Exercise.** Write at least one page in your journal about what you guessed correctly, where you were incorrect, and any surprises. Write about areas that need more of your time, less of your time, and time wasters you want to eliminate. Also, address the extent to which your actual time spent supports your goals and values. Conclude by discussing changes, you will make to more effectively use your time.

> ## Student Comment
> "The main benefit I got was to use my time wisely, separate the important from the unimportant, and calculate use of my time."
> —BIANCA HERNANDEZ

## AUTHOR'S NOTE

Many of my students become angry and upset after doing the time assessment activity because they learn how they are actually spending their time. Some have been shocked at the differences between categories of their estimated and actual time. The shocks come when they realize that their time spent did not support their goals and priorities. For example, I mentioned that one of my students discovered that she watches forty hours of TV a week and studies two to three hours a week. This came as a rude awakening and shock to her, even though she decided not to change these habits.

I explain to my students that their disappointment, anger, and shock can serve as a motivator for positive change. The first step is for a student to be willing to see reality, instead of remaining blind to what is really happening. Secondly, once a student sees how he or she is actually using valuable time, it is possible to make changes. I encourage you to spend your time (life) in a way that takes you to your goals.

## Success Story Paper

The following paper was written by a student of mine who is a single mother of three children. She works full time and began college later in life. Needless to say, she has a lot on her plate. Finding enough time for her many priorities is a challenge.

### Time Monitor Paper

#### By Lynn Carpenter

The time monitor paper is difficult for me to write. The reason is I do not have enough spare time to even think about where my time goes. I was actually exhausted when looking at this assignment because it made me realize how much I do on a day-to-day basis.

During this assignment I realized that there are definitely areas that can be improved. The way I spend my time at home is one of the things that can be adjusted. For instance, I could use the small amount of time that I watch TV and use it for more quality time with my kids and doing homework. Instead of waiting until the last minute to do my assignments I could get it done before it is actually due. I spend a lot of time working and going to school which affects my kids and managing my time better would give me more time with them.

During the week I spend an average of 75 hours on school and working, 56 hours sleeping, and 11 hours driving which adds up to 142 out of a 168 hour week. This leaves 26 hours a week for my kids and any time I might actually have for myself which is not much.

At this point in my life I realize that I am stretched about as far as one person should be, but in the long run this sacrifice will pay off. It will pay off because I am bettering myself working toward a goal that will improve my life and the lives of my children. The education that I am receiving will help me to put my kids through college and create better opportunities for me later.

I do plan on changing a few things like the time in front of the TV and focus more on the most important things in my life.

ACTIVITY 3.2  **Goal for the week:**

_____

Three steps to achieve my goal:

1. _____

2. _____

3. _____

## WHY IT IS IMPORTANT TO TAKE GOOD CARE OF YOUR BODY, TOO

Your physical and mental health are connected and affect your ability to succeed in college, career, relationships, and other areas your of life.

Without good health, it will be difficult to make your dreams come true. Vitality and energy are byproducts of good health and are needed to succeed in college, your career, maintain excellent relationships, and accomplish many other goals.

You probably know, from your own experience, that your physical and mental health affect each other. When you are physically ill, your mind is less clear, and it's easy for you to feel down. When you're depressed, you have less energy. You will need to keep your brain healthy to think clearly, to focus your attention, and to retain and recall information. Let's look at some of the benefits of good health.

## Benefits of Good Health

↗ Increases your odds living a longer life

↗ You will have more energy

↗ Positively influences your mental health

↗ Increases your sense of well-being

↗ Improves your self-esteem

↗ Improves your overall quality of life

↗ Gives you more energy and stamina to pursue your goals

## Tips For Maintaining Excellent Health

Genetics play a role in your health and longevity, but lifestyle plays an even bigger role in affecting your overall state of health.

There are no guarantees, but here are some ideas for increasing your odds of having a long and healthy life. These tips will benefit both your brain and your body.

### 1. DRINK PLENTY OF WATER

Much of your body and brain are made up of water. You need water to stay hydrated, to flush out toxins, to get nutrients from food, and for your brain to work well. Drinking plenty of water also keeps your skin from becoming dry and prematurely wrinkled from dehydration.

How much water do you need a day? Rule of thumb is to drink one half your weight in ounces each day. For example, if you weighed 130 pounds, you would need 65 ounces or about two quarts of water a day. If you do strenuous exercise or work, you will need even more water.

If you are dehydrated, you probably have lost your thirst signals, which let you know when you need water. Once you start drinking enough water, your thirst signals will return. Then you can get enough water by drinking it when you feel thirsty.

Coffee, tea, and soda are not substitutes for water. Actually, they are dehydrating. If you drink them, you will need more water. Even fruit juice is not a substitute for water because it comes from a food source, and it's not a real solvent. A true solvent is something that dissolves and cleans poisons out of your body.

Drinking tap water is better than not getting enough water, but it is best to drink water which has been purified naturally or through reverse osmosis or distillation. Only some of the bottled water meets these conditions.

### 2. YOU NEED A LITTLE SUNSHINE

It is true that you can get too much sun, but you need some sunshine. Ten to twenty minutes of daily early morning or late evening sun is good for you.

Sunshine gives you vitamin D which you need so your bones can absorb calcium. Without enough vitamin D, your bones can become brittle and break. It is unnatural to spend all of your time indoors. You need fresh air and a little sunshine to maintain excellent health.

### 3. EXERCISE IS IMPORTANT

Your body needs movement and physical activity. Proper exercise can slow down your physical deterioration. Your brain needs oxygen and exercise will provide more of it for your brain and other vital organs. Your brain requires about 25% of the total oxygen that you need.

You need three types of exercise: flexibility, aerobic, and strength training.

**A. Flexibility exercise.**

Your body will become stiffer as you age. Yoga, swimming, tai chi, or just doing stretching can help you to maintain flexibility.

**B. Aerobic or cardiovascular exercise.**

Walking, biking, jogging, dancing, and sports which help you to stay in your working heart rate for twenty to thirty minutes are good for your heart. Charts are available to determine the working heart rate for your age bracket.

**C. Strength training exercise.**

This type of exercise keeps your muscles firm and strong. When combined with proper nutrition, it also keeps your bones strong. This exercise includes: weight lifting (it can be light weights), calisthenics, and machines, which provide resistance.

Unless you are an athlete or compete in sports you don't need to spend a large amount of time exercising. Like anything else, you can overdo exercise and then you will receive less benefit from it. It is better for you to exercise in moderation.

## 4. DON'T SMOKE

If you are serious about maintaining excellent health, it is important to stop smoking or to never start. It is damaging to your health.

## 5. EAT WELL

Fresh fruits and vegetables are among the most important foods you can eat. A variety of colors in fruits and vegetables are better for you because they contain different types of antioxidants. Antioxidants strengthen your immune system and slow the aging process. Fresh produce is best, frozen is second best, and the least nutritious are canned fruits and vegetables.

It is good to eat some raw foods such as vegetables, fruits, nuts, and seeds. They contain enzymes which are frequently destroyed when the food is cooked. Enzymes help with your digestion and increase your energy. If you eat a salad with one or two meals a day, you will be creating a great and healthy habit. When you eat raw food, know your sources to avoid bacteria contamination. Whole grains, beans, seeds, and nuts are good for you. Raw nuts, seeds, fruits, and vegetables give you energy and contain vitamins and minerals. Your brain also requires nutrients to function well. For example, your brain uses glucose which you can get from fruit and whole grains.

It's best for your health for you to avoid or reduce fast foods, foods high in salt, saturated fat, and sugar. Following these simple and common sense health tips can increase your chances of living a healthy and enjoyable life.

## 6. GOOD DENTAL HYGIENE

Many dentists say that brushing and flossing your teeth at least once a day may add a few years to your life. Many forms of bacteria, which cause illness, start in your mouth. Good dental hygiene reduces the amount of harmful bacteria in your mouth and prevents it from entering other organs in your body. The loss of teeth is often due more to gum disease than problems with the teeth themselves. Taking a few minutes a day to brush and floss your teeth is a healthy habit that will keep you smiling.

## 7. GET ENOUGH SLEEP

Getting enough sleep is important for staying healthy. If you are not getting enough sleep at night, try a power nap during the day. Lack of sleep over time can damage your health. It also can reduce your ability to concentrate, impair your memory, and lower your energy, which you need to succeed. Use good time management principles discussed earlier so you can find enough time to get the sleep you need. Sleep benefits both your brain, body, and soul.

## 8. ALCOHOL AND DRUGS CAN DAMAGE YOUR HEALTH

Alcohol is a depressant and destroys brain cells. It impairs your physical and mental functioning. Alcohol also contributes to many accidental deaths, illnesses, and unsafe sex and violence. If you drink alcohol, then drink in moderation. Avoid binge drinking. If you think you have a serious drinking problem, then seek help.

Drugs are as damaging as alcohol and some do greater harm. If you are arrested you can go to prison, damage your reputation, have problems finding a good job, lose valuable relationships, and destroy your peace of mind. If you have a problem with drug use or addiction, seek counseling and help from detoxification centers or support groups like Alcoholics Anonymous (AA) and Narcotics Anonymous (NA).

**Student Comment**

"I became motivated to improve my health habits. Thank you for the inspiration."
—LUZ SANCHEZ

ACTIVITY 3.3  **Rate your health habits. Check those that are true.**

① ____ I avoid unhealthy foods containing lots of salt, fat, and sugar most of the time.

② ____ I eat several servings of fruit and vegetables every day.

③ ____ I drink plenty of water each day.

④ ____ I brush and floss my teeth daily.

⑤ ____ I very seldom eat fast foods.

⑥ ____ I have a regular exercise program.

⑦ ____ I do some aerobic, flexibility, and strength training exercise each week.

⑧ ____ I get enough sleep almost every night.

⑨ ____ I avoid situations that put me at risk of injury or harm.

⑩ ____ I don't abuse alcohol or use illegal drugs.

____ Total score for health habits.

ACTIVITY 3.4  **Rate your mental health. Check all that are true.**

① ____ I feel happy and grateful most of the time.

② ____ I am rarely depressed.

③ ____ I manage stress well most of the time.

④ ____ I do not expect perfection from myself.

⑤ ____ I have wonderful relationships where I both give and receive love.

⑥ ____ I can and do express my feelings often.

⑦ ____ My sense of self-worth and self-esteem are good.

⑧ ____ I am able to forgive myself and others for past mistakes.

⑨ ____ I don't abuse drugs and alcohol.

⑩ ____ I bounce back from tragedies and life's difficulties.

_____ Total score for mental health.

Make an investment today in your physical and mental health to increase your energy, ability to concentrate, and your feeling of well-being. Your state of health will affect your ability to learn, succeed, and make your dreams come true.

MAYO CLINIC
Stress Assessment

mayoclinic.com/health/stress-assessment/sr00029

## SUMMARY OF MAIN POINTS IN CHAPTER 3

↗ Time is your most precious resource because it is irreplaceable, and as it goes by, so does your life.

↗ Focus more of your time and energy on 20% of the activities that bring you the best results.

↗ Planning, prioritizing, and using time management tools will help you to manage your time wisely.

↗ By spending more of your time doing what you think is important, but not urgent, you will reduce stress and accomplish more.

↗ Your physical and mental health affects each other and every other part of your life.

↗ Exercise and good nutrition will improve your physical health and increase your energy, which is needed to achieve your dreams and goals.

↗ Good physical and mental health are attainable for you and will improve your concentration, ability to learn, and your chances for success in college.

## QUESTIONS TO ANSWER IN YOUR JOURNAL AND DISCUSS WITH OTHERS

↗ What are five of my biggest time wasters? How can I reduce or get rid of them?

↗ What is my most common time management mistake? How can I correct it?

↗ Why do I procrastinate? Name three ways that you can overcome procrastination.

↗ What are my three top priorities to get done tomorrow? Name three small steps that you can take for accomplishing each of these priorities.

↗ What benefits have I received from exercise in the past?

↗ What is one new activity I am willing to do to improve my physical health and energy level?

↗ What is one new activity I am willing to do to improve my mental health?

↗ What am I willing to do to main my good health as long as possible?

In Chapter 4, you will be learning strategies to use when reading and taking notes so you can get the most from your textbooks and class lectures.

TIME
MANAGEMENT
TIPS

timemanagement.com

# Make Learning Easier ... Discover How to Read, Study, and Understand Textbooks

**Y**our reading ability and comprehension are strongly related to succeeding in college. You need good study skills for purposeful and worthwhile learning to occur. Effective study skills are centered on your reading and writing ability. If you can't read well, you will not do well in college. Not only will you need to understand words, but you must be able to get the hang of ideas, meaning, theories, and concepts.

The key to your being a good reader is for you to be an active, not a passive, learner. If you are a passive learner, you just read the words in a textbook without focused attention and without thinking about what you're reading. If you are an active learner, you think, question, and take notes when you read. As an active learner, you read important passages from the textbook and write the main points down in your own words. You use study skill strategies as an active learner to make sense out of what you are reading.

In this chapter, you will learn about strategies of active learners and how to understand and remember more of what you read.

## Benefits of Excellent Reading Skills

↗ Increases your retention and comprehension

↗ Improves your ability to focus

↗ Improves your self-esteem and self-confidence

↗ Increases your learning satisfaction

↗ Stimulates and develops your critical thinking skills

↗ Improves your self-management skills

```
                        Be an active reader

    Create study                              Break
    guides and                                reading periods
    practice tests                            into chunks

                     Reading
                     Strategies

    Explain paragraphs                        Annotate and ask
    to yourself out loud                      questions

                       Preview chapters
```

*"Learning without thought is labor lost."*
—Confucius

↗ Learning becomes more enjoyable for you

↗ Attain higher levels of achievement

↗ Reduces your test anxiety

Now let's look at strategies you can use before, during, and after reading.

## Strategies You Can Use Before Reading

❶ **Create and use the right study environment.** Choose a location where you can eliminate or reduce distractions, have enough room for your materials, and won't have constant interruptions.

❷ **Choose a time when you feel rested and alert.** If you are sleepy, take a short nap before studying. Eat a healthy snack if you need some energy.

❸ **Ask yourself what you already know about the subject.** Connecting what you're already familiar with to the new material will make learning easier for you.

❹ **Set goals and know the purpose of your study session.** Ask yourself what is it you are trying to learn. For example, are you preparing for a test or to write a paper? These are different purposes, and you will study for them in different ways.

⑤ **Preview the chapter(s).** When you preview chapters before reading them, you will gain a comfort level with the material that you are going to read. You will know what the chapter is about and where you are going. It's like you are looking at a map before you take a trip. When you look over the chapters, form the habit of turning headings and sub-headings into questions. This will help you to focus and to get a better idea of what the author is saying.

When you preview chapters, glance at:

❶ Chapter headings and sub-headings, introductions, questions, pictures, charts, bold or italicized words, and summaries or conclusions.

It will only take you a few minutes to preview a chapter and this provides a good overview. This overview will help you understand and retain more material when you read the chapter.

## Strategies You Can Use During Reading

**READING STRATEGIES**

emmanuel.edu/Documents/Academics/ARC/Reading%20Strategies.pdf

❶ **Break up your reading and ask questions.** Read a section of the chapter and then ask yourself questions about what you read. Check your understanding of the material. This process will help keep your attention focused on what you are reading. If your mind wandered while reading, you will know it when you pause to ask questions. If you lost focus, you can go back and reread the section.

*Reading one section at a time will increase your comprehension and retention of the material.* While reading each section, anticipate and guess questions that might be on your next test. Jot down these questions and make them part of a practice quiz that you will take before the actual exam is given.

*Read in chunks followed by taking small breaks.* For example, read for about thirty to forty minutes and then break for a few minutes. You will retain more information this way. Studies have shown that you will remember more at the beginning and ending of a reading session. So you can purposely create many beginnings and endings by breaking up your reading. Many people find that their concentration begins to fade after thirty to forty minutes. Use this knowledge to your advantage.

❷ **Look up words you do not understand.** Keep a dictionary and a thesaurus handy. A good vocabulary will increase your success in school and life. Many high level executives and CEOs have vocabularies second only to college English professors. If you do not understand individual words, it will be difficult to comprehend the meaning of the sentence that contains those words.

❸ **Write summaries of what you are reading.** You can do this in a separate notebook or in a section of the notebook you use for class notes. Write a brief summary in your own words after reading the chapter - or after reading each major section of the chapter.

❹ **Create study guides.** Here are examples of study guides to help you study effectively:

A. **Create flash or study cards.** Use 3 x 5 cards for learning and memorizing vocabulary words, definitions, and the meaning of scientific and other terms. Write the word or question on one side of the card and the definition or answer on the other side.

Study cards are great for helping you memorize information, but you still need to understand the concepts. One advantage of study cards is that you can take them with you to use when you are waiting at the doctor's office, waiting in line, or when you are in other situations where you have small chunks of time available.

EXAMPLE OF A STUDY CARD

What is annotation?

Front

Writing key ideas in the margin of the text in your own words.

Back

B. **Create outlines.** Outlines are a good way to organize your thoughts and the material you are reading. They are especially effective if you like to structure material in a sequence or linear fashion.

ACTIVITY 4.1 Outline the main points in the article below.

## Using Dissatisfaction to Find Work That Matters
### By Raymond Gerson

One clue for discovering work that matters to you can be found by noticing your own dissatisfaction with problems you see in the world. Are there problems that inspire compassion for others? Do you see problems or needs that make you feel sad or angry? Is there a need that you would like you fulfill if you had the power to make a difference?

Dissatisfaction can be positive if you use your discontentment to make a contribution. How can you use your talents and skills to help fill a need you see in the world? Aristotle put it this way, "Where your talents and the needs of the world meet, there lies your vocation."

Now fill in the numbers and letters below with what you consider to be the main points:

1. Main point here:
   a. Supporting point: _____
   b. Supporting point: _____
2. Main point:
   a. Supporting point: _____
   b. Supporting point: _____
   c. Supporting point: _____

C. **Create idea maps.** These are especially good for visual learners. An idea or mind map (also referred to as "think link") is a picture of the main lessons that shows how they are connected to each other. Idea maps are diagrams used to represent ideas linked to and arranged around a central idea. Ideas branch out from the central idea, and there is no limit to the number of branches and connections that you can create. See Figure 4.1.

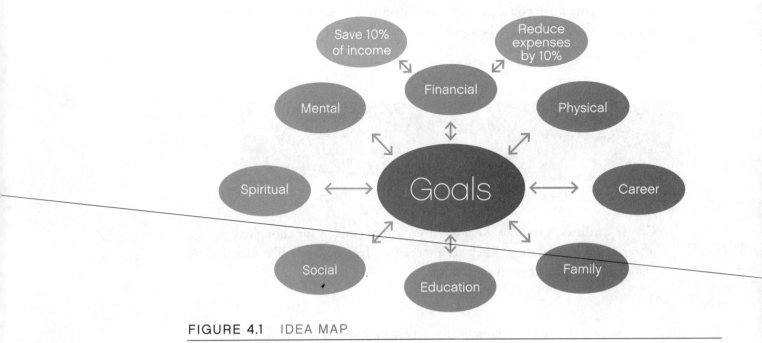

**FIGURE 4.1   IDEA MAP**

*Source:* Developed by Raymond Gerson. Based on Tony Buzan. *Use Both Sides of Your Brain: New Mind Mapping Techniques.* Plume, 1991.

ACTIVITY 4.2 **Create an idea map for the seven goal categories, but also expand each of them into another branch as in the financial goal example.**

D. **Create timelines.** This study aid involves putting events in chronological order or in a sequence of events, usually in the order they occurred. It is a good study guide for courses like history where you can list historical events in order of occurrence and prominent people who were associated with those events. Table 4.1 is an example of a timeline of major losses in the life of Abraham Lincoln.

E. **Practice annotating and annolighting. Annotating** consists of **writing key ideas** in the margins of the textbook in your own words. **Annolighting** consists of **highlighting key words** and phrases and annotating these highlights in the margins. In other words, you are explaining the highlighted words and phrases.

| Table 4.1 Abraham Lincoln's Major Losses and Failures ||
|---|---|
| **Year** | **Temporary Defeats** |
| 1832 | Defeated for state legislature |
| 1833 | Failed in business |
| 1835 | Sweetheart died |
| 1836 | Nervous breakdown |
| 1838 | Defeated for speaker |
| 1854 | Defeated for U.S. senate |
| 1856 | Defeated for V.P. nomination |
| 1858 | Defeated for U.S. senate |
| 1860 | Success—elected U.S. president |

It is best not to highlight on the first reading. Skim a section after you have read it; then, highlight only key words and phrases instead of whole sentences. When students highlight on the first reading, they tend to highlight too much and this defeats the purpose of highlighting. Highlighting helps to identify main ideas and bypass less important information. This increases comprehension and retention of material. It is best to highlight only 15%–25% of the material.

**Determine your purpose; then highlight.** For example, is your purpose to identify main ideas or were you asked to understand the author's philosophy on a particular subject? Your purpose and goal for the text will determine what is best for you to highlight. You should only highlight words you think are necessary to understand important ideas in a sentence.

## Example of Annolighting

Note: The *italics* on the right represent written comments in the margins.

### Work as an Art Form and You as the Artist

By Raymond Gerson

Anyone who responds to an inner calling to fulfill a worthy purpose, envisions their goal, and then brings this vision into reality and form is an artist. In this way your work can be a form of art. Gibran said, "Work is love made visible." When you love what you do, your work becomes an expression of love. It is natural to desire to express the best of yourself in the world through your vocation. This is how the inner (that which needs to be expressed from within you) becomes the outer visible form of your work.

*Follow heart, see goal, make happen and you're an artist.*

An architect envisions a building, draws it on paper, and eventually it takes the form of a building. A teacher sees the results he or she wants the students to achieve, conveys this expectation to the students, and inspires them to rise to the level of expectation. Both the architect and the teacher are like artists who paint their masterpiece. Laurence G. Boldt, in his wonderful book.

*Be an artist. Picture what I want and bring into form. Be inspired! Create.*

*Zen and the Art of Making a Living* put it this way, "You can experience your everyday life as art by bringing inspiration and absorption, creativity and resourcefulness, play and delight." When you are inspired and in the flow, your work becomes a form of art.

ACTIVITY 4.3 Annolight the Following Article from Chapter 1.

## Small Habits Can Transform Your Life

### By Raymond Gerson

Your day-to-day habits have an increasing effect over time. Positive habits bring positive results and negative habits bring negative consequences.

Small, positive habits done on a regular basis can give you large benefits over enough time. For example, walking a mile a day might seem like a small habit, but in one year you would have walked 365 miles and in ten years you would have walked 3,650 miles. Imagine the benefits to your heart and respiratory system after ten years of walking just one mile a day.

On the other hand, let's say you drink one can of soda a day. This gives you the equivalent of ten teaspoons of sugar a day. What effect will this have on your weight and long-term health compared to a healthy habit like walking?

Your habits may seem small, but they can have big effects. Habits tend to be difficult to break and can easily follow you through life. So doesn't it make sense to replace your negative habits with positive ones and to add new positive habits to your life? You can use small positive habits to maintain excellent health, to achieve your dreams, and to live a fulfilling life.

*Student Comment*

"What I liked was how many different techniques there are to help me read better."

— ELIZABETH ELLIS

## Combining Questions and Annotation

You can add questions on one side of your text and annotate on the other side, if your book has enough margin space. If there is not enough space you can use your notebook. People usually think in questions and answers. When you read a section in your book certain implied questions are answered by the author. You can ask questions which were answered by what you read. This practice will engage you with your reading. You will become an active reader, and it will help you to stay focused and to understand what you read. And, it makes reviewing for your test easier.

**Annotation** is even more powerful as a strategy when you combine it with asking questions. When you prepare for your test, you can review your questions on one side and your answers (annotation) in your own words on the other side. You can cover your answers while looking at the questions and use them as a self-test.

Let's look at an example where I used this strategy for an article I wrote about taking small steps to your goals.

### Small Steps to What You Want

| Questions | | Annotations |
|---|---|---|
| What is **kaizen**? | Lao Tzu said, "A journey of a thousand miles must begin with the first step." The Japanese word *kaizen* means small steps for continued improvement. | Keep stepping up. |
| How can I make the journey to my goals manageable? | Any large goal or project can be broken into small steps which leads us to the achievement of the goal. | Break down large goals into smaller ones. |
| How can I over-come fear of big goals and remain self-confident? | According to Robert Maurer, author of **One Small Step Can Change Your Life,** taking small steps helps us to bypass fears that often arise when we are facing big changes. An overwhelming task does not seem daunting when we break it down into small steps. Fear and anxiety restrict our ability to think clearly and to be creative. When we take small steps to large goals we remain relaxed, confident, and think more clearly. | Take small steps. |
| What is an example of using small steps to reach a big goal? | I started weight lifting when I was eighteen years old. I could only bench press 75 pounds. Two of my weights were a quarter of a pound each. I would often tell myself that I should be able to lift a half pound more weight and I would add these small weights to the barbell. In a few years, I was able to bench press 300 pounds at a body weight of 145 pounds. This is an example of using small incremental steps to accomplish a big goal. I kept increasing the weight by a small amount, consolidated my gains, and in a few years was lifting 225 pounds more than when I began weightlifting. It is amazing what can be accomplished with small incremental steps.<br><br>You can decide what you want in life, whether it is a great relationship, career, or any other goal. Then begin taking small steps toward your goal until you achieve it. | Weight lifting. Keep adding small weights to make big gains in strength. |
| How can I make my dreams and goals come true? | Now you have a combination of two simple, but powerful strategies to increase your understanding and memory of what you read. Try combining questions with annotation and you will learn faster, easier, and better. | Decide what you want and go one step at a time. |

ACTIVITY 4.4 In the following article, write questions on one side and your annotated comments on the other.

## Listen to Your Life and Discover the Work You Were Born to Do

"Is the life I am living, the same as the life that wants to live in me?" These are the words of Parker Palmer from his book, *Let Your Life Speak: Listening for the Voice of Vocation.*

Are you living your life based on "oughts" and "shoulds" or on what your life and inner voice are calling you to do? It is easy to fall into the trap of pursuing a career because you or others believe this is what you "ought" to do. And yet, to "follow your bliss" and to discover the work that you were meant to do, you must listen to your heart.

Parker Palmer spent years in vocations, which were not aligned with his true nature and best talents. This resulted in his being depressed for many years of his life. Eventually, he returned to teaching and helping educators. This work was in harmony with the life that wanted to be expressed through him. Greater job satisfaction and the ability to make a positive contribution was the result.

One of my college students was depressed and was self-sabotaging by missing classes and turning his school work in late. For years, he and others believed that he "should" become a nurse. More self-reflection helped him to realize that nursing would not be fulfilling. He had worked in hospitals before and did not enjoy it. Recalling the joy of being an athletic trainer's assistant while in high school made him realize that he wanted to go in a different direction. For example, he remembered patching up the quarterback who went back into the game and scored the winning touchdown. This experience made him feel joy and a sense of purpose and accomplishment.

My student changed his college major and began pursuing the goal of becoming an athletic trainer. His depression disappeared, papers were turned in on time, and he attended every class. He was inspired, happy, and self-motivated. His grades began to improve, and he seemed like a different person.

This is an example of what can happen when you stop living your life according to "oughts" and begin living the life that wants to live in you. The clues to a career that is right for you are in your life. Let your life speak and then listen to your own inner voice. This is one way to discover the work you were born to do.

The following two articles were blogs that I wrote for one of my websites. They are about a simple reading comprehension strategy that has done wonders for many of my students.

### Reading Comprehension Strategy Makes Student Scream

**Why did a student in a college psychology course let out a loud scream of delight, leap out of her chair, run down the aisle, and then give her professor a big hug? Read on for the rest of the story.**

A friend of mine is a professor of psychology who is also helping his students to improve their reading comprehension. He gives tough exams, and many of his students fail the tests, unless they understand the concepts and principles.

Last semester, he started advising a few students, who were failing, to read each chapter three times. He advised these students to stop after reading each paragraph and explain it out loud to themselves. Instructions were not to go to the next paragraph until they could explain the meaning of the preceding one. This strategy was being offered to the students to help them become active readers in which they thoroughly engaged with the material for understanding and then through repetition stored the information in their long-term memories.

Several students who used this strategy went from making "Fs" to making "As." One of the students was so excited when she received her grade of "A" that she hollered out loud, bolted from her seat, ran down the aisle toward her professor and then gave him a big hug. Prior to this experience, she was failing all of her college courses in spite of reading the chapters in her textbooks.

Now, my friend has decided to conduct an experiment and do some action research to find out which of three different strategies will improve reading comprehension and test scores the most.

One group of students plans to read the chapters once before the next test, but will also pause after each paragraph and explain it out loud. They are not to go to the next paragraph until they understand the meaning of the preceding paragraph. Group 2 will read the chapters three times, but will not pause and explain the paragraphs. Group 3 will read each chapter three times and will also explain each paragraph three times.

Which of these three strategies will work best and in what order? Which group will make the highest scores? Which one will prove to be the most effective reading comprehension strategy? Read the following article to find out.

> ### Student Comment
>
> "I have always had problems with reading comprehension and keeping my attention on what I am reading. After I started using the reading strategies in this chapter my test scores went from Fs to As."
>
> — ADRIANNA VASQUEZ

## Reading Comprehension Strategy Makes Student Scream (Part 2)

**I promised to give you the results of my friend's study. Before I share his comments and results, I want to share what has happened with a few of my students.** A couple of my students made failing grades on two of my quizzes. I asked them to prepare for the next exam by reading the chapter once, but to stop after each paragraph and explain it out loud. The latest brain research indicates that most people can remember 90% of what they teach or explain compared to 10% of what they hear and 20% of what they both hear and see. Both of my students tried this strategy, and they made As on the next quiz. Another student improved from a D average on previous quizzes to a B after using this technique.

My friend is Lynn Skaggs, PhD and professor of psychology, at Central Texas College. Here are his results in his own words:

"The results were really good. I had 25 students participate and were pretty evenly distributed among the three groups: Group 1 – read once, summarizing each paragraph out loud before going to the next paragraph; Group 2 – read the chapter three times; Group 3 – do both.

I compared their grade with the average on their previous two tests.

Group 1 – grade increased 23%

Group 2 – grade increased 21%

Group 3 – grade increased 24%

There is really no significant difference in performance among the groups. The increase is the equivalent of a student averaging 75 increasing to a 92.

A confound was that almost all of Group 3 had good grades on their previous two tests, so their ability to improve was very limited. So, I looked at only students who had D or F averages:

Group 1 – increased 28%

Group 2 – increased 28%

This is the equivalent of a student with a 60 average increasing to 77 – from failing to passing.

Group 3 – There was only one student with D or F in this group, but his grade increased 57%!

Since there is really no difference between the study techniques, it probably comes down to a student finally studying, period, and using almost any technique that requires lots of involvement with the text.

The main technique error is in barely studying the text and focusing on notes taken from the text instead. That seems to be a recipe for failure.

Read the text, read the text, read the text is the recipe for success. However, the most important ingredient for success is for the student to make the effort to study and stop texting friends!"

---

Permission was granted by Professor Skaggs to use his comments.

**ACTIVITY 4.5** **Read the following article** one paragraph at a time. **Explain each paragraph out loud to yourself or to another person.**

## Focused Attention Is a Key to Success

One of the secrets of successful people is their ability to focus on the task at hand. Concentrated attention is the key to achievement in sports, school, relationships, and in your career.

Concentrated attention is similar to the power of focusing the rays of the sun through a magnifying glass on to a piece of paper. It burns a hole through the paper because the sun's rays are magnified. Similarly, you can magnify your results with concentrated attention.

Make a list of your priorities for each day. Tackle these tasks, which you identified as important one-by-one. Treat each task that you are doing as the most important activity of the day. This will help you to be totally present in the here and now. Do each activity with enjoyment and enthusiasm, if possible. If you are unable to be enthusiastic, at least do the activity with your attention until you have completed the task or reach an appropriate stopping point. Then, scratch it off of your to-do list (if it is unfinished, add it to tomorrow's list) and approach your next priority in the same way. This may not sound cool in this age of multi-tasking, but it will give you excellent results.

Be like a scientist and try this approach of focusing your attention on one task at a time as an experiment to see if it works for you. I think that you will be pleased with the results.

## Strategies You Can Use after Reading

❶ **Review the text.** Pay special attention to your highlights and annotations. The more often you review, the more you will remember. Review again as close to the time of the test as possible. If you can review in the morning before you take the test, this will ensure the material will be fresh in your mind.

❷ **Review your study guides.** If you haven't created any study guides, it is not too late to do so as you read. You can also create study guides after you have completed reading the chapters. Use whichever study guides seem best for the situation. Use the ones that work best for you.

❸ **Review your notes from the textbook reading and from class lectures.** Note taking will be discussed later in the next chapter.

❹ **Create a practice test with anticipated questions.** This can be a powerful study method. You can do this alone or - even better - with a couple of your classmates. Each of you can develop questions.

You can come up with more questions together than by yourself. If you anticipate even half of the questions that will

be on the test, it will be a big advantage for you. You will be able to answer those questions quickly and easily; then you can concentrate on the questions that you didn't anticipate. This will reduce your test anxiety and increase your level of self-confidence during the exam.

**❺ After you have read each chapter in the text, write a final summary.** Distill the material into the main points and ideas.

**❻ Teach others what you have learned.** The teacher learns as much or more than the student. When you teach the material you learn and retain it better. You strengthen what you already know and gain new perspectives or ways of looking at the material.

You can teach lessons to younger brothers or sisters, to friends, or if you have children who are old enough, you can teach them. Getting together with a couple of classmates offers an opportunity for you to teach each other. Each one of you can be responsible to teach different parts of the material to each other.

**❼ Seek help if anything is not clear.** If you are having difficulty understanding anything from the text or class notes, seek assistance. For example, see if tutoring is available. You can also seek assistance from a classmate or from your instructor.

ACTIVITY 4.6  Review the main points of what you have read in this chapter. Create a brief practice quiz. Write five multiple choice questions in your notebook with four possible answers for each question. Only one choice will be correct. Here is an example:

The key to effective reading is to be:

    A.     An active learner.

    B.     A passive learner.

    C.     A genius.

    D.     A speed reader.

Correct answer is A.

Now you have a variety of reading strategies to use. Be systematic, like a scientist, and experiment with these different strategies to find out what works best for you.

## JOURNAL ASSIGNMENT

Try out one of the reading strategies discussed in this chapter. Write at least one page in your journal describing your results and what you learned from using the reading strategy.

## AUTHOR'S NOTE

I had a student in one of my classes who was reading at seventh grade level according to her score on the Texas Success Initiative. This was the lowest reading level of anyone in my college success course. She failed my first two quizzes with scores of 40 and 50. I asked her to try the strategy of reading a paragraph in the text and then explaining it (teaching it) out loud to herself. I asked her not to go to the next paragraph until she understood the previous one. On the next quiz she made a 100.

On every quiz after that, she continued to make A' s. When I asked what she was doing to go from Fs to As, she said that she was following my advice and explaining each paragraph in the book to herself out loud. As a result of practicing this strategy, she was consistently out scoring other students with higher reading scores. She told me that using this one strategy transformed her life, helped her to develop a success mind-set, and gave her the confidence that she can succeed in college.

I suspect that her low reading score on the Texas Success Initiative was at least partially due to a reading attention problem. When she learned a way to focus and keep her attention on what she was reading, better comprehension was the result.

## Student Success Story

In one of my courses, I ask the students to write a paper about their educational journey from elementary, middle school, and high school, which led them to college. The paper usually reflects their learning experiences, obstacles, and what it took to get them to college. In the following story, a former student shares part of her educational journey.

### My Educational Journey

#### By Angelica Rubio

As I began my education years ago, I entered with high hopes. My future was bright and I was ready for the adventure. Somewhere along that journey, my promising future tumbled right before my eyes. It didn't happen over night; it was more of a slow deterioration of everything I had dreamed of becoming.

Looking back on those early years, I remember who and what I once wanted to be. I was a typical child who dreamt of being a veterinarian. It seems a little silly to me now, but then I believed it was within my grasp. I had all the potential to become anything I wanted because of all the effort and determination I put forth. It was amazing how learning came so natural to me even at this early age. I was always a straight A student and was very involved in my education.

Then, junior high came along and I was so thrilled. I was ready for the bigger and better challenges that came along with it. Although it was a big transition from elementary I never once allowed it to prevent me from always giving 100%. While there, I explored my learning abilities, which ultimately led to many achievements and awards. So many people around me believed that if I continued on this path, I was sure to succeed in a college career. As my junior high years came to an end, I was ready for the next challenge – high school.

High school, to me, was a whole different ball game. In a way, I guess you could say that I let the glamour of it all get the best of me. There were so many new things to experience, and I took the phrase, "have the time of your life" a little too literal. I used to think these four years were the best times of my life; boy how I was wrong! Somehow my love for school became just one big social occasion for me. My grades quickly dwindled down to ones that I could never have imagined. I took a long, hard drop to the bottom of the pit; it was such a disappointing feeling. Toward the end, I tried to make up for all the time lost, but I was a little too late. So, eventually, I quit and let down all those people who for years believed so strongly in me. Overall, what hurt the most was letting me down. Deep down I still had faith that somewhere, somehow, I would be somebody.

With all said and done, here I am today, a new Angelica who's ready to conclude that journey that I cut short so long ago. It may have taken me a little while, but I see it as better late than never. When I finally decided to start where I left off, I met someone who made me believe again. This woman not knowing anything about me had so much confidence in my ability. Today, I am thankful for her faith. I am at a point in my life where all I want to do is succeed. I am so determined, it has become my passion. My whole educational experience to this point is a lesson learned. I hope to never look back at what I once was or could have been. Like the saying goes, "You live and you learn." My outlook now is to live and learn another day for my future.

ACTIVITY 4.7  **Goal for the week:**

_____

Three steps I will take to achieve my goal:

1. _____

2. _____

3. _____

## SUMMARY OF MAIN POINTS IN CHAPTER 4

↗ Your reading ability and study skills are strongly related to college success. Be an active, not passive learner.

↗ Use study strategies such as: previewing, breaking up your reading, creating study guides, and annolighting to help you to be an effective reader.

↗ Ask yourself questions as you read and use them for self-testing.

↗ Explaining each paragraph in your own words and out loud will enhance your reading comprehension.

## QUESTIONS TO ANSWER IN YOUR JOURNAL AND DISCUSS WITH OTHERS

↗ What are my greatest strengths and weaknesses as a reader?

↗ Which of the reading and study strategies discussed in this chapter appeal to me the most? How will these strategies benefit me?

↗ What is one reading strategy that I will use right away and how will I use it?

↗ What was the most important lesson that I gained from the student success story in this chapter?

In Chapter 5, you will be learning systems for taking notes in class and better writing skills which can improve your grades on objective tests and the quality of your papers.

READING STRATEGIES

mindtools.com/rdstratg.html

## CHAPTER 5

# How to Take Good Notes and Write Well to Maximize Your Performance

### Note-Taking Skills

#### TAKING GOOD NOTES FOR SCHOOL SUCCESS

The information presented in your classes by teachers and professors usually contains important ideas and material, which will be included on exams. Most instructors include questions on exams that come both from the textbook and the class lectures. Many students do not realize the importance of listening in class with focused attention and taking good notes.

If you are not in class, you cannot listen to the instructor, cannot pick up verbal and nonverbal cues as to what is important, and cannot take notes. So, a major key to your success is attending class.

Note-taking helps you to concentrate on what your teacher or professor is saying. It helps you understand and organize the information in your textbook that is related to the lecture.

It is important for you to take good notes and review them often because you will forget information rapidly after you hear it. The Ebbinghaus Forgetting Curve reveals (Table 5.1) how much information you will remember with the passage of time. Hermann Ebbinghaus found that we tend to lose more than half of our memory of newly learned knowledge in a matter of days and weeks. This tends to happen unless you review the learned material.

So, you can see that if you do not attend your classes, listen attentively, take good notes, and review them; you will retain less and less of the material over time.

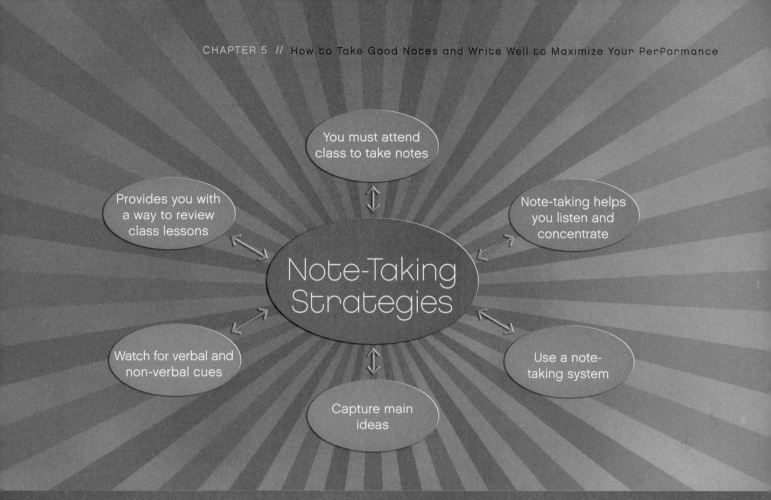

"*True ease in writing comes from art, not chance.*"
— Alexander Pope

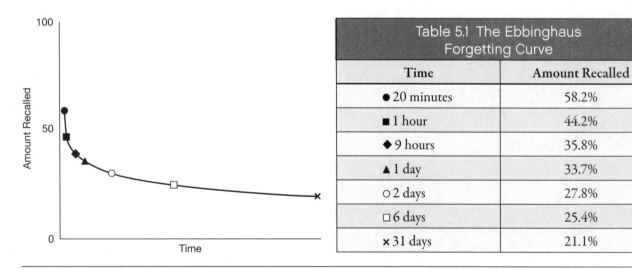

| Table 5.1 The Ebbinghaus Forgetting Curve | |
|---|---|
| **Time** | **Amount Recalled** |
| ● 20 minutes | 58.2% |
| ■ 1 hour | 44.2% |
| ◆ 9 hours | 35.8% |
| ▲ 1 day | 33.7% |
| ○ 2 days | 27.8% |
| □ 6 days | 25.4% |
| ✕ 31 days | 21.1% |

*Source:* Hermann Ebbinghaus, *Memory: A Contribution to Experimental Psychology,* (1885). Translated by Henry A. Ruger & Clara E. Bussenius (1913). Originally published in New York by Teachers College, Columbia University.

## Benefits of Effective Note-Taking

↗ Important information is recorded and available to you for review instead of forgotten

↗ Helps you to concentrate in class, stay alert, and be an active learner

↗ Helps you organize information

↗ Complements and makes information in the textbook easier for you to understand

↗ Improves your grades on exams and class assignments

↗ Builds your critical thinking ability

↗ Builds your listening skills

↗ Provides you with information to study that may not be in the textbook

↗ Improves your overall learning

## Active Listening Is Important For Effective Note-Taking

Active listening means that you are engaged with the lecture. You can do this by:

↗ **Listening with your focused attention.** This means being fully present.

↗ **Asking questions both silently and out loud.** You can ask questions silently within your own mind and also ask your instructor questions to stay engaged.

↗ **Watching for verbal and nonverbal cues.** You will find what information is important by listening and watching your instructor's verbal cues and body language.

↗ **Writing what you are hearing in your own words.** You will understand and remember your own words better than the words of others. Translate your instructor's lectures into your own words so it makes sense to you.

↗ **Evaluating what you are hearing.** Analyze and evaluate the information presented to separate the important from the unimportant

ACTIVITY 5.1 Think about the internal and external distractions that interfere with your ability to listen well. List three of these distractions and brainstorm ideas for reducing them.

1. _____

   _____

   _____

2. _____

   _____

   _____

3. _____

   _____

## NOTE-TAKING ASSESSMENT

Decide to what extent each statement applies to you. Circle the rating that fits you best at this time.

| | | Rarely | Sometimes | Often | Almost always |
|---|---|---|---|---|---|
| ❶ | I attend my classes. | 1 | 2 | 3 | 4 |
| ❷ | I pay attention and listen with focused attention. | 1 | 2 | 3 | 4 |
| ❸ | I take notes. | 1 | 2 | 3 | 4 |
| ❹ | I take notes in my own words. | 1 | 2 | 3 | 4 |
| ❺ | I ask questions silently and out loud. | 1 | 2 | 3 | 4 |
| ❻ | I use a specific note-taking system. | 1 | 2 | 3 | 4 |
| ❼ | I review my notes soon after class. | 1 | 2 | 3 | 4 |
| ❽ | I compare my notes to the textbook. | 1 | 2 | 3 | 4 |
| ❾ | I write down main points and use abbreviations. | 1 | 2 | 3 | 4 |
| ❿ | I review my notes often before my test. | 1 | 2 | 3 | 4 |

ACTIVITY 5.2 **List your three biggest note-taking problems. Brainstorm several possible solutions to each problem.**

1. _____

   _____

   _____

2. _____

   _____

   _____

3. _____

   _____

   _____

## TIPS TO HELP YOU TAKE EFFECTIVE NOTES

1. **Attend your classes.** You cannot take notes if you are not in class. It is also important to be rested and alert when you take notes. Take your textbook, notebook, pens, and other materials that you will need to class so you can take good class notes. It will really help if you read chapters ahead of time before your instructor discusses them in class.

2. **Pay attention to verbal and nonverbal cues.** Your instructor will often give you hints as to what is important.

   **A. Verbal cues** – The instructor's voice becomes excited, slows down or speeds up, pauses before and after a comment and she varies pitch, repeats something, says "listen to this" or "an important point is", or other comments, which indicate that an important idea is being stated.

   **B. Nonverbal cues** – The instructor's eyes or face lights up, gestures become animated, he paces back and forth, looks to see if students are taking notes, points to information on the board or to a handout or PowerPoint slide.

3. **Sit close so you can see and hear well.** Obviously, you need to be able to hear the instructor. Sit close enough to watch the instructor's expressions so you can pick up nonverbal cues.

4. **Write legibly.** You want to write neatly enough so you can read your notes later.

5. **Leave a couple of lines between topics.** This allows you to fill in what you missed after class.

6. **Compare notes with a classmate.** Each of you may have written and missed something different from each other. "Two heads are better than one."

7. **Do not try to write everything down.** Take down what you feel is important, not too much or too little is a good rule of thumb.

8. **Annotate your notes after class when you have time.** Use the same process of annotating or annolighting your class notes that you learned for textbooks.

9. **Date and number your pages and identify the subject.** This keeps your notes organized, and it will be easy to find the notes from class lectures when you need them.

10. **Review and edit your notes soon after class.** The sooner you review your notes, the easier it will be to fill in missing information. It will be fresh in your mind. Every time you review your notes, you will retain more information.

11. **Read or skim chapters before the instructor discusses them in class.** If you do this, you will be familiar with the material and will be able to take better notes.

12. **Ask questions in class.** You can ask the instructor questions for a better or clearer understanding of the lecture and material. This also allows you to slow the instructor down so you will have more time to capture important points. You can also ask questions silently in your mind, which can help you to stay focused and alert.

13. **Create study guides and anticipated test questions from your notes.** This is something you can do soon after class. You can create study guides, which you learned earlier in this chapter, and make up practice quizzes from your notes.

14. **Compare the text to your class notes.** The text and your notes will usually complement each other. Both usually make more sense to you when you compare them.

*Student Comment*

"I learned how to take better notes and writing skills. I learned valuable skills that I can use in my other courses and in my life."
— JOSE PALICIOUS

15. **It is better to write on one side of the paper.** This allows you the opportunity to place your notes side by side for easier reviewing.

16. **Include examples and facts, which illustrate important points.** This allows you to say and understand more of what is in your notes.

17. **Rewrite key ideas in your own words.** Summarize what you think are the most important ideas.

18. **Use abbreviations and symbols.**

    For example:

    - Write "psy" instead of "psychology".
    - Put a star sign by important points.
    - Use symbols like equal (=) instead of writing out the word.
    - Shorten words like "continued" and write "cont'd" instead.

    These are just a few examples of how you can abbreviate and shorten words to save time when writing notes. You can create and use your own abbreviations, symbols, and shortcuts that work for you as long as you can understand what you have written. This will increase your speed at taking notes.

19. **Review your notes soon after taking them and before exams.** This is as important as reviewing your textbook. It is important to review your notes within a day after taking notes and at the end of the week to help get this information into your long-term memory. Then, review again before your quiz, but first, self-test. Create a practice quiz, give it to yourself, and test your understanding and recall.

20. **Use a note-taking system.** There are several note-taking systems to choose from. For example, you can use an outline method to emphasize major topics. Under the major topics, you can add subtopics and under these, list supporting points, examples, and illustrations.

## Examples of Note-Taking Systems

You can use an idea map, which was discussed earlier, as a note-taking system. This is especially useful, if you are a visual learner.

One of the most popular note-taking systems is the Cornell Method. In this system, you divide the page into three sections (See Figure 5.1). The largest section is on your right (usually about six inches wide); you use this space for taking notes during class. You can also use this space while taking notes when you read the text. Use the left section (about two and a half inches wide) after class to write in questions or make statements that are addressed in your notes. Use bottom section (about two inches deep and eight and a half inches wide) for summarizing what you think are the main points.

## Cornell System of Note-Taking

Figure 5.1 is an example of the Cornell Method being used to take notes on the subject of How to Write Essay Papers.

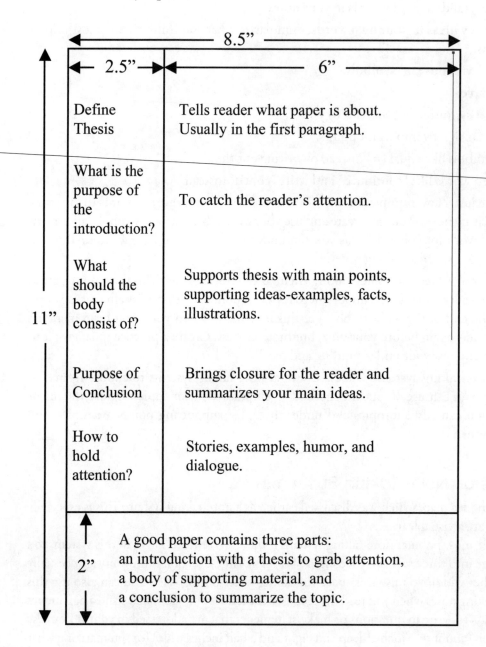

FIGURE 5.1    CORNELL NOTE-TAKING SAMPLE: HOW TO WRITE ESSAY PAPERS

Now you can see the value of note-taking and how taking good notes will contribute to your success in school.

## Outline Method

An outline method of note-taking works well for linear thinkers who like to take notes in an organized and logical sequence. It is similar to using other outline formats that you have probably used before (See Figure 5.2):

---

I. **Main idea #1.** Knowing how to plan a research project is the first step.

   1. **Supporting point.** Identify sources and where to look for information.

      A. Example: World Wide Web or library databases.

      B. Example: Information that is recent and reliable versus old and unreliable information.

II. **Main idea #2.** Keyword searching is different from subject searching.

   1. **Supporting point.** Key word searches usually bring up many more documents and irrelevant items than a subject search.

      A. **Example:** "Time management" is a keyword phrase that will bring up many documents.

      B. **Example:** "Time Management for college students" will bring up less documents, but they will be more relevant.

---

**FIGURE 5.2**   OUTLINE SAMPLE: LIBRARY RESEARCH

## Idea Map

You have seen an example of an idea map used for reading comprehension. The principle is the same for taking notes and is especially appealing to visual learners and students who are strong in Visual-Spatial Intelligence. Idea maps are also referred to as mind maps or think links. See Figure 5.3 sample below.

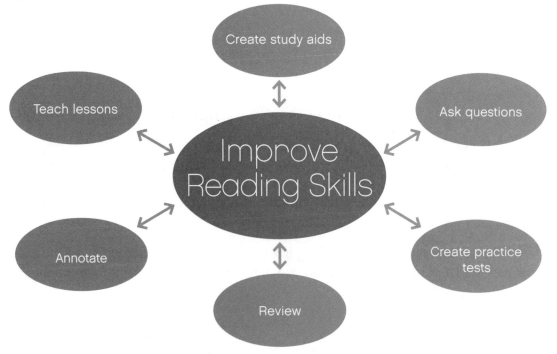

**FIGURE 5.3**   NOTE-TAKING IDEA MAP SAMPLE: IMPROVE READING SKILLS

## Parallel Note-Taking System

If your instructor provides you with lecture notes before the topic is covered in class, you can use parallel note-taking. This is an excellent system for taking advantage of online notes.

This system works best with a three-ring binder. On one side are your instructor's lecture notes and on the other side is a blank sheet of paper for your notes. During the lecture, record your notes on the blank paper with the instructor's lecture notes in front of you. In other words, the instructor's notes and the paper for your notes will be parallel to each other (See Figure 5.4).

| How to Get Your Priorities Accomplished | How to Get Your Priorities Accomplished |
|---|---|
| **Instructor's notes** | **My notes** |
| Make a list of your priorities for each day. Tackle these tasks which you identified as important one-by-one. Treat each task that you are doing as the most important activity of the day. | Each day, I list my priorities in order of importance and do them one at a time. |
| This will help you to be totally present in the here and now. Do each activity with enjoyment and enthusiasm, if possible. If you are unable to be enthusiastic, at least do the activity with your attention until you have completed the task or reach an appropriate stopping point. | Doing them with enthusiasm is best, but at least with attention. |
| Then, scratch it off of your to-do list (if it is unfinished add it to tomorrow's list) and approach your next priority in the same way. This may not sound cool in this age of multi-tasking, but it will give you excellent results. | Complete the task and scratch off my list. |

FIGURE 5.4   PARALLEL NOTES SAMPLE:
HOW TO GET YOUR PRIORITIES ACCOMPLISHED

## CONNECT NOTE-TAKING TO YOUR BEST MULTIPLE INTELLIGENCES

In Chapter 2, you identified your three strongest multiple intelligences. You can use these intelligences for effective note-taking. For example, if you are strong in musical intelligence, go over your notes after class and translate important ideas into a rap, rhyme, or song. If you are strong in logical-mathematical intelligence, use an outline method, put the main ideas into a logical order, and analyze the connection between these ideas.

ACTIVITY 5.3   Identify three note-taking strategies that match your top three multiple intelligences. Think about how you can use these intelligences to take better notes.

Best Multiple Intelligences                    Best Note-Taking Strategies

1. _____          _____

2. _____          _____

3. _____          _____

As you practice taking notes and use at least one note-taking system, you will see an improvement in your grades if you edit, study, and review your notes. Using good note-taking skills is one of the keys to college success.

Now you have four different note-taking systems from which to choose. You may prefer to use one system, a variation of a system, or to use different systems when appropriate for the situation.

## Writing Skills

### BENEFITS OF WRITING WELL

↗ Increases your job opportunities

↗ Improves your grades and college achievement

↗ Helps you to do better on essay tests

↗ Allows you to write articles in your career field

↗ Communicates your level of professionalism and expertise

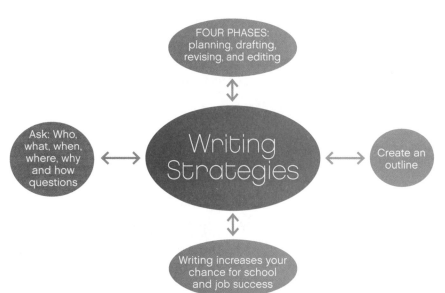

## Tips for Writing Good Papers

There are four main phases or stages of writing.
They are: 1) planning 2) drafting 3) revising, and 4) editing. Let's look at the purpose of each stage.

### STAGE 1: PLANNING

In this phase, you will be deciding on your topic (unless your instructor gives you one). You will be thinking about what you want to say about your topic. Even if your instructor chooses your topic, you will write about it in your own unique style. The planning phases consists of the following steps:

**1. Choose a topic you are passionate about.** If you didn't choose the topic, you should still look for parts of the topic that interest you. Write about what you know.

**2. Brainstorm.** Jot down topic ideas as fast as they come into your mind. If the topic was chosen for you, then write down ideas about what you already know and want to say about it in your own way.

**3. Determine your audience.** Who are you writing this paper for? Have an audience in mind for whom you will be writing, even if only the instructor will read your paper.

**4. Narrow down your topics and ideas.** Identify the topic you will write about. Narrow down the main ideas you want to cover.

**5. Write your thesis statement.** Write "The purpose of my paper is" and complete the sentence. What is your paper going to be about?

**6. Ask questions like a journalist.** Who? What? Where? When? Why? How?
Answer these questions for yourself.

Below are examples of using journalistic questions to write a paper. I will show you a sample paper at the end of the Writing Tips section.

1. **Who?** Who has had bad experiences that had a benefit?

2. **What?** What are examples of these experiences?

3. **When?** When did these events happen?

4. **Where?** Where did these events take place?

5. **Why?** Why were these experiences important?

6. **How?** How was good found in these bad experiences?

7. **Create an outline.** Make an outline before writing your paper. Include your introduction and thesis statement, at least three main points for the body of your paper to support your thesis, and your conclusion. Let's look at a sample outline below:

## Sample Outline

Title:  The Hidden Benefits in Life's Difficulties

**❶** Introduction.

    **A.** Napoleon Hill opening quotation.

    **B.** Thesis statement– "Every bad experience has a benefit."

**❷** Body.

    **A.** Supporting paragraph and idea #1.

        **1.** Overcoming adversity can lead to greatness.

        **2.** Abraham Lincoln example.

    **B.** Supporting paragraph and idea #2.

        **1.** Good is often hidden in what seems to be bad.

        **2.** Story of wise persons in India.

    **C.** Supporting paragraph and idea #3.

        **1.** There is opportunity in crisis.

        **2.** My personal health crisis story.

**❸** Conclusion and summary.

    **A.** Adversity can lead to greatness.

    **B.** Benefits are hidden in bad experiences.

    **C.** Opportunity can be found in crisis.

    **D.** Good is hidden in bad experiences.

ACTIVITY 5.4 Think of a paper that you will be writing for one of your classes. Write out the thesis statement. Answer the six journalistic questions.

## STAGE 2: DRAFTING

This is the second phase of writing your paper. The first draft is your first actual writing of your paper. Here are steps for the drafting phase:

    1. **Freewrite your first draft.** Write with your heart (later you will edit with your mind). Let the ideas flow without criticizing or judging what you are writing. Try to write

without lifting your pen from the page or your fingers from the keyboard of your computer. Let it flow.

2. **Research.** After freewriting, is a good time to gather facts, stories, and examples to support your thesis and main idea. Some people advise doing research sooner. My personal experience has been that it is better to freewrite first to say what you think and feel, then do research to support your thoughts.

3. **Introduction.** Include your thesis statement and attention grabbers in your introduction. Your thesis tells your audience the purpose of your paper. You can grab the reader's attention by using a quotation, a startling statement, a good question, humor, or a human interest story.

4. **Body.** Develop each supporting paragraph. Every paragraph in the body of your paper should support your main points. A good rule of thumb is to have at least three points or ideas that support your thesis. Use a separate paragraph for each of these points.

5. **Write clear and simple sentences.** Write as if you are having a conversation with one person in your target audience.

6. **Stay focused on the main topic.** Move from sentence to sentence and from paragraph to paragraph so it flows and makes sense.

7. **Conclusion.** This is where you summarize your main points. You can end with a call to action, a story, or with a great quotation, if any of these are appropriate for your paper and audience.

## STAGE 3: REVISING

In this third phase, you evaluate your paper to see what you need to improve, reshape, and rewrite. In the drafting phase, you did freewriting from your heart without making any revisions. Now you have the opportunity to fill in details and improve your first draft.

Ask yourself:

1. Does your thesis, your thesis sentence, and paper meet your writing purpose?

2. Is it clear and simple to understand?

3. Will it grab the reader's attention?

4. Does the body contain ideas which support your thesis?

5. Does it flow?

6. Do you have a strong conclusion?

Answering these questions will help you to know what needs revising.

This is the phase in which you take a look at the overall structure (big picture) of your paper. Then, look at your paragraphs. See if they are organized well, flow easily from one to another, and if they are too short or too long. Rearrange your paragraphs, if necessary, so that they are in a logical sequence. Do the same thing with your sentences. When you finish revising, the content and structure of your paper should be in good shape.

Eliminate words and information that are unnecessary. For example, remove sentences or words that you have repeated unnecessarily. Replace words with different ones that will make your writing clearer, more interesting, and more believable.

## STAGE 4: EDITING

This stage involves correcting grammar, punctuation, and spelling errors. Use a computer to spell-check. Also, manually check for spelling errors that the computer might miss. Check your commas and periods to make sure that they are in the best place. Do you need any exclamation marks, colons, or semicolons? This is the phase to make grammatical improvements and to proof and polish your work.

One approach you can use is to proofread your paper from back to front. When you read your sentences from the end of the paper to the beginning, it will help you to focus and catch errors that you would normally miss.

Read your paper out loud. If you run out of breath while reading a sentence, it is probably too long and may need to be shortened. Seek assistance if you need someone with good grammatical skills. Learning labs at colleges usually have assistants who will look over your paper to point out grammatical errors and to make suggestions for improvement.

Wait a while before looking over your paper for the final time. Proofread your paper one more time, and complete the final draft of your paper before turning it in to your instructor.

Now let's look at an example of a paper that I wrote from the outline you saw earlier.

## Sample Paper

### The Hidden Benefits in Life's Difficulties

By Raymond Gerson

"Every adversity, every failure, and every heartache carries with it the seed of an equivalent or greater benefit." These are the words of Napoleon Hill who spent his life studying successful people and the obstacles they had to overcome. Based on Napoleon Hill's experience interviewing hundreds of successful people, he concluded that every bad experience has a benefit. I believe that you also can find something good and benefit from difficult life experiences.

You can become a greater person by overcoming adversity. Take the example of Abraham Lincoln. Lincoln's sweetheart died, he had a nervous breakdown, was demoted while serving in the military, failed in business, and lost several elections. Many historians agree that he was one of the finest human beings and presidents we have had in the United States. Lincoln's many adversities seemed to only make him stronger and more determined.

Good is often hidden in experiences that seem to be bad. There is a story that illustrates this idea. Long ago in India, there were no matches and people covered their cooking fires with ashes. The ashes kept the fires alive. In a particular village, all of the fires mysteriously went out. The villagers were upset because they had no way to cook. They went to see the wise one of their village and told him about their problem. He replied, "This is something good." This sounded crazy to the villagers, but the wise one just said, "Wait and see." A couple of days later a cruel king passed through the country with his army of soldiers. They killed people and destroyed villages. One night when the king came to the village with no fires, he thought that no one must live there. So the king ordered his soldiers to go on to the next village. This story illustrates how something good can lie hidden in something that appears to be bad.

The opposite side of crisis is often opportunity. When I was in high school, I became ill because I was not taking good care of myself. I had to be out of school for six weeks. At first, this seemed like a terrible crisis to me. I was so bored that I began to study for the first time in my life. When I returned to school, I had to take many make-up tests, but to my surprise I made As and Bs. Because of this experience, I made the decision to go to college. I am still enjoying a wonderful career because of my decision to attend college. I also realized that my health was important and began taking good care of myself. I am still experiencing the payoff today. What seemed like a crisis at the time turned out to be an opportunity to attend college and become healthy.

In conclusion, there is a benefit and something good in every bad experience. Overcoming adversity can make you great, good is often hidden in bad experiences. There is opportunity in every crisis. Look for the good in your difficulties and you will find it.

> *Student Comment*
>
> "The Hidden Benefits in Life's Difficulties made me realize that through all my pain I can still come out on top. This book is powerful because it gives you information that benefits not only college success, but your life in general."
> — BETTY HALL

## THINK LIKE AN ARTIST WHEN YOU WRITE

When you have a paper to write, think of yourself as an artist who is going to create a sculpture. The planning phase is similar to an artist coming up with the idea for creating the sculpture. In the drafting phase, you are taking chunks and shaping them into a general outline. The revising phase is where you add details to make your sculpture look better. In the final editing phase, you polish your work, add any finer details, and smooth out any errors. Do your best to turn your writing into a memorable work of art!

## JOURNAL ASSIGNMENT

List the two most important note-taking strategies and two most valuable writing tips that you learned from this chapter. Reflect on and write your ideas for applying these strategies and tips to maximize your performance in school.

## AUTHOR'S NOTE

In the early stages of my college success courses, I always notice that several students aren't taking notes. Even when I say, "Be sure and study these ideas (which I name) because there will be questions about them on the test," some students still don't take notes. This never ceases to amaze me. In time, I am able to convince most of these students to take notes in class. It has been my experience that if you don't take notes, you are likely to do poorly in class or dropout.

## Student Success Story

The following paper was written by Tomas Carrizales-Rodriguez. He got off track, dropped out of high school, and spent some time in trouble with the law. Fortunately, with the right type of support and through his own effort, Tomas turned his life around.

## From Dropout to Graduate

By Tomas Carrizales-Rodriguez

The biggest accomplishment in my life was finishing high school at the age of 16 and enrolling in Austin Community College. This was important for me because I am the first in my family to attend any type of higher education.

I had trouble in high school because I went to DAEP. This is a school where the bad students go and I was there for a year. I hated it there so I stopped going to school. For the next two years, I was a dropout. I was just doing drugs and not going home. I would get in trouble with the cops and my mom just got tired of it. So she went up to the high school for help and she found Mr. Day, one of the principals. He told my mom to bring me up to the school so he could talk to me.

I had always felt judged by high school principals because no matter whether I was good or not, I was blamed and sent to DAEP. So I didn't want to go back to school or talk to this new principal. Mr. Day said, "I can help you if you let me Tomas." I asked, "How can you help me?" "Well, first you need to get back in school, then I can help you a lot more." I said, "I don't want to go back to DAEP." Mr. Day said, "Well, you have to go for two weeks and you will be out. Then, I can help you get your credits that you need to finish high school and, hopefully, you can go to college."

I think one of the biggest steps I had to take was to quit feeling sorry for myself. I feel I had a pretty tough life. I grew up without a dad and that was tough on me. My family struggled to get by and this fuelled my anger at the world. Once I started to mature, I looked back and thought, "All I am doing is hurting me. If I don't want this to keep repeating, I have to fix it now or I will have no future."

I knew I could not do this all on my own. If I had not had the support of my mom who never gave up on me and the guidance from the Opportunity Center, I'm scared to think where I would be now.

When Mr. Day put me in Atlas, I had no credits and I was about to turn 15 so I was pretty far behind. I met with Mr. Day and the counselors and set up a plan for me to get caught up and graduate early. It was up to me to make it happen. I had to stay focused and attend school everyday. The Opportunity Center was a great place to be. The teachers will help you one-on-one and they don't look down on you if you act up a little bit. They just want to help you. I was getting my credits faster than I thought and they told me that I could graduate early. I needed help on my reading and writing so Mrs. Horton helped with that as well as with my college paperwork. She is a huge influence in my life. A lot of people from Del Valle Opportunity Center helped me turn my life around and to become a success.

I learned many lessons from this experience. I know the importance of having faith in myself. You have to believe in yourself first before anyone can help you. Also, no matter how tough your life is, someone else has it just as bad or even worse than you. I learned that it is important to be at school everyday and be on time. This is a habit you will need throughout your entire life. I learned that there are a lot of good people out there who care about students and people no matter how messed up they are. I know to set goals and dream big because if you work hard anything can happen. I feel I picked up good study skills and work habits. I think all these things apply to everyday life. Because school is not just about knowledge, it is also a guide to the rest of your life. When I get a job, I know I need to be there on time and have good attendance. I have to be able to pick up what they are teaching me and I might have to do extra at home so I can get ahead at my job.

I know I still have a lot to learn, but life is one big lesson in failure and success. I am proud that I graduated from High School and am attending ACC. This by far is the biggest success of my life. It has taught me study and note-taking skills or I would not have been able to graduate early because it is not easy to pick up all those credits as quickly as I did. It has taught me to be prepared. It has also taught me to believe in myself. I hope with what I learned in the past, combined with this course, I can achieve my next success and that is graduating from college.

ACTIVITY 5.5 **Goal for the week:**

_____

Three steps I will take to achieve my goal:

1. _____
2. _____
3. _____

## SUMMARY OF MAIN POINTS IN CHAPTER 5

↗ Use a note-taking system to capture important points and take better notes to study and review.

↗ It is important for you to take good notes, review them within twenty-four hours, again in a week and again before the test because otherwise information is quickly forgotten after you hear it for the first time.

↗ Asking and answering journalistic questions and preparing an outline will help you to write better papers and in less time.

↗ A good paper will include an introduction and thesis which grabs the reader's attention, a body with strong supporting ideas, and a conclusion, which brings the topic to closure and leaves the reader wanting more.

## QUESTIONS TO ANSWER IN YOUR JOURNAL AND DISCUSS WITH OTHERS

↗ What does the Ebbinghaus Forgetting Curve reveal to me about the importance of taking notes in class?

↗ What are my strengths and weaknesses as a note taker? Which note-taking strategies will help me the most—and why?

↗ How can I best apply the four stages of writing to write better quality papers?

↗ What three strategies will I use to improve my writing ability? Why do I think they will improve my writing?

In Chapter 6, you will be learning test-taking and memory strategies, which can boost your grade point average, increase self-confidence, and reduce test anxiety.

DARTMOUTH ACADEMIC SKILLS CENTER
Note-taking tips

dartmouth.edu/~acskills/success/notes.html

COLLEGE WRITING TIPS
collegewritingtips.net

# What Students Ought to Know About Memory and Test-Taking Strategies

In this chapter, you will learn several memory techniques that you can use to remember more of what you study and learn. Later in the chapter, you will learn many different test-wise strategies that will improve your skills and confidence when preparing for and taking tests. Also, you will learn ways to reduce or eliminate test anxiety. Having a better memory plus effective test preparation and test-taking skills are a powerful combination that will help you achieve success during your college career.

## How to Remember More of What You Want to Retain and Recall

A better memory will help you to retain and recall more information from the text and class lectures for your tests and papers. A better memory can help you to achieve greater success in school. Even on exams that have questions, which require an understanding of concepts and principles, you will not do well, if you don't remember information related to those principles. Good recall will make it possible for you to use information in school, your career, and in your life when it's needed.

Your short-term memory stores information for a few seconds up to a few minutes. Your long-term memory contains information that requires you to use more effort to retain it and your conscious effort to recall it.

There are a variety of memory aids known as **mnemonics,** which you will be learning in this chapter. **Mnemonics** are memory aids that help you to quickly and easily remember information.

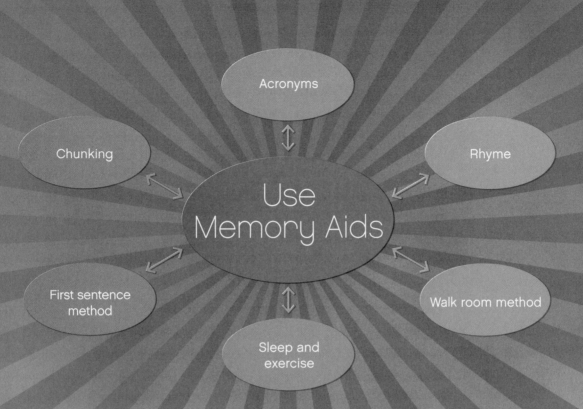

"*An education isn't how much you have committed to memory, or even how much you know. It's knowing where to go to find out what you need to know, and it's knowing how to use the information you get.*" —William Feather

## Benefits of Memory Aids and Having a Good Memory

↗ You can learn and recall facts, names, and figures more easily

↗ Your brain functioning improves because you stimulate parts of your brain

↗ Your test scores will usually improve

↗ Improves your concentration

↗ You will be able to recall more information when writing papers

↗ You will be better at remembering people's names, which improves relationships

## HERE ARE SOME WAYS TO HAVE A BETTER MEMORY

1. **Exercise.** It increases oxygen to your brain.

2. **Get enough sleep.** If you are in your teens or early adulthood, you need eight to ten hours of sleep a night. Studying before getting a good night's sleep can help you to remember more information.

3. **Keep stress levels low.** High stress will interfere with your concentration.

4. **Don't smoke.** Smoking will reduce oxygen to your brain.

5. **Drink enough water.** Your brain is made up of a high percentage of water, and you need it to function well.

6. **Eat well.** A healthy diet helps your brain to be healthy and function well.

## STRATEGIES TO IMPROVE MEMORY

1. **Use several of the study strategies you learned earlier.** Break up your study periods, review often, organize your materials, and create study aids such as flash cards and idea maps. All of these are memory aids, which will improve your success in school.

2. **Pay attention.** You cannot remember material that you never noticed or learned.

3. **Create memorable images.** Word pictures aid your memory. For example, to remember Pat's name, you can picture her in your mind patting her shoulder. For someone named Mike, you could picture and associate him with a microphone in his hand.

4. **Use your preferred learning style.** If you prefer auditory learning, then tape-record what you want to remember and play it back. If you are a visual learner, use pictures, charts, graphs, idea maps, and things you can see.

5. **Use as many senses as possible.** Learn a poem while seeing the words and any pictures associated with these words. Read the poem out loud so you can hear it, and move around while reading. In this way, you will use several of your five senses at the same time.

6. **Create interest.** You will remember more material if you can make it interesting. Material that bores you is more difficult to remember.

7. **Associate what you are learning with something humorous.** Anything you find to be funny or even ridiculous will be easier for you to recall.

8. **Associate or relate the new material to something already familiar.** A student of mine remembered that he gets vitamin D from the sun by picturing himself walking his dog (D for dog) outside in the sun. He said he will probably never forget which vitamin we get from the sun because of the association he created.

9. **Rehearse, recite, and overlearn.** If you are learning a poem or quotation, recite it over and over. It will go into your long-term memory, and you will eventually be able to repeat the poem without thinking about it.

10. **Use mnemonic techniques.** Examples of these memory aids and shortcuts are listed and explained below:

    A. **Acronyms** – These are initials that create pronounceable words such as NBA for National Basketball Association. Another example is Roy.G.Biv so you can remember the colors of the rainbow.

    B. **Acrostics or first letter strategy** – Take the first letter of each of the items you want to remember and make a word or phrase out of these letters. A popular example is "Please excuse my dear aunt Sally." This is a mnemonic for "Parenthesis, Exponents, Multiplication, Division, Addition, and Subtraction." This is the order in which operations in algebraic expressions are to be evaluated.

    C. **Rhyme** – Jingles and rhymes will aid your memory. For example, "In 1492, Columbus sailed the ocean blue" or "30 days hath September, April, June, and November."

    D. **Chunking** – When you arrange a list such as numbers into smaller units, this becomes a memory aid. For example, 19531825 can be chunked into 1953 and 1825 or 1953_18_25.

    E. **Method of loci** – Associate what you want to remember with a familiar route or path. Let's say you need to remember parts of the body in a particular order such as heart, brain, lungs, and kidneys. Picture a walk through your house and associate parts of the house with each part of the body. For example, when you enter the house you could picture a photo of a loved one in the living room (heart), a picture of Einstein (brain) in the hallway, an exercise machine (lungs) in the master bedroom, and a can of kidney beans (kidneys) in the kitchen. When you see this question on a test, you will easily recall the correct order of these body parts by recalling your walk through your house.

Keep in mind that just memorizing information by itself will not be enough for success in college. You need to combine memorization with learning and understanding the concepts.

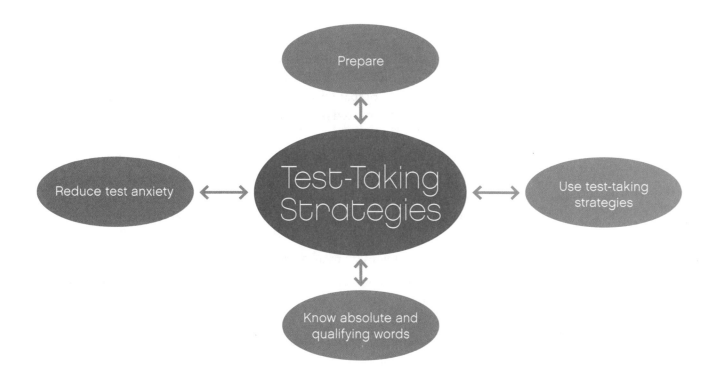

## Test-Taking Skills

Learning a variety of test-taking strategies is an important part of your academic success. You will be taking exams throughout your education. These tests usually account for a high percentage, if not all, of your grade in each course. No matter how much you study, you will not do your best unless you know how to prepare for and take tests.

## Benefits of Test-Taking Skills

↗ Reduces your test anxiety

↗ Increases your self-confidence

↗ Makes good use of your types of intelligence

↗ Improves your test scores and grades

↗ Increases your self-confidence for other evaluations and exams that you take later in your career

↗ Improves your self-esteem

↗ Gives you more motivation for pursuing your education

↗ Gives you greater ability to focus on learning due to less anxiety about tests

## General Test Preparation Strategies

Here are some general strategies that will help you: prepare for tests, while you are taking a test, and useful tools after taking a test. I will also cover specific test-taking strategies for the various types of tests that you will be taking. First, here are some tools and strategies you can use to prepare for a test.

### TEST PREPARATION STRATEGIES

1. **Find out what kind of test you will be taking.** Will you be taking an essay, a multiple-choice test, fill-in-the-blank, or some other type of test? You need to answer this question to prepare properly for your test. Talk with your instructor to find out what will be covered on the test. Learn as much as possible about your upcoming test.

2. **Set a goal test score you want to achieve.** Study with your goal in mind.

3. **Use the reading and study strategies you previously learned.** One way to prepare for the test is by applying the strategies you learned in the last chapter. Create study guides that will help you prepare for your test and which use your preferred learning style.

4. **Use the memory strategies that you learned earlier in this chapter.**

5. **Apply test anxiety reduction techniques (discussed later in this chapter) to reduce your anxiety before the test.** Picture yourself in your mind taking the test and being relaxed and successful.

6. **Be positive.** Use positive self-talk in the days and hours before you take the test.

7. **Get a good night of sleep.**

8. **Build up your energy.** Eat something nutritious before the test so that your blood sugar and energy level are in good shape. Remember that your physical condition affects your state of mind and vice versa.

9. **Review your notes and highlights as often as possible.** Just before your test, review your notes one last time so the material is fresh in your mind.

10. **Develop a practice test.** Anticipate test questions and give yourself the practice quiz. As you learned in the last chapter, it is helpful to study with and teach others.

11. **Finish reading assignments a few days before the test date.** This leaves you time to spend reviewing the material that you consider most important.

12. **Talk with students who have already taken the course.** You can look at old exams if other students have them. Ask the former students what you can expect and for any advice they can give you for succeeding on the test.

13. **Remind yourself of your long-range goals.** Refresh your memory about why you want an education and the importance to you of succeeding in school. Remind

yourself of the benefits you will receive. This will keep you motivated to prepare for the test.

14. **Arrive a little early to relax and review.**

15. **Bring all of your necessary materials to class.** Bring your pens, Scantrons, #2 pencils, and blue books, if required.

ACTIVITY 6.1    Take a few minutes to sit quietly by yourself and take some slow, deep breaths.. Relax your mind and body. In your mind's eye, see yourself taking the test. In this relaxed state, see yourself taking the test while feeling clear-minded and positive. Picture yourself successfully completing the test with a big smile on your face.

## SUCCESS STRATEGIES TO USE DURING THE TEST

1. **Before you start the test, jot down information on the back of the test that you are concerned you might forget.** Get your instructor's permission to do this.

2. **Look the test over to find out what it covers.** For example, let's say you see that the test has thirty multiple-choice questions and two essay questions. You should decide how much time you need to spend on both sets of questions. If you have forty minutes to take the test and need twenty minutes on the essay questions, then you will know that you have twenty minutes to complete the multiple-choice questions. When you look over the test in the beginning, you will also be able to see which questions will be easier for you to answer and which ones will be difficult for you and will require more time.

3. **Answer questions that you know and the easier ones first.** This will allow you more time to concentrate on the less familiar and difficult questions.

4. **Read the instructions and questions thoroughly.** The questions will often provide you with clues for the correct answer on objective tests and for what your instructor wants you to write about on essay tests.

5. **Answer every question.** If there is "no penalty for guessing," it's best for you to answer every question, even if you have to guess.

6. **Make sure the test questions and your answers match.** If you are using a Scantron or separate answer sheet, it is very important that you make sure the questions and answers match up.

7. **Keep track of time.** You will need to stay aware of how much time you have left during the test. This will allow you to pace yourself, and it increases your chances of completing the test.

8. **Use all of the available time.** Go over your test to check for accuracy. Make sure you answered every question and make any changes you think are needed.

*Student Comment*

"I cannot begin to tell you how scared I was of college classes at first because I was afraid of failure. Studying for tests was my weakest spot in school. Every time it was test day I would try to cram as much information as I could before the test. Then when it was time to take it I would always go blank. I am no longer worried about my tests. I have seen improvement in my test-taking ability and test results and now I have a positive mind when tests come along."
—ASHLEY LEMLEY

9. **Ask for clarification.** If you don't understand a question, ask your instructor to make the question clearer.

10. **Be honest.** Do not cheat. Cheating will keep you from learning and can result in your expulsion from school.

11. **Reduce anxiety.** If you start feeling nervous and worried, then use the techniques you learned to reduce your test anxiety. Breathe.

## SUCCESS STRATEGIES TO USE AFTER A TEST

1. **Reward yourself for the preparation and work you did.**

2. **Get correct answers from the instructor.** You need to be in class when the instructor gives feedback and correct answers. If the instructor does not go over the test in class, you can ask for a private meeting to find out the correct answers to any questions that you got wrong.

3. **Use the test as a learning and feedback tool.** Determine what you did well and what needs improvement. Learn from your mistakes. Analyze your strengths and weaknesses on the test questions and answers.

4. **After two or more tests in a course, look for patterns.** Is there a pattern to your mistakes? Do you keep making similar mistakes on every test? You can also look for any patterns in the test questions that the instructor uses. For example, let's say you noticed on multiple-choice questions that the answer "all of the above" is usually correct and "none of the above" is usually the wrong answer. By being aware of your instructor's pattern, you can watch for questions which contain these possible answers.

5. **Make a plan for the next test.** What changes will you make while preparing for your next test and taking the test itself? You may also have a better idea how to pace yourself so you have extra time to spend on difficult questions and to complete the test.

## SUCCESS STRATEGIES FOR MULTIPLE-CHOICE TESTS

The majority of tests in college will be multiple-choice tests so you want to be especially test-wise when taking them. Multiple-choice tests usually include a phrase, stem, or question followed by three to five possible answers from which you can choose.

Here are some strategies for taking multiple-choice tests:

1. **Read the directions carefully.** Make sure you know what you are being asked to do on the test.

2. **Read the entire question or statement to make sure it is asking what you think is being asked.** Be clear in your mind about what you are looking for or supposed to do.

3. **Answer easy and familiar questions first.** You can go through the test several times like this.

4. **Treat your choices like they are true/false statements.** Ask yourself for each choice, "Is this true or false?"

5. **Eliminate choices you know are wrong.** Narrowing your choices to two instead of four increases your odds of making a correct choice. You will have a fifty-fifty chance, even if you guessed. Make an educated guess when you are unsure of the answer.

6. **Answer every question.** If there is no penalty, then do not leave answers blank.

7. **Look for keywords in the statement or question that provide you with clues to the correct answer.** Choose the answer that is similar or harmonious with the keyword or phrase. See the following example:

**Monica is a visual learner.** She would probably prefer to learn by:

A. **Listening to lectures.**

B. **Watching a PowerPoint presentation.**

C. **Participating in a field trip.**

D. **Playing a book on tape.**

What was the keyword in the statement about Monica? The answer is visual. So before looking at the choices you already know the answer will involve the sense of sight. The answer is obviously B.

8. **Pay attention to negatives or questions which are asking you for an exception.** Here is an example:

The following is not a soft skill:

A. Mathematics.

B. Persistence.

C. Time management.

D. Self-discipline.

The negative is the word "not." So if you were using the true/false approach, you would ask for each possible answer, "Is this a soft skill, true or false?" The correct answer is mathematics. Even if you did not know what a soft skill was, you could see that one answer stood out as different from the others and must be the correct answer. If you had been asked which **are the** soft skills, the correct answer would have been different. Your choice would be b, c, and d.

9. **Make sure your test and answer sheet are lined up.** Make sure you do not mark answers that go with different questions.

10. **Pay attention to "All of the above" and "None of the above" choices.** More often than not "All of the above" is the correct answer. More often than not "None of the above" is an incorrect answer. This is not always true, but if you have to guess, the odds will be in your favor if you answer this way.

11. **Look for similar answers.** Usually one of two similar answers is the correct one. Sometimes both choices are available such as an answer like A and B or A and C. These choices are more often correct than incorrect.

12. **When there are contradictory answers, one of them is often the correct answer.** If you see that two possible answers on your test are saying the opposite of each other, then one of them must be incorrect.

13. **Look for the best answer, even if two choices could both be correct.** Choose the one you think is the best choice.

14. **Specific answers are more often correct than vague or general answers.**

15. **Words that are repeated often** in the test will often be a right choice in one of the questions on your test.

16. **Choose answers that agree grammatically with the statement or question.**

17. **Choose logical answers over those that do not make common sense to you.**

18. **Pay attention to qualifying and absolute words and statements.** Words like frequently, sometimes, and probably are qualifying words. They leave room for an exception or for you to doubt the answer. Words like "always," "never," and "all" are absolute words and leave no room for doubt or an exception. For example, "The grass is usually green" uses the qualifying word "usually." Qualifying words and statements are more often correct answers. If we said, "The grass is always green," the word "always" is an absolute word. Isn't the grass sometimes brown? Absolute statements are more often an incorrect answer on multiple-choice tests.

19. **Determine how much time you can spend on each question.** Don't spend too much time on any given question so that you will have enough time to complete the exam.

20. **Review the test.** Change answers, if you think your first choice was incorrect and you see a better choice.

ACTIVITY 6.2  Try these two multiple-choice questions. Choose the best answer.

1. The correct order for previewing a chapter in a textbook is which of the following?
    A. Read a section, create an outline, review the chapter, and check for understanding.
    B. Preview the chapter, read a section, check for understanding, and create an outline.
    C. Create an outline, read a section, preview a chapter, and check for understanding.
    D. Check for understanding, read a section, create an outline, and preview the chapter.

2. Talking out loud as you read is an excellent study strategy and especially appealing for which learning style?
    A. Visual.
    B. Aural or auditory.
    C. Kinesthetic.
    D. None of the above.

What was the keyword in question number one that provided you with a clue to the correct answer? The keyword was "Preview." This keyword gives the answer away because the first step is to preview the chapter.

In question number two, what was the key phrase in the question? If you replied "Talking out loud," you were correct. Before you looked at the choices available, you should have known that the answer would involve which of the five senses? If you answered "Sense of hearing," you are correct. The correct answer is B. It's the only choice which involves hearing.

## STRATEGIES FOR DOING WELL ON ESSAY TESTS

Essays are more subjective than objective tests and offer you the opportunity to express more of your knowledge. Here are some strategies for answering essay questions:

1.  **Read the entire question and make sure you understand what is being asked.** Ask for clarification, if you don't understand the question.

2.  **Identify and interpret directive words.** These are action verbs which indicate what you are being asked to do. Here are examples:

    A.  **Analyze** – Break into separate parts and discuss each one.

    B.  **Compare** – Write about how two or more things are alike.

    C.  **Contrast** – Write about how two or more things are different.

    D.  **Critique or evaluate** – What are the positive and negative aspects? What is the value?

    E.  **Describe** – What are the qualities or characteristics?

    F.  **Discuss** – State the pros and cons.

    G.  **Illustrate** – Give examples and supporting explanations.

    H.  **Outline** – Organize into a structure with main ideas and supporting points.

    I.  **Summarize** – Briefly restate the main points.

3.  **Brainstorm ideas** and jot them down on a scratch pad.

4.  **Create a brief outline** to organize what you want to cover before you start writing.

5.  **Use the writing principles discussed in the last chapter.** Use a strong thesis statement in the introduction, supporting ideas in the body, and summarize main points in the conclusion.

6.  **Write neatly** so your instructor can read it.

7.  **Make sure most of the information you write comes from the text or your class notes.**

8.  **Reword the question and make it your first sentence in the form of a statement.** For example, let's say you were asked to contrast visual and kinesthetic learning styles. You could begin by saying, "Visual and kinesthetic learning styles are different in the three following ways." Then you would complete the sentence and say how they are different. This would be a good opening sentence.

9.  **Budget your time.** Don't spend too much of your time on one essay question at the cost of your other questions. You will want to write more, if some essay questions are worth more points than other questions.

10. **Focus on writing one main idea per paragraph.**

11. **If a question asks you for facts, do not give personal opinions.** You should provide some factual information.

12. **Review, proofread, and revise your draft.**

## Overcoming Test Anxiety

One reason that you might not do as well as you are capable is because of test anxiety. **Test anxiety** is a feeling of stress that happens when you are over-worried about your performance on a test. It is possible for you to be so nervous that your mind can go blank during a test or your thinking can become unclear.

The good news is that your test anxiety can be reduced or eliminated. If you have a small amount of anxiety about a test, this is natural and it is usually not a problem. On the other hand, if you have high test anxiety, it can prevent you from having success on tests and in school.

### HERE ARE SOME WAYS FOR YOU TO OVERCOME TEST ANXIETY

1. **Prepare well for your test.** Find out what the test will be like from your instructor. Use the reading and study skill strategies you learned in the last chapter. The more prepared and confident you feel before the test, the less anxiety you will experience.

2. **Change how you see tests.** You can try to see the test as a learning and feedback tool. Tests provide feedback as to what you are doing well and reveal where you need improvement.

3. **Understand the relationship between your body, your thoughts, and your feelings.** Your negative thoughts create tension in your body and unpleasant feelings in your mind. By changing your thoughts, you can change how your body feels and how you feel emotionally.

4. **Use positive self-talk.** Tackle your negative thoughts by replacing them with positive ones. When you hear yourself thinking thoughts like, "I might fail" come back with "I can and will succeed."

5. **Put the test in perspective.** It's not life and death for you. It's just a test. Even if you fail a test, it's not the end of the world. You are not a failure as a person because you failed an exam. Refocus and do better next time.

6. **Exercise before coming to class to take the test to relieve your tension.** Doing some exercise or listening to relaxing music on the drive to class may relieve your anxiety before taking the test.

7. **Recognize that you are not helpless.** You have choices and you can take control over how you feel and think.

8. **Arrive to class a little early.** Give yourself a few minutes to relax before the class begins. Rushing to class at the last minute can increase your stress level.

9. **Visualize success.** Practice mental imagery like the athletes do before they participate in a real sports event. See yourself in your mind's eye taking the test and being relaxed, cool, and confident.

10. **Be present in the moment.** Anxiety comes when you worry about the future or remind yourself of your past failures. One way to be present and to relax is to observe your breathing. When you get anxious, you will naturally start breathing faster and shallower. When you are relaxed, you will naturally start taking slower, deeper breaths.

You can purposely take slow, deep breaths before and even during the test. Observe your breathing and you will automatically be focused on the present. When you change your breathing, your thoughts and feelings will become more positive.

Another relaxation technique is to tense all of your muscles and then let go. You can repeat this several times to lessen tension in your body.

## JOURNAL ASSIGNMENT

Create a multiple-choice test of ten questions which covers the material in this chapter. Test yourself. Write in your journal what you learned from this activity. 1) What were the benefits for you of doing this exercise? 2) How can you create an even better practice test next time? 3) What insights did you gain?

## AUTHOR'S NOTE

I had no idea when I was in high school and college that there were so many test-taking strategies. I could have really benefited from this information. I did stumble upon the idea of creating practice tests, and this was a great help to me. It was a wonderful feeling when I was taking a test and over half the questions had been on my practice test. It allowed me to breeze through the familiar questions and then spend time concentrating on questions that I didn't anticipate.

I memorized several poems years ago by reciting them repeatedly and overlearning them. It amazes me that I can still quote these poems word for word automatically without much thought.

I make it a point to learn the names of my students as soon as possible. Using some of the memory strategies which were discussed in this chapter makes it possible for me to know all of my students' names by the second or third class.

The test-taking and memory aids discussed in this chapter have worked for me and my former students. And, I believe they will work for you.

## Student Success Story

The following student paper is different from the previous ones because it is about the benefits, including test-taking skills, that this student gained from taking my Transition to College Success course. This was an eight-week course, and she learned many of the same college success strategies that are in this book.

### Final Thoughts about the Course and Its Benefits

By Rhonda Guidry

At first I thought, "Why is this course so important? Why do I need this class? Well, once this course was explained, I got excited and signed up for it. I thought the course was awesome.

The most valuable part of the course for me was the test-taking strategies and study skills. Taking this class has helped me to study smarter, not harder. It helped me with test success and also with test anxiety. I learned that if I did fail a test, it would not be the end of the world, and I became more relaxed about test-taking. The test-taking and study skills helped me to be better prepared to succeed in my other college courses.

Time management also helped me to manage my time more productively. I am better at using a daily planner and using a semester calendar. Also, I learned how to avoid procrastination and how to balance academic and social demands.

I have learned necessary skills for doing college-level work. This will prepare me for college success. Now, I believe that this class is an excellent way to help new students that are entering college. It helps by teaching active listening, note-taking, and other strategies for success in college. I am better now with taking notes, highlighting, and studying. I learned to highlight a chapter and study it to get ready for class discussions and tests.

I plan on using knowledge of my aural learning style and study skills in all of my future courses. I discovered that talking out loud really helps me to remember the lessons. I also go back over every test and look for any careless errors. All of the many skills I learned in this class will help me with the other college courses I will be taking.

ACTIVITY 6.3  **Goal for the week:**

_____

Three steps I will take to achieve my goal:

1. _____

2. _____

3. _____

## SUMMARY OF MAIN POINTS IN CHAPTER 6

↗ Memory techniques alone are not enough for you to succeed in college. It is also necessary for you to understand concepts and principles.

↗ Memory strategies and mnemonics can often help information transfer from your short-term into your long-term memory. This is important for college success.

↗ See and use tests as feedback, which can reduce your test anxiety and improve your test results.

↗ Knowing and using test-taking strategies will increase your academic success.

## QUESTIONS TO ANSWER IN YOUR JOURNAL AND DISCUSS WITH OTHERS

↗ What are three memory strategies that I will use to prepare for my next test? How will I use each of them?

↗ What is an example of something I once overlearned and still can remember today?

↗ What are three test-taking strategies that I will use to study for my next test? How will I use them?

↗ Which anxiety reduction strategy appeals to me the most and how can I use it for best results?

In Chapter 7, you will be identifying some of your skills, interests, and values which you can use in different careers. You will begin thinking about careers of possible interest to explore for more information.

**LUMINOSITY**
Improving Memory and
Cognition Brain Training

luminosity.com

**TEST-TAKING
STRATEGIES**

testtakingtips.com

# Preparing for Career Success . . .
# Discover Your Skills, Values, and Interests

At this point in time, you may or may not know the exact career that you want after college graduation. Even if you do know, you might change your mind when you gain more self-knowledge.

Self-knowledge should be the starting point for making career choices. If you don't know who you are, which includes your skills, values, and interests, how can you choose a career that is a good match for you? Self-knowledge is the way you can determine a good match. Many people make the mistake of looking outside of themselves at career choices, before they look within to discover what they are about. In this chapter, you will discover more about yourself so that you can make wise career choices. The answer to what works best is within you, and you will discover the answer by getting to know yourself better. In this chapter, you will learn several memory techniques that you can use to remember more of what you study and learn. Later in the chapter, you will learn many different test-wise strategies that will improve your skills and confidence when preparing for and taking tests. Also, you will learn ways to reduce or eliminate test anxiety. Having a better memory plus effective test preparation and test-taking skills are a powerful combination that will help you achieve success during your college career.

By the end of this chapter, you may not know the exact career you want to go after, but you will have some careers that you want to explore and learn more about. Even beginning to think about career goals will motivate you to do well in school because you will see the relationship between getting a good education and getting the job you want.

When I ask my students, "Why are you going to college and what do you hope to gain from a good education?", they usually answer, "a good career." They want a career that pays well, is

```
                              Skills

        Holland Code                          Values

                    Career
                    Success
                    Preparation

        Problems of                          Personal
        interest                             strengths

                         Interests
                         and special
                         knowledge
```

*"Your life's work is the work you were born to do—the most appropriate vehicle through which to express your unique talents and abilities."*
—Laurence Boldt

enjoyable, and one in which they are successful. Most of my students realize that a good education can open doors of opportunity to rewarding careers so that they won't have to work in low-paying and back-breaking jobs for the rest of their lives.Chapter 7

## A Student Learns the Hard Way

One of my best students told me that he had returned to college after dropping out in his freshman year three years earlier. When he first came to college, his only interest was partying, and he did almost no studying. He said he worked for three years in a physically demanding, low-paying job. One day, he told his boss that he no longer wanted to do this type of work. His boss asked, "What other kind of work can you do with so little education?" My student said these words from his supervisor felt like a knife stabbing him in his heart. He said the words were painful because he knew they were true. He thought, "Yes, what else can I do if I don't get a better education." He returned to college as a more mature and serious student because he had learned the value of a good education in the "school of hard knocks."

## Career Satisfaction Improves Life Satisfaction

Research shows that life satisfaction and happiness increase when you are happy with your job. Your quality of life is affected by what you do for a living. After working for over forty years in career counseling and job placement, I observed that about 75%–80% of employees feel unhappy in their jobs. This is tragic, considering the amount of time we spend working and the influence our careers have on our lives. It does not have to be this way.

You have talents which are waiting to be discovered. It is your responsibility to find your gifts and to use them in your life's work. This is one of the secrets to job fulfillment. You can make a positive difference and contribution by discovering your talents and how to use them to fill a need in the world. Such a career will give you a sense of purpose in life. According to Fred Buechner, your true vocation will be, "The place where your deep gladness and the world's deep hunger meet." In other words, you will experience joy when you use your talents to fill a need for others that you are passionate about. Ask yourself, "What is my life calling me to do? What is my life asking of me and how can I give it my best?" This chapter will help you begin searching for answers to these questions.

## Benefits of Career Exploration and Planning

&#8599; You get to know yourself and what you want in life

&#8599; Discover your skills, interests, and values

&#8599; Explore career choices that match you

&#8599; Teaches you how to do a job search

&#8599; Reduces the chance of wasting time in college majors and jobs that are not right for you

&#8599; Increases your self-confidence

&#8599; Discover a purpose in life that motivates you

## Your Life Provides Clues to Your Natural Gifts

The following section contains some ideas from another book I wrote called, *Create the Life You Want*.

You will discover your special talents by observing:

&#8599; Enjoyable activities you do well

&#8599; Repeated feedback from others about what you do well

&#8599; Behaviors and skills that are so natural that you rarely notice them

&#8599; Activities you do where time seems to fly

&#8599; People whose work you admire

&#8599; Activities that make you come alive

*Source:* Developed by Raymond Gerson. Based on *Create the Life You Want* by Raymond Gerson. Inspirational Works, 2006.

Richard Bolles wrote a best-selling career book called, *What Color Is Your Parachute?* In his book, Bolles asks his readers to identify their motivated skills. These are skills you are motivated to use and would enjoy using in a job. You can identify your motivated skills and talents by examining your most enjoyable accomplishments.

I love teaching and counseling others. Some years ago, I began to notice the way I naturally share ideas, information, and inspiration with others. This happens whether I am with a group of people or one-on-one. Without thinking about it, I had been doing this from my childhood, beginning with my younger sister and brothers. Before I began teaching, I noticed that movies or books about great teachers inspired me and had a powerful affect on my emotions. These are examples of how your life can provide clues to the right work or vocation.

Pay attention to yourself. Notice what you naturally do so well that you may have overlooked strong abilities. You may not think of them as skills or talents. Notice what inspires you and makes you feel most alive.

Observe yourself in your daily activities. Recall past behaviors and experiences. (Look at jobs or volunteer work you have done. Decide which you liked and in which you did well.) Consider subjects you are good at in school. What do you do well and what is difficult? Write in your journal to help you get clear about your strengths and weaknesses. Briefly review it each evening before going to sleep. Write down observations about yourself from the day just past. Listen to yourself. Listening carefully to the advice you give others will help you get in touch with your beliefs and what you care deeply about. For example, a friend of mine used to advise me to teach psychology. Eventually, he returned to school and got his PhD in psychology. He has been a college professor of psychology for years and loves it.

**ACTIVITY 7.1** Name three things that you naturally do well:

1. _____

2. _____

3. _____

## Discovering Your Greatest Gifts

Finding your greatest gifts and natural career path will come from answering the question,

1. Who am I?
2. Who is the real you?
3. What is natural for you to do?
4. Are there some things you do so well that you have heard about it many times from others?

If feedback from others is similar and repeated often, it is worth thinking about. Over and over again, I heard from others that I had a gift for inspiring people. It is such a natural part of who I am that I took this gift for granted for many years. Do you have talents you've ignored or overlooked? Ask those who know you well to tell you what they believe are your greatest strengths and talents. Weigh the feedback against everything else you know about yourself. See if it fits and is supported by your own observations and life experiences.

Activities during which you lose all sense of time can provide important clues to your natural vocational tendencies. You may get so focused on what you are doing that you don't notice time passing. When you're bored, time drags, but time flies when you're doing something you enjoy.

Who do you admire for their work, talents, or accomplishments? Do you know anyone whose job you would love to have? What about their job appeals to you? Each of us has lots of ability and special talents that can be developed. Your talents, combined with a positive

*Student Comment*

"This course helped me to get a better understanding of my career and my life. I learned more about myself in this course than in any other course I have taken. This course has reassured me that I have a bright future."

— JOSEPH GONZALES

regard for yourself and others, can be a powerful way for you to make an important contribution. Using your special gifts to accomplish a worthwhile purpose will improve your life and those lives of others.

You will do well and enjoy your work when it uses your best and favorite skills, matches your top interests, and supports your highest values.

In the following activities, you will be identifying your favorite skills, interests, and values.

## IDENTIFYING YOUR SKILLS

Rank the following skills and talents on a scale of 1 to 10. A 10 represents exceptional skill, a 5 is average, and a 1 is very little or no skill. Determine your top 10 skills. Use a dictionary for words you are unsure about.

| | | |
|---|---|---|
| 1. Acting____ | 2. Adapting____ | 3. Analyzing____ |
| 4. Appraising____ | 5. Arranging____ | 6. Assembling____ |
| 7. Assessing____ | 8. Building trust____ | 9. Calculating____ |
| 10. Carving____ | 11. Coaching____ | 12. Compiling____ |
| 13. Computing____ | 14. Constructing____ | 15. Consulting____ |
| 16. Counseling____ | 17. Creating____ | 18. Dancing____ |
| 19. Designing____ | 20. Developing____ | 21. Diagnosing____ |
| 22. Drawing____ | 23. Editing____ | 24. Establishing____ rapport |
| 25. Evaluating____ | 26. Executing____ | 27. Growing things____ |
| 28. Healing____ | 29. Initiating____ | 30. Inspiring____ |
| 31. Interviewing____ | 32. Inventing____ | 33. Leading____ |
| 34. Managing____ | 35. Mediating____ | 36. Music ability___ |
| 37. Negotiating____ | 38. Operating____ Machines | 39. Organizing____ |
| 40. Painting____ | 41. Performing____ | 42. Persuading____ |
| 43. Physical____ ability | 44. Planning____ | 45. Producing____ |
| 46. Recruiting____ | 47. Repairing____ | 48. Researching____ |
| 49. Resolving____ problems | 50. Sculpting____ | 51. Selling____ |
| 52. Serving____ | 53. Sewing____ | 54. Speaking____ |
| 55. Strategizing____ | 56. Supervising____ | 57. Synthesizing___ |
| 58. Teaching___ | 59. Working with____ animals | 60. Writing____ |

Now go back over your list and identify your top ten best and favorite skills. List then below:

1. _____    6. _____

2. _____    7. _____

3. _____    8. _____

4. _____    9. _____

5. _____    10. _____

_____

*Source:* Developed by Raymond Gerson. Based on *How to Create the Job You Want* by Raymond Gerson. Enrichment Enterprises, 1996.

There are many ways to get new skills and develop them such as working at a job, going to school, volunteering, and internships. Volunteering is a great way to find out if a particular type of work appeals to you and to develop new or current skills.

## IDENTIFYING YOUR INTERESTS
In this section, you will consider:

↗ Subjects that interest you and which you know a lot about

↗ Problems or needs in the world which you feel passionate about

The subjects of interest may have been learned in school, at work, doing volunteer work, from hobbies, or from reading or training you did on your own.

*Student Comment*

"The most valuable thing that I learned from this book and course is that in life you have to do what you love to be happy. I learned that when you're good at something you should really look into how you can do that in a career. When you do something you love you are more likely to be successful at it. Even though we might achieve something great without loving what we do, it is also important to be happy in that work."
— AMANDA FIGUEROA

**List your top five areas or subjects of interest below:**

1. _____

2. _____

3. _____

4. _____

5. _____

## Problems or Needs in the World

Every job tries to solve certain problems or to fill particular needs. For example, a nurse works with illnesses, injuries, and patients who need to get well.

There are millions of problems in the world needing your energy and creativity to solve them. Problems actually create opportunities for solutions, and this often means they create new jobs.

What problems do you feel deeply about? What do you feel passionate about? Which needs would bring you joy if you could fulfill them for others?

There are many different jobs using a variety of skills to solve the same problems. Say you decide to contribute to the need of affordable housing in your community. You could do this as a carpenter, a builder/developer of houses, or a real estate salesperson. All of these jobs can help solve the problem of too little affordable housing.

Perhaps you want to help young people grow up to be healthy and strong adults. You might consider teaching, coaching or counseling, becoming a health care provider, or physical fitness trainer. There are many different jobs, dealing with similar needs, to consider when seeking a match for your skills.

To decide which problems are of greatest interest to you, ask yourself, "What contribution do I want to make? If I were rich and didn't have to work, what would I do? What type(s) of people in the workplace do I admire? When I solve a problem or fill a need, which ones bring me the greatest joy? If I had two years to live and decided to work, what would I do? How do I want to be remembered?" Answering these questions can put you in touch with your strongest interests.

Let's look at some examples of problems and needs in the world that can become careers, if you choose to solve them.

## EXAMPLES OF POSITIVE ACTIONS TO FILL NEEDS AND/OR SOLVE PROBLEMS

- ↗ Reduce crime
- ↗ Increase affordable housing
- ↗ Improve technology for persons with disabilities
- ↗ Build better teams and relationships
- ↗ Improve the economy
- ↗ Match people to appropriate jobs
- ↗ Design better technology
- ↗ Reduce illiteracy
- ↗ Provide relief for victims of natural disasters
- ↗ Improve quality of products
- ↗ Improve physical or mental health of others
- ↗ Reduce costs
- ↗ Improve efficiency and make things work better
- ↗ Provide recreation and entertainment
- ↗ Improve the lives of children
- ↗ Improve communication
- ↗ Develop training and development programs
- ↗ Improve education
- ↗ Raise funds for worthy projects
- ↗ Organize and improve work flow
- ↗ Help people to save time
- ↗ Improve transportation services
- ↗ Identify problems before they happen
- ↗ Provide financial planning for others
- ↗ Increase sales

↗ Reduce environmental problems

↗ Improve services or products

---

*Source:* Developed by Raymond Gerson. Based on *How to Create the Job You Want* by Raymond Gerson. Enrichment Enterprises, 1996.

If the list above leaves you uninspired, think of other problems that interest you. Below, list at least five needs or actions you think would be challenging and enjoyable to do, whether or not they come from the above list.

1. _____

2. _____

3. _____

4. _____

5. _____

Now decide which of your favorite skills and interests are the best match for the actions or needs you think are important. Then, prioritize and arrange these needs in order of importance to you. What are your top three?

1. _____

2. _____

3. _____

Student Comment

"I was able to learn what my skills, values and interests are and what jobs fit me based on them. I now have the tools I need to get my dream job."
— DESTIN KOZOJED

Consider preparing for a career that will allow you to fill the need or solve the problem that is most important to you.

## IDENTIFY YOUR VALUES

There is a saying that "a person who stands for nothing will fall for anything." What is important to you in life? What are your most important values? Upon what values do you stand?

The following exercise will give you a way to examine some values and to consider which of them are most important to you. Feel free to add any to the list that are not included, if they are important to you.

Check each value below that is very important to you. Review the list, and write down your five most important values below the list. Use a dictionary for words you do not know.

| | | |
|---|---|---|
| 1. Abundance___ | 2. Accomplishment___ | 3. Appreciation___ |
| 4. Adventure___ | 5. Affection___ | 6. Attractiveness___ |
| 7. Balance___ | 8. Belonging___ | 9. Calmness___ |
| 10. Capability___ | 11. Challenge___ | 12. Compassion___ |

13. Confidence___       14. Contentment___      15. Courage___

16. Creativity___       17. Dependability___    18. Determination___

19. Discipline___       20. Excellence___       21. Expertise___

22. Faith___            23. Fame___             24. Family___

25. Fidelity___         26. Financial___        27. Fitness___
                            independence

28. Flexibility___      29. Generosity___       30. Gratitude___

31. Happiness___        32. Helping others___   33. Honesty___

34. Humility___         35. Inspiration___      36. Integrity___

37. Justice___          38. Kindness___         39. Knowledge___

40. Leadership___       41. Love___             42. Make a contribution___

43. Motivation___       44. Nonviolence___      45. Optimism___

46. Persistence___      47. Popularity___       48. Power___

49. Punctuality___      50. Recreation___       51. Relationships___

52. Respect___          53. Self-control___     54. Skillfulness___

55. Solitude___         56. Spirituality___     57. Success___

58. Teamwork___         59. Thoughtfulness___   60. Variety___

61. Virtue___           62. Wealth___           63. Wisdom___

1. _____     4. _____

2. _____     5. _____

3. _____

## IDENTIFY YOUR PERSONAL STRENGTHS OR TRAITS

When you become aware of your strengths, you believe more in yourself. You can then develop and use these strengths in your career and your life.

Review the list of personal traits and positive qualities below. Select and write down the five you think are your greatest strengths and fit you best in the numbered list. If your greatest strengths and needs are not listed, feel free to add them. Please use a dictionary for words you do not know.

| | | | |
|---|---|---|---|
| Kind | Disciplined | Honest | Self-reliant |
| Friendly | Persistent | Inspiring | Neat |
| Positive | Caring | Energetic | Self-aware |
| Trusting | Gentle | Helpful | Humorous |
| Calm | Creative | Charming | Fair-minded |
| Stable | Considerate | Self-directed | Flexible |
| Ambitious | Tactful | Tolerant | Competent |

| | | | |
|---|---|---|---|
| Poised | Reliable | Dependable | Strong-willed |
| Faithful | Motivated | Unselfish | Compassionate |
| Overcoming | Cooperative | Dedicated | Open-minded |
| Courageous | Trustworthy | Consistent | Imaginative |
| Independent | Sociable | Determined | Efficient |
| Confident | Talented | Hard working | Cheerful |
| Thoughtful | Forgiving | Expressive | Enthusiastic |
| Persuasive | Affectionate | Accepting | Understanding |

1. _____
2. _____
3. _____
4. _____
5. _____

You can also look at these strengths as self-management skills, as they are important to employers who will hire you. These strengths also can be thought of as soft skills, which are different from the hard skills, that are needed to do a particular type of job.

An additional activity you can do is to ask people who know you to make a list of five of your best personal traits.

## SKILLS MOST WANTED BY EMPLOYERS

This list was based on a study by Michigan University Placement Services. It was compiled from a survey of five hundred employers in the United States.

1. Ability to get things done
2. Common sense
3. Honesty/integrity
4. Dependability
5. Initiative
6. Good work habits
7. Reliability
8. Interpersonal skills
9. Enthusiasm
10. Good judgment
11. Motivation
12. Decision-making skills
13. Intelligence
14. Adaptability
15. Oral communication
16. Energy
17. Problem-solving ability
18. Good work ethic and habits
19. Mental alertness
20. Emotional control

### Student Comment

"I always thought that you don't necessarily need to work in something you enjoy because life is not perfect and sacrifices may be needed. Reading this chapter helped me see that you can at least try to get an opportunity to do so." "I also felt inspired by the author sharing stories about struggles he faced in school. Even though he struggled like any other student, he was able to become a college professor and writer. This gives hope to me and to all of us."
— JESSICA LOZANO

*Source:* Reprinted from Lawerence Boldt, *Zen and the Art of Making a Living* (New York: Penguin Group, 1991), p. 492.

Consider which of the above skills you already have and which ones you need to develop.

## PERSONALITY TYPES AND WORK ENVIRONMENTS

According to John Holland, there are six different personality types, and people usually look for careers and work environments that match their personality.

The six personality types are:

❶ Realistic (R) – Practical, love to work outdoors and with their hands, enjoy building things, and using tools. Examples of matching occupations: carpenter, chef, auto mechanic, industrial arts teacher, and pilot.

❷ Investigative (I) – Good at math and science, problem solving, research, and curious about how things work. Examples of matching occupations: biologist, doctor, chemist, and veterinarian.

❸ Artistic (A) – Creative, attracted to the arts such as music, art, dancing, and acting. Enjoy being innovative. Examples of matching occupations: graphic designer, writer, musician, and fashion designer.

❹ Social (S) – Helping others is most important. Attracted to teaching, social work, counseling, and other direct helping relationships. Examples of matching occupations: counselor, teacher, nurse, and dental hygienist.

❺ Enterprising (E) – They like to influence others and are goal and results driven. Good communicators who often are attracted to business and management. Examples of matching occupations: lawyer, business owner, salesperson, and hotel manager.

❻ Conventional (C) – They like things orderly and organized. Good with details. Enjoy routine and working with data and numbers. Examples of matching occupations: accountant, secretary, banker, and bookkeeper.

In the order of your preference, which of these personality types you think best fit you? Most people feel a match with two to three of them, but they have an order of priority.

My preferences are:

1._____

2. _____

3. _____

**HOLLAND CODE**
For more information

self-directedsearch.com

For a more complete and accurate assessment of your Holland Code, (three letters) you can go to http://www.self-directedsearch.com to take the online Self-Directed Search Assessment.

Keep in mind that a career decision should be made based on many factors and not just on one or even several tests or assessments.

ACTIVITY 7.2 **Careers to explore.**
List three occupations that you would like to research, explore, and learn more about.

1. _____

2. _____

3. _____

## How to Choose A College Major

You are ahead of the game because of the work you have already started doing in this chapter. Once a student identifies careers that are a good match, the next step is to find college majors that are a good fit for those careers.

**You have started the career development process by:**

↗ Assessing your interests, skills, and values

↗ Considering your personality type and appropriate working environments

↗ Identifying occupations to explore

↗ Reading about those occupations and requirements in the *Occupational Outlook Handbook*

**You can also:**

↗ Consider what were your best and worse subjects in high school

↗ Consider which parts of any jobs you have done were enjoyable and which parts you disliked

↗ Take an online career assessment. For example, many colleges offer career assessments such as "Discover." It allows you to search by occupations to find appropriate college majors.

**Here are more tips:**

↗ Talk with a high school guidance counselor, if you are in high school

↗ See an academic advisor or counselor, if you are in college

↗ Talk to students in majors that interest you

↗ Talk to professors who teach in departments of interest

↗ Interview people who work in careers that interest you for their advice and find out what were their majors

↗ Do internships, volunteering, and part-time work in career fields of interest to find out if they are for you

↗ Consider degree requirements for majors that interest you. Are you willing and able to meet these requirements and to go to school that long?

↗ Consider labor market projections. Will jobs in this field be in-demand in your preferred geographic locations?

↗ Consider earning potential. Will it be enough to meet your needs and desires?

↗ Use college catalogs as a resource to find descriptions of majors

↗ Look at books on how to find a college major

↗ The *Princeton Review* online can be a resource. Go to: http://www.princetonreview.com/majors.aspx to do a college majors search. You will see profiles of over 200 majors.

↗ Students often change majors as they take courses, do research, learn more about possible occupations, and/or realize that career opportunities will develop regardless of the major/degree that is earned. So don't panic if you decide that your first declared major or career choice is not the one for you.

THE PRINCETON
REVIEW

www.princetonreview.com

**OCCUPATIONAL OUTLOOK HANDBOOK**

bls.gov/ooh

You can find out more about these careers through written or online research. Both the library and the Internet can provide good sources of information. Your school librarian can help you.

One good source is the *Occupational Outlook Handbook* (OOH) which you can find in most libraries or online at www.bls.gov/ooh.

Another great way to learn more about careers that interest you is to talk with people who work in these occupations. This is called "informational interviewing." Usually people who you already know can refer or introduce you to the people who you want to interview. One of the counselors at your school can help you to think of some questions to ask. You can also find questions by reading more about informational interviewing online. Take advantage of the resources at your high school or college because this can make a difference between success and failure in school. Resources include counselors, tutors, learning labs, librarians and libraries, and more.

## ONLINE JOB SEARCH STRATEGIES

**JIBBER/JOBBER**

jibberjobber.com

➚ Use search engines to include searches for: job banks, job listings, job sites, and job opportunities listed by location and careers.

➚ Use keywords on your resume to highlight your skills.

➚ Use jibber/jobber to track resumes you have sent out and jobs for which you applied.

➚ Use social media sites such as Linkedin, BeKnown (a professional social networking application for Facebook), Twitter, and others.

**LINKEDIN**

linkedin.com

## TIPS FOR JOB SEEKERS USING SOCIAL MEDIA WEBSITES

➚ Linkedin - Search the jobs section by keywords and location. Search for employer contacts. Search previous employers and schools and seek recommendations to be included in your profile. Create a profile, include keywords in your resume, connect and network, and use the answer section to ask and answer questions.

**TWITTER**

twitter.com

➚ Twitter - Use Twitterchats (live conversations) and learn job search strategies from jobhuntchat, H Chat and Careerchat. Network, find job leads, show your expertise, and follow employers of interest.

➚ BeKnown - Professional Social Networking for Facebook. This was created by monster.com. It uses some of the features of Linkedin as part of Facebook. If you are already on Facebook, BeKnown will appear as an application. You can follow companies and see jobs which are matched against your BeKnown profile.

**BEKNOWN**

beknown.com

## What is Your Life Calling You to Do?

The word "vocation" comes from the Latin word for "voice." It means a calling that you hear. A calling comes from within you and inspires you to move in a certain direction. Finding the right career is a process of self-discovery. Who are you and what are your natural tendencies? Answering these questions will lead you to the right career.

I believe, based on my over forty years of doing career counseling with hundreds of people, that each of us is born with a purpose. You can say it is a mission, avocation, calling, or whatever name you prefer to call it. Discover and line up with your purpose, and you'll find work that gives meaning to your life. You will experience joy when you find a purpose beyond or greater than yourself. Happiness tends to be unattainable when you live only for yourself. Your ability to make a difference will be obvious when you perform the work you love and do best.

When you give the best of yourself, using your natural ability and holding back nothing, you will get much joy in return for your efforts.

## Express Your Own Unique Song and Music

You have only a little time to use your ability and make your dreams happen. Life passes quickly. Your life will be over before you know it, so time is too valuable to waste. Becoming aware of your limited life span can be a motivator for you to take positive action. Now is the time to go for your dreams. You can't change the past, but you can take action now!

Ask yourself:

❶ What do I really want out of the rest of my life?

❷ What are my highest priorities?

❸ What dreams have I not yet achieved?

❹ Have I sung my special song and used my best talents?

❺ What contribution would I like to make?

The answer to these questions is inside you. It is a matter of self-reflection and self-discovery.

No one wants to die with their song unsung and with their ability unused. You have your own special talents and the ability to make a difference in the world. Let your life speak to you. Notice what it is that lights you up inside with fire, aliveness, and passion. Look for clues to your life's purpose. You can discover and use your greatest and most natural gifts and talents. You can make a difference!

> ## Student Comment
> "I realized that a career doesn't have to be a high paying one for me to enjoy it. A career that includes your interests can be fun."
> — DUSTIN HALL

## JOURNAL ASSIGNMENT

Use the *Occupational Outlook Handbook* (OOH) to research the three occupations that you listed as being of interest.

In your journal, write a brief summary of what you learned from the OOH about these careers. Write about what you liked and disliked about these occupations.

## AUTHOR'S NOTE

Earlier, I mentioned that I did poorly in school until my last year of high school, when I started getting more serious about my education. During those years, I had no goals and felt lost. I had no idea what my skills, interests, and values were, what careers I was suited for, and I had no sense of purpose. At this time, school had little meaning because I couldn't connect the value of an education with where I wanted to go in life. It's no wonder I was doing badly in school.

I desperately needed career guidance with someone that could help me discover that I actually had natural gifts and potential. Unfortunately, this type of guidance was not available in my school.

I teach a full semester college course in career exploration and planning. High school students can also take the course as part of the Early College Start Program. The course helps a student to discover skills, values, and interests, determine an appropriate major and career goal, how to research the job market, and how to use job search strategies.

It is my belief that every high school and college should offer a course in career development and planning. A student who learns both study skills and discovers a career direction will gain the motivation and know-how to do well in high school and college.

## Student Success Story

The following paper was written by a former student of mine who completed my college career course while she was still in high school. Her paper provides an excellent example of how many of the ideas and exercises in this chapter can help a student to discover an appropriate career direction and purpose.

### Case Study Paper for Career Exploration and Planning Course

By Tracy Rocha

I am a high school senior, and a few weeks ago I had no idea what I wanted to do after graduation. I knew I wanted to go to college, but I wasn't sure what I was going to study. My counselor at school mentioned this career exploration course to me and after taking the course my situation changed from being stuck to just the opposite. Now I have a pretty good idea of what I want to do and this is all because of this class.

This course is one of the few classes that have actually benefited me in realizing what I want to do for the rest of my life. I enrolled into the class with low expectations, but came out of it with a lot of valuable knowledge. This class not only helped me learn how to be a good job-hunter and narrow my career choices to either becoming a medical social worker or a physician's assistant, but it also taught me a lot about myself.

I never would have imagined that the number one rule to be successful in life is to "know thyself." You need to realize what strengths, values, weaknesses, and interests' you have and to think of the steps needed to achieve the goals that will help you create a better future. This is what I did throughout this course.

With the help of the professor, the Discover program, and the *What Color is Your Parachute* book, my accomplishments during this semester have been many. First of all, I took the time to evaluate myself and thought really hard about what I wanted. I learned that my mission in life is "to care for and be of service to others, helping people overcome situations by informing them of unknown possibilities, and influencing their decisions to live a better life," and that is exactly what I plan to do. I am going to let my mission guide me from now on, and with the help of God, I believe I will get to where I want to be.

During this course, I also set goals for myself that will hopefully keep me on the right track. I learned that goals have to be realistic and at the same time short-termed enough to stay focused on them. Some steps I have taken toward my career goals are to research my career choices and learn in depth about them. The two careers I mentioned earlier fit me perfectly. Both careers allow me to do what I love, how I want to do it, and where I want to do it. They are both jobs that are in high demand and will let me live my life as I want. I will not be superrich, but I will not have to worry about money. Last but not least, I made a resume, cover letter, and thank you note during this semester which gave me the opportunity to practice for the future and improve my skills.

From when I started this course to where I find myself now, I feel I have come a long way and have made much progress. I'm more confident in where I am headed with my life and have a lot of hope. Even though life is full of surprises that might cause change, I am following my heart in what I want to do and will have no regrets. I know I will feel good about myself and live life with a positive attitude. I will be happier and feel I have lived my mission like God wanted me to do.

My plan after ending this course is to make a final decision about which of the two careers I will pursue. I want to keep striving to accomplish my goals and try my best always. Even if that means sacrificing certain things and learning how to balance my life, this is something I want to get better at. The key for me now is just to take "baby steps" because they are what will lead me to big achievements.

I have big expectations for myself now and to tell you the truth I am not scared of meeting them or other people's expectations. As I mentioned before, this class has really prepared me for what is ahead of me and I believe I can do what ever I put my mind to. I am willing to step up to the challenge.

I just want to take this time to thank you, Mr. Gerson, for having such a huge impact on me. I appreciate everything. I am inspired to make something out of my life. The things I learned during this class, I will take with me forever.

**ACTIVITY 7.3  Goal for the week:** _____

_____

Three steps I will take to achieve my goal:

1. _____

2. _____

3. _____

DANIEL POROT
Career expert:
Information
and games for
identifying your skills

careergames.com

## SUMMARY OF MAIN POINTS IN CHAPTER 7

↗ Your life provides clues to your natural ability.

↗ You will do well and enjoy your work when it matches your skills, interests, and values.

↗ Many different jobs can fill the same need or can solve similar problems.

↗ Within you is a special song—a form of expression waiting to be discovered and communicated.

## QUESTIONS TO ANSWER IN YOUR JOURNAL AND DISCUSS WITH OTHERS

↗ What are five enjoyable activities that I do well?

↗ What strengths and talents do others repeatedly tell me I have?

↗ How can I use my strengths to overcome my weaknesses?

↗ Who are three people whose jobs I would like to have and why?

DISCOVER ACT
CAREER PLANNING
(Check with your
school or college to
find out if they can
give you Discover
or another online
career assessment.)

act.org/discover

You have learned many ideas and skills so far, which will improve your academic performance, if you apply them. In the final chapter, you will be learning how to create the life you want so that you can make your dreams come true and make a positive difference for others.

## CHAPTER 8

# How to Create the Life You Want and Make a Positive Difference in the World

You began this book by thinking about your life dreams and turning them into goals with deadlines. Your goals provide a vision of where you want to go in life. Deciding what you want is the first step to creating the life you want. The second step is to manifest your vision – to make it happen.

An architect envisions a house in his or her mind, draws it on paper, and then it is built. This is how thoughts become things. You start with a thought, desire, vision, and goal, and they become a physical reality. In the same way, you can create the life you want by turning your dreams into physical reality. Not only is it possible to make many of your dreams come true, but you can help others to fulfill their needs and dreams. You can create the life you want and make a positive difference in the lives of others.

## Benefits of Creating What You Desire and Making a Contribution to Others

↗ Your life becomes more fulfilling and enjoyable

↗ Your self-worth and self-esteem increase

↗ You grow as a person

↗ Your self-confidence increases

↗ It is good for your physical and mental health

Create the Life You Want

- Define successful life
- Determine your mission
- Develop your self-image
- Awaken your greatness
- Leave a legacy
- Build character

*"To the extent that your work takes into account the needs of the world, it will be meaningful; to the extent that through it you express your unique talents, it will be joyful."*
— Laurence Boldt

↗ You get a sense of well-being and purpose

↗ You know yours is a life well lived

↗ You get the joy that comes from making a difference

## What is a Successful Life?

I wrote this book to help you succeed in college. It can also help you to do well in your courses and to prepare for college success even if you are still in high school. This book's secondary purpose is to help you succeed in your career and life.

In addition to the specific success strategies for college success, here are some general success principles to help you achieve more in your college, career, and life.

Success means different things to different people. For example, a person may need to make a lot of money to feel successful. Another person may feel successful helping others and making much less money.

In the beginning of this book, I defined success as "Making progress toward your goals." Your goals will be different from many others because each person decides what goals are important for him or her to achieve. It will be difficult, if not impossible for you to feel successful, if you are not moving in the direction of your goals.

Success will often come when you least expect it in the most ordinary moments. Keep making the effort and continue moving forward and results will happen. You might ask, "What if I feel like I am in a fog and can't see where I want to go?" Just start moving in the general direction you want to travel and try to see the next step in the fog. With each step you take you will see and decide on the next step. In this way, you keep moving forward one step at a time.

## GENERAL LIFE SUCCESS PRINCIPLES

1. **Know yourself.** Be aware of your strengths and weaknesses. Build and use your strengths to excel, overcome weaknesses, and to improve.

2. **Know the outcome you want.** Set goals and have a definite purpose. Visualize your desired outcome.

3. **Ability to focus.** One key to success is your ability to concentrate on the task at hand. You will achieve greatness from doing small things with care and attention. Be in the present moment, focus, and do whatever you are doing as well as possible.

4. **Self-discipline.** Manage yourself and your time to get the best out of yourself.

5. **Self-motivation.** Focus on your goals to maintain motivation. Visualize your success.

6. **Go the extra mile.** Be willing to do more than is expected or being asked of you. Take action and provide more value than you are getting paid to do. Employers will want to hire and keep you, if you are willing to go the extra mile.

7. **Persistence.** This is your ability to hang in there even, when the going gets tough. Persistence is your ability to persevere and not give up easily. You also need to know when to change course.

8. **Complete tasks and avoid procrastination.** Do what you need to do now and follow through on tasks until completion.

9. **Willing to risk failure.** This is your ability to take reasonable chances and to learn from your mistakes. This takes courage and a belief in yourself.

10. **Ability to delay gratification.** Your going to college is an example of delayed gratification. You are sacrificing some pleasure now for future benefits.

11. **Communicating and relating well with others.** Many employers will want to hire you if you can work well with others. Your ability to listen and to understand how others are feeling are important communication skills.

12. **Enjoy helping others.** Success often doesn't happen, at least not for long, if a person is selfish and only cares about their progress. If you are willing to help others, you will probably become a successful leader.

13. **Master mind alliance.** This is where you get with others and help each other reach your goals and their goals.

### Student Comment
"I like this book because it's a starting point for my success. It is sort of like a manual on how to be great. You may fail, but it tells you how to get back up and succeed."
—MATHEW CASTILLO

ACTIVITY 8.1 **What will it take for you to feel successful? Write your definition of success in the space below.**

_____

_____

## Building a Strong Foundation for Your Inner Growth

Your inner growth will determine the person you become and are becoming. Your inner development is even more important than just getting material things. The good news is that when you become a better and better person, you will also usually do better in your relationships, career, and finances. Your inner growth can bring you the happiness that you might miss out on, if you focus only on going after material things. You will enjoy the material things more if you are happy with yourself.

Steven Covey, in his book, *The 7 Habits of Highly Effective People*, discovered something interesting when he read success literature written during the last two hundred years. The success literature of the last fifty years was about the importance of personality and skill development. The literature of over fifty years ago by writers such as Emerson and Thoreau and others was more about character and inner development. What happens if you do not build a strong inner foundation? You have probably seen stories on the news about politicians, ministers, athletes, and others with great talents and communication skills that ended up in disgrace and/or in prison. What was missing? *The foundation was missing.* Character, which has to do with inner qualities, is the foundation upon which your skills, talents, and strategies must be built. Without good character, you will not be able to handle the temptations and obstacles that come your way and this can hurt you and others. Without strong character, you would likely misuse your talents. If a house has a weak foundation, it can easily fall down. If a person has weak character, he or she can easily fall also. So, it is important to keep improving yourself and becoming a better and better person.

Here is a partial list of character traits to develop:

↗ Honesty and integrity. Honesty builds your self-respect and the respect you get from others. It takes time for you to earn trust and you can lose it overnight, if you are not careful. Integrity includes honesty and includes your values and principles.

↗ Forgiveness. You can find the courage to forgive yourself and others. This will bring you peace of mind.

↗ Responsibility. This means you respond to the situation before you that needs to be done.

↗ Courage. You will need courage to do what you feel is right and to go ahead in spite of your obstacles. Courage does not always mean you have no fear, but it also means you go ahead and do the right thing, even if you are afraid.

↗ Compassion. You can feel for others who are suffering and take action to help them.

↗ Humility. You can be humble and self-confident at the same time. To be humble means you are not full of yourself and your own self-importance. A humble person does not think he is better than others.

↗ Love. When love is awakened in you, other good qualities such as joy, inner peace, and courage, develop automatically. Love helps you to see that we are all interconnected and worthwhile.

ACTIVITY 8.2  List three more character traits below that you want to develop further.

1. _____

2. _____

3. _____

A person may be brilliant, highly educated, personable, and have awesome talents, but without good character, he will not have true success. Strong character traits are the foundation upon which you and others can build a successful and fulfilling life.

Your choices and actions reveal your character and who you are as a person. When you piece your small habits together, it shapes who you become. By changing your thoughts, you can change and improve your habits or actions, which are creating the person you are becoming.

## The Power of Self-Image and Your Success

Maxwell Maltz's book, *Psycho-Cybernetics,* which was mentioned earlier, contained major breakthrough information at the time it was published about self-image.

What was so significant about this book? Dr. Maltz was a plastic surgeon who improved the physical appearance of thousands of people, especially those with facial deformities. Some of his patients went through positive changes after surgery in how they saw themselves. Others felt no different about themselves; even though photos showed they had major improvements in how they looked following surgery. Why? They still saw themselves the same way because their self-image did not change. For example, some people who felt ugly before surgery still saw themselves as unattractive after major improvements were made to their appearance. Dr. Maltz realized that your self-image or picture of how you see yourself is extremely important.

The bad news is that your self-image defines and limits what you will achieve in life. You cannot outperform what you believe to be true about yourself. Your self-image determines your degree of happiness and fulfillment, success in relationships, and career accomplishments and satisfaction. It also impacts your physical, emotional, and mental health.

The good news is you can change and improve your self-image. Dr. Maltz found that 90% of people could use at least some improvement in their self-image. His book provides practical exercises for improving your self-image and for managing your inner critic or what could be called "the negative voice inside your head." As your self-image improves, so does your self-confidence and self-esteem, which are important for any type of success in life. A strong and healthy picture of yourself can help you to overcome many of your self-imposed limitations and beliefs.

See Figures 8.1 and 8.2.

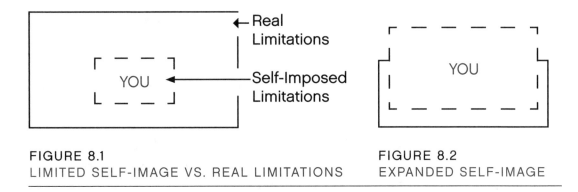

**FIGURE 8.1**
LIMITED SELF-IMAGE VS. REAL LIMITATIONS

**FIGURE 8.2**
EXPANDED SELF-IMAGE

There is a difference between self-imposed and real limitations.

Some of your limitations are real. For example, you can't lift a house weighing thousands of pounds over your head. In the figure above and to the left, the outer boundaries of the box represent your real limits. The smaller box represents your self-imposed limits.

Self-imposed limitations such as "I will always be a poor student" can be changed and improved. Real limits can't be changed, but you can go beyond the self-imposed limits so they do not hold you back from achieving your dreams. The box to the right obviously represents an expanded self-image and what is possible for you.

## HOW TO IMPROVE YOUR SELF-IMAGE

Your inner critic can be a major obstacle to your achieving a successful and fulfilling life. All of us hear the voice of this critic at times. It takes the form of inner dialog and negative self-talk. This is the voice that says, "I can't do it" or "I'm not worthy of achieving my dreams."

As you strengthen and improve your self-image, you also lessen the power of your inner critic. This will help you to overcome your inner resistance (which is often at a subconscious level) to achieving your dreams. As your self-worth increases, your limiting beliefs will be changed into positive beliefs. When you can start believing in your worthiness and great potential, it will change your life.

Is there something practical that you can do to improve your self-image? Yes! Dr. Maltz suggested that you go into what he called "The theater of your mind" each day and play mental movies. Picture yourself sitting in a theater looking at a large white screen. Then, see yourself on the screen acting and feeling like the person you want to be. For example, you might picture yourself cool and relaxed while taking a test. Also, replay movies of yourself reliving past successes. Your self-image is influenced more by pictures than words.

> *Student Comment*
> "I learned how to improve my self-image and discovered my mission."
> —CLAUDIA GUERRERO

You will become what you think about most of the time. By reliving your success experiences often, you will reinforce an image of yourself as a successful person. Also, when you play mental movies of yourself acting as the person you want to become, you begin to see yourself in that way. You will behave like the person you believe yourself to be. When you improve your self-image, your life improves from inside out. This is one of the great secrets for you to find happiness and fulfillment.

ACTIVITY 8.3 **Practice going into the theater of your mind that Dr. Maltz talked about.**

Sit down and relax. Imagine a big blank movie screen and you are the only one in the theater. Now, for a few minutes, see yourself on the screen being the person you want to be. See yourself calm and confident.

If you are going to a job interview or any situation that causes you anxiety, practice this method. You can practice seeing yourself in the interview doing well. This is one way to improve your self-image. Your self-image is a mental picture of how you see yourself. Keep improving this picture so that it supports your success.

## Your Thoughts and Words are Powerful and Can Make a Difference in Your Life and Others'

How you feel about yourself makes a big difference. Your thoughts have the power to weaken or strengthen you. Scientific experiments show that if you think about Mother Teresa or have loving thoughts, it will make you feel more compassionate, and your immune system will get healthier and stronger. This study was done with college students and published in the *Journal of Advancement in Medicine*. The researchers also discovered that thoughts of Hitler or of hatred weaken the immune system. Negative thoughts and self-talk can make you weaker and less healthy. Your positive self-talk supports and strengthens your self-image. You'll have a much better influence on others, if you develop a healthy self-image.

### THE POWER OF POSITIVE EXPECTATION

Many studies have been done to show that your expectations will influence how things turn out. What you strongly expect will happen often does happen. This is called a self-fulfilling prophecy.

Studies have been done in the schools that show that a teacher's expectations can influence a student's performance. There are examples in which teachers were told that one group of students were the smart ones and another group of students were the dumb ones, when both groups were actually of similar intelligence. The students performed according to the expectations of their teachers. The students, who were considered the smart ones, performed much better than the group who had been labeled unintelligent. The teachers verbally and nonverbally communicated their expectations to the students who then performed according to the teachers' expectations.

*Student Comment*

"I know now that if you dream big, then you have to reach as far to the stars as you can. I know that it is up to me to make my dreams come true."
—ROSLYNN RICHARDSON

In a review of the research on the effects of teachers' expectations on student performance by Kathleen Cotton, she concluded that "the most important finding from this research is that teacher expectations can and do affect a student's achievement levels and attitudes."

You will often rise to the level of the teacher's expectations because it changes your mental picture of yourself and your own expectations. When your self-image supports your success, you will perform in a way that is likely to bring it about.

How you think and what you choose to think about, shapes your character and influences your self-image. This is one reason why what you are thinking about and doing (your actions) in the present is so important—you are creating your future now!

ACTIVITY 8.4 **Identify a time in your life when your expectations (negative or positive) influenced your outcome.**

Reflect on this and write your insights and thoughts about it below.

_____

_____

_____

## The Power to Make a Difference Comes From Within

The kind of person you are and are becoming determines how you see others. How you see yourself and others is influenced by your own inner qualities. Also, how you perceive others will determine what influence you will have on them. Remember the power of expectation. Do you see people as worthwhile human beings with great potential or as con artists who want to take advantage of you? Your perception determines your influence and is even more powerful than what you say, although what you say will be an expression of who you are.

Mother Teresa saw others through eyes of love; Hitler, through eyes of hatred. Each acted according to his or her perception. One had a positive influence on the lives of many people. The other left a path of destruction, suffering, and death. Mother Teresa's and Hitler's levels of consciousness – their widely different perceptions – led to entirely opposite historical legacies or what they left behind. What do you want your legacy or mark or footprint on the world to be? What is your purpose and mission?

### INNER AND OUTER PURPOSE

In his book, _A New Earth: Awakening to Your Life's Purpose_, Eckhart Tolle tells us that human beings have an inner and outer purpose. The inner purpose is to fully awaken and know yourself.

Your outer purpose may be different from others and it can change with time. According to Tolle, you will be most effective when your inner and outer purposes are connected. You will be able to bring more of yourself and who you really are into your work in the world. He says you can bring more of your self and true power to make a difference into your outer purpose by enjoying what you do. If you cannot enjoy your work, he says, at least accept it. In other words, don't fight and resist what is, but go ahead and do the work with care and attention. This doesn't mean that you don't look for new work. According to Tolle, even better than enjoying your work is to add enthusiasm to your enjoyment. This happens when you not only enjoy what you do, but you add a vision or goal to the work you are already enjoying. Your goal, combined with enjoyment of your work, gives you a strong outer purpose.

### DISCOVERING YOUR MISSION AND WORK THAT MATTERS

The world is facing major problems today such as global hunger, poverty, economic problems, global warming and other environmental challenges, health care problems, educational issues, weapons of mass destruction, overflowing prisons, crumbling infrastructures, and the list goes on. You can either feel discouraged by these problems or see them as a map of possibilities for change. As I mentioned earlier, problems call for solutions and crisis is the flip side of opportunity. Many people have discovered work that they feel really matters, and even their personal mission, by deciding to tackle a particular problem. You can do the same.

Edward Everett Hale said, "I am only one, but still I am one. I cannot do everything but I can do something, and I will not let what I cannot do interfere with what I can do." Your life can make a difference for others. You can leave the world a little better because you lived and took positive action.

❶ What is life calling you to do?

❷ Do you have a great idea and vision that can bring out your best?

❸ Do you have a special gift you want to share with others?

This can be your personal mission. It will be the vehicle by which you express your unique abilities to make a positive difference.

*Student Comment*

"The most valuable part of this course and book for me was the last chapter on 'How to Create the Life You Want and Make a Positive Difference in the World.' This chapter, well, the whole book, in fact, helped me to better myself in many ways. I learned how to be more responsible, how to overcome hard times, and to forgive myself and others for past mistakes. I know one day I will make a difference in someone's life. This course and book helped me to find out more about myself and to think better about myself. Honestly, I'm a whole new person inside and out."

—ALEXANDRA MARTINEZ

An individual mission is a calling or higher purpose that you feel inspired to fulfill. It includes your goal, vision, and your main purpose. A mission will take you beyond yourself to a greater sense of purpose. When you discover your mission, your life will take on new meaning, and you will automatically feel motivated to fulfill your mission.

A mission may take the form of a career, volunteer work, parenthood, or a hobby. One person's mission may be to add beauty to the world through art, music, or some other means. It could involve helping young people to get off of drugs, or to help them acquire a quality education.

A mission is any worthwhile purpose for which you feel a deep sense of commitment and connection. It usually involves a cause you feel deeply about and uses talents that bring you joy.

You may not know your mission yet, but it is not too early to begin giving it some thought. It also may change and develop as you get older. Think about how you would like to make a contribution to others. Is there a problem, need, or dream others have that you feel passionate about? A need you would love to fulfill?

Think about your goals and skills you want to use. Think about the types of populations you would most like to help.

Here is an example of a brief mission statement that I wrote. "To teach others to discover their talents, potential, and calling so they can fulfill their dreams and make a positive difference in the world." Now give it a try in the activity below.

ACTIVITY 8.5 **Write a brief mission statement in the space below. Keep in mind that it can change as you become clearer about your personal mission.**

_____

_____

_____

## Where Does Greatness Lie and wHow Can It Be Awakened?

What follows is a brief article I wrote and would like to share with you called, "How to Awaken the Greatness within You."

### How to Awaken the Greatness within You

#### By Raymond Gerson

The power to make a positive difference comes primarily from within. It has more to do with who we are than what we say. This is why Mahatma Gandhi said, "My life is my teaching" and "Be the change you want to see in the world." Our example speaks louder than words, but our words are also a reflection of who we are as a person.

Gandhi is a great example of someone who transformed himself and the lives of many others when he shifted from self-consciousness to other-consciousness. From childhood to early adulthood, Gandhi felt awkward and self-conscious. He was shy and had many fears. Only when he became captivated by a passionate mission — a sense of purpose larger than himself — was he able to go beyond his fears.

Gandhi's compassion for the Indian people and his desire to free India from British rule became a burning desire that changed Gandhi into a man of great courage, love, and inner strength. His life's purpose took him beyond his petty self-concerns and self-imposed limitations. He became a great leader who inspired a nation to fulfill his mission.

Success and happiness that escapes us when we seek them directly will frequently come when our focus is on contributing to others. We need to get out of our own way and allow the power within to be expressed.

Many of you want to make a positive contribution. You want to know that your having lived on this earth made a positive difference in the lives of others. Your positive actions can inspire others to glimpse their own potential and to become what they are capable of becoming. This brings joy, meaning, and fulfillment to your life.

You may be wondering, "Okay, fine, but how am I supposed to find a great purpose that overcomes my fears and self-concerns"? First, take a look at the many problems and needs in the world. Which ones do you feel passionate about? Are there problems in the world that make you angry or sad? What inspires you to act? What impact do you want to have on the world? How could you use your talents to contribute to humanity? Answering questions like these can help you to discover how you want to be of service.

Many psychologists have said that most people use only a small percentage of their brain power and creativity. Enormous resources are within you, but they often remain dormant until you find a purpose that is bigger than yourself. You move then from self-centeredness to focusing on your unique way of helping others. Like Gandhi, you can also rise above your weaknesses and awaken your dormant potential when you decide how you want to be of service. This is the secret for awakening the greatness within you.

## WHAT WILL BE YOUR DESTINY AND LEGACY?

The interesting thing about Gandhi was that he was shy, awkward, and lacking in self-confidence as a young man. Once he became passionate about a mission and focused on helping others, he was transformed. He rose above his petty fears and self-consciousness and discovered a mission which brought out his best.

One source of happiness is being of service and helping others. This does not mean you must become a social worker, nurse, or counselor to be of service to others. A business person, architect, auto mechanic, medical lab technician, and people in almost any profession can be of service directly or indirectly.

When you use your best skills in a profession that you love, you also experience joy. Your education can be the key that unlocks the door of opportunity leading you to this work and allowing you to fulfill your mission.

## JOURNAL ASSIGNMENT

In your journal, name the three most important ideas you learned from this book and discuss how you will use them to succeed in college.

## AUTHOR'S NOTE

It is possible to create work or a job for yourself that doesn't exist in the form of an advertised job opening. If you can sell an employer on the value you can bring to the company, it is possible to create a job that doesn't yet exist or where there is no opening available. I have done this in my life and have taught others how to do it.

My book, *How to Create the Job You Want*, explains how. The book is available as a free gift at www.successforcollegestudents.com.

So many wonderful events are happening for me late in life. The same can be true for you, and this is why I encourage you to take care of your health. You will fulfill dreams and new ones will replace them. In your 60's and 70's or 80's, you might decide to remarry or retire and travel, write a book, return to work, start a business, do volunteer work, or who knows what. You will need the health and energy to pursue your dreams.

Life goes by quickly. As I was writing the first edition to this book, I received an invitation to attend my 50th high school reunion. It seems like only yesterday that I graduated from high school. The last fifty years went by so fast that it boggles my mind.

Realize how quickly time is passing and how precious it is so you will use it wisely. Ask yourself, "If I was hundred years old and today was my last day on earth, what regrets would I have? What would I like to have accomplished? Who is the person I became?" Then, realize that there is still time to live the life you want to live.

CREATE THE JOB
YOU WANT

successforcollegestudents.com

## Student Success Story

The success story by Melinda Medina is a great example of unconditional love and how clues to your mission can come from your life experiences.

## My Future in the Making

By Melinda Medina

I would have to say caring for my grandmother when she had cancer would be my biggest accomplishment in my life.

It was early November 2002, when my best friend, my other mom, my grandmother was formally diagnosed with pancreatic cancer. I had taken her to several appointments before that and I had no idea what to expect because she just had abdominal pain for the past few months. Once she got a medical specialist who was experienced in that field, it was clear that it was cancer and very serious.

I needed to make a plan for her and the remainder of the time she had left with us. At first, I don't think she had a clue about what she would be going through. As I looked in her eyes while explaining what the doctor had discovered, it was clear to me she was scared. I remember telling her that no matter what happened, I would never leave her side. At that point, I told myself any attention she needed I would give her. I would stay nights and eventually moved in with her. This was to prevent her from going to a nursing home. I had made a promise that I would be there to the end and that was what I intended to do.

I can remember my grandmother asking if there was any way she could beat the cancer and without a doubt, there was no way. However, I would not take away whatever hopes she may have had. I mentioned to her there was a surgery she could have that may help or just give her added time to what the doctor thought she had left. With that said, she underwent a surgery that in reality bought her only a couple of months. After the unhelpful surgery, she also had the option of chemotherapy. Chemo required several hours for more than a couple of days out the week. These appointments, as well as travel time, getting her ready, and taking her to other errands the doctors had her doing would keep me from home for hours or even long days. My personal life had come to an end. I was her personal assistant, driver, chef, and companion.

I decided one day, after commuting twenty-five minutes from my home to hers, that I would move in. I wanted to be at her call whenever she needed me without having to wait. I could see the happiness in her face when she woke up, and I was there at her bedside, or in my twin bed that I had set up right beside her. Everyday that I was with her was special to me. I would take time out after her feedings, medications, etc. to talk, laugh, cry and just about anything to keep her mind off the pain she was going through. When she was up to it some, I would record her on my video camera, just to have memories for myself and my family. I would also comb her hair, give her nice hair hairdos, paint her nails, and just remind her that I had such a beautiful, fun-loving, good-hearted grandmother. I always told her that taking care of her was such a joy, and that I wouldn't trade it for the world.

She once sat up and cried and said how embarrassing and depressing it was that she couldn't take care of herself because the disease made her so weak and she was in lots of pain. She once told me that I would be a great nurse, that I had lots of personality and love for people. I knew that my grandmother had a lot of pride. This was a woman who started to work at the age of nine and, with no education, she was able to raise six kids, buy a home, and retire from a job she had for over fifteen years. She still found time to take care of me since I was born. There was no way I could repay her, so I was against hospice and home health aides. I knew that they would do a good job in helping her and giving my grandmother what she needed. But I wanted to be the one who helped her in every way possible. So, every day when I fed, bathed, washed her clothes, cleaned her wounds and made sure she was well rested or hydrated, it made a big difference in my life.

There were days that I prayed this wasn't happening. When I came back to the reality, it was clear I had to do the best I could for her during the days we had left. I had never thought what I had done for my grandmother might become a profession and had not thought of becoming a nurse. After my son was born, (he is two years old now), I decided I needed a career and a future for him. I enrolled in college. When they asked me what my major would be, I thought about it awhile. Then, I remembered my grandmother and how much I helped her live her days in complete happiness. I said I would like to become a nurse so I can provide others with my willingness to care for people, my friendliness, and my love for a job that never ends.

I believe that you learn different skills in your life, and it's up to you to use them. I think nursing is my skill and I plan to be the best nurse I can for myself and others.

ACTIVITY 8.6 **Goal for the week:**

_____

Three steps I will take to achieve my goal:

1. _____

2. _____

3. _____

## SUMMARY OF MAIN POINTS IN CHAPTER 8

↗ Deciding what you want and making it happen are steps to creating the life you want.

↗ Character is an important foundation for you to build success upon.

↗ Visualize what you want, associate positive emotions with your goal, and then let go, and don't worry about how or when it happens.

↗ Your power to make a difference lies within you. When you find a purpose larger than yourself, you will create a life that is fulfilling and helps others.

## QUESTIONS TO ANSWER IN YOUR JOURNAL AND DISCUSS WITH OTHERS

↗ Which success principles discussed in this chapter appealed to me the most and how will I use them to succeed?

↗ What are my three strongest character traits? Which three character traits mentioned in this chapter do I need to work on the most?

↗ What is one self-imposed limitation that is part of my self-image and how will I over-come it?

↗ What are three things I would like for people to be able to say about me and my legacy when I am gone?

CREATE THE LIFE
YOU WANT

successforcollegestudents.com

# Post-Course Assessment

Now take the Post-Course Assessment below and compare your scores to the Pre-Course Assessment you took before you started Chapter 1.

This questionnaire is not a test, but is an opportunity for you to find out what you know and don't know about the topics in this book. It will help you to see your strengths as a student and in which areas you need improvement. So be honest where you see yourself now.

Read the statements below and give yourself points for each one. Use the point system below and then add up your total points for each of the eight topics. Then, add up all of your points for an overall total score.

↗ 5 Points     The statement is mostly or always true

↗ 4 points     The statement is often or frequently true

↗ 3 points     The statement is sometimes true

↗ 2 points     The statement is rarely true

↗ 1 point     The statement is never or almost never true

## POST-ASSESSMENT

**❶ Goals**

A. __ I have clear goals for what I want to accomplish in life.

B. __ My goals are written down.

C. __ My goals have deadlines or dates for completion.

D. __ I have short, medium, and long-range goals.

E. __ I have goals for all major areas of my life: education/career, physical, mental, spiritual, financial, social, and family.

F. __ I practice visualizing my goals as if I have already achieved them.

Total _____

**❷ Learning Styles and Types of Intelligence**

A. __ I am familiar with different learning styles.

B. __ I know which is my preferred and best learning style.

C. __ I am familiar with theories of different types of intelligence.

D. __ I know my strongest types of intelligence and how to use them.

E. __ I know how to use my preferred learning style and types of intelligence to overcome my weaknesses.

F. __ I take good care of my body and my brain.

Total _____

**❸ Time Management**

A. __ I have a clear picture of how I spend my time.

B. __ I know several time management strategies and use them regularly.

C. __ I know how to prioritize, I make a daily list of my priorities, and do them most of the time.

D. __ I am able to get my class assignments done on time.

E. __ I use time management tools such as planners and calendars.

F. __ I know how to balance my activities so there is enough time for work, fun, school, and family.

Total _____

**❹ Reading and Studying**

A. __ I know and use reading and study systems.

B. __ I know how to create and use study aids.

C. __ I break my study periods into small chunks.

D. __ I know and use annotation while reading.

E. __ I am skilled in the art of using questions to be engaged with what I am reading.

F. __ I know and use strategies before, during, and after reading my textbooks.

Total _____

**❺ Note-Taking and Writing**

A. __ I use a note-taking system.

B. __ I regularly take notes in my classes and when I read textbooks. I review and study my notes shortly after taking them and before tests.

C. __ I use a writing system, and I know how to write good papers.

D. __ I know the Cornell Note System and how to use it.

E. __ I know what a thesis statement is and how to use it.

F. __ I ask and use journalistic questions before I write my essays.

Total _____

**⑥ Memory Strategies and Test-Taking**

A. ___ I know and use several techniques for improving my memory.

B. ___ I create memory aids to prepare for tests.

C. ___ I know how to use my preferred learning style to aid my memory.

D. ___ I know and use several strategies to reduce test anxiety.

E. ___ I know several strategies for taking objective and essay tests.

F. ___ I predict questions that may be on the tests and create practice quizzes to take before the actual exam.

Total _____

**⑦ Career Development**

A. ___ I have identified and know my strongest values, skills, and interests.

B. ___ I know my strongest personal traits.

C. ___ I know how to research occupations.

D. ___ I am familiar with Holland's six personality types and work environments.

E. ___ I have identified needs and problems in the world, which I would like to help with or solve.

F. ___ I know how to pick majors in college or jobs that would be a good match for me.

Total _____

**⑧ Create the Life You Want**

A. ___ I know my purpose and mission in life.

B. ___ I know and use many success principles and strategies.

C. ___ I am improving myself and my character on a regular basis.

D. ___ I understand why my thoughts are powerful and how to use positive self-talk.

E. ___ I know ways to create the life I want and how to make a positive difference.

F. ___ I understand the importance of my self-image and how to improve it.

Total _____

## Overall Total Score _____

How did your scores compare to the first time you answered these questions? This Post-Course questionnaire gives you one way to measure your progress and to see how much more you know about topics in the book and what it takes for college success.

# Conclusion

You have covered a lot of ground since beginning this book. You have learned much more about yourself. You have learned:

- ↗ How to turn your dreams into goals
- ↗ How to determine your learning styles and types of intelligence
- ↗ Time management and good health strategies
- ↗ Reading comprehension techniques
- ↗ How to write well and take good notes
- ↗ Memory and test-taking strategies
- ↗ Career development ideas
- ↗ How to create the life you want and make a positive contribution to others

Young people are the future and can create a better world. As a young person who has the opportunity to receive a good education, you are one of the fortunate ones in the world. You can use the knowledge and skills contained in this book to do well in school and succeed. Your education is a powerful means to make a positive difference in the world.

Consider how you can give something back from what you learned. You can teach some of these ideas and strategies to a younger brother or sister, to your friends, or you can become a mentor to younger students. By teaching others, you will learn the lessons better yourself and will help others at the same time.

I would love to hear how this benefited you. You can contact me at raymond@raymond-gerson.com. I leave you now with my best wishes for a successful and fulfilling education, career, and life.

# Examples of Student Papers

In my eight-week "Transition to College Success" course which is based on Achieve College Success...Learn How in 20 Hours or Less, I require several reflection papers. These papers include the following: Pre-Assessment, Goal Setting, Time Management or Time Monitor, and Success Story.

Examples of Student Success Story papers are in Chapters 1 and 8. An example of a student Time Management paper is in Chapter 3.

The Pre-Assessment paper is a reflection by students about what they learned about themselves from taking the Pre-Assessment Questionnaire. The Goal Setting paper is about a one-week goal each student created, steps taken to achieve it, the outcome, and what was learned from it.

Examples of a Pre-Assessment and Goal Setting paper are provided below:

## Pre-Assessment Paper

### By Maria Moreno

The pre-assessment questionnaire was an unpleasant wake-up call for me. I was surprised and disappointed to find out how little I knew about what it takes to succeed in college. It showed me that I really do need to learn the topics that will be covered in this course.

I scored low in career development, learning styles and intelligence, reading, studying and note taking, test taking and memory strategies, and creating the life I want. I really don't know much about these subjects. I scored about average in goal setting. I do have goals, but not in all of the categories. I plan to set more goals and to start writing them down. My time management and health and fitness scores were pretty good. I do use a planner and I write down my important things to do. I exercise several times a week and eat pretty good most of the time. I can still improve on these, but I was happy to see I am doing something well.

Even though I felt upset at first with my results, the assessment helped me to see what I need to work on and why I need this course. This is funny because I didn't think I needed a course like this.

I look forward to taking this assessment again at the end of this course and I think there will be big improvements. This motivates me to study and learn these topics because I really want to do well in college.

## Goal Paper

By Sugey Zavala

My short and small goal that I achieved was to at least pass my biology test on Friday. To achieve this goal, for the first time I worked really hard and I did everything I could to pass my test. All of my hard work at the end it paid off because I got an outstanding grade on my biology test.

The steps that I took to achieve my goal were a little difficult because I couldn't do other things that I like to do. One step was staying after school almost every day of the week so I could understand everything clearly. Also in my free time, I would study everything we learned that day in class to make sure I understood it. That week I paid extra attention to the teacher, because I didn't wanted to miss on anything we were learning each day.

While doing these steps to achieve my goal, I had to overcome some obstacles too. One obstacle was not playing my favorite sport, soccer, like always because I stayed after school for about two hours almost every day. Another obstacle was that in my free time I couldn't go out with my mom to the stores because I stayed home studying really hard to achieve my goal.

Finally, it was Friday and I was doing my biology test that I worked so hard to at least pass it. By my surprise the test was very easy, so I was the first one to finish. When everybody was finished, the teacher gave us back our tests already graded and I was very happy because I had gotten my first hundred in biology and I was the only one that got a hundred in my class. At that moment I was so happy because I had not only achieved my goal but I overcame it with the best grade in my class.

From working on this short and small goal I learned that when you work on something really hard, you can achieve or overcome anything you want. In order to achieve my goal I had to overcome some obstacles, but at the end everything was all worth it.

# Distance Learning/Distance Education

## Is online learning right for you?

Online classes, distance learning, and distance education all refer to the same thing, that is, taking a class by signing up for it through a college or university, logging onto a computer, reading materials, accessing and completing activities and papers, participating in discussions, and taking tests. You may never meet your instructor in person, and you may only know your peers in the class by their online presence.

And, while the traditional way of attending class and taking notes, participating in discussions, turning in paper assignments is still an integral part of the higher education system, it is also true that one can complete an education wholly online at some institutions.

Most colleges and universities are now offering online classes in most areas. But is taking an online class right for you? Let's look at an overview of what the requirements of taking an online class might be.

First, online classes require the use of a computer and Internet access. Do you have easy computer access? This could mean having a not-too-old computer at home with Internet access and word processing software (such as MS Word). Or you might have access to a computer through work that you could use when you are off the clock. There are also computers available to you on school campuses during open hours. One benefit of taking an online class is that you can enroll and participate in a time frame that works for you, even if you have to come to campus to use a computer. For example, if you work during the day, and the only time a class is offered on campus is during your work hours, you might be happy (willing) to drive to campus after work and take that same class online, if that means completing the class.

Second, the time required to attend an online class is generally equal to attending a traditional on-campus class. A three-hour class may still require three hours of "in-class" time no matter if online or "face-to-face" learning happens. Also, consider that you will need two hours of homework time for every hour of in-class time, so a three-hour online class may require nine hours of total time per week.

Finally, online classes often have requirements that have you "check in" several times per week (often five different times per week), and not on the same day. Usually, this is broken down between:

1. Attendance and participation, and;

2. Lecture, discussion on discussion boards, and coursework requirements.

Plan on regular class activity throughout the week, and not just sporadic attention to course requirements every so often.

So, what makes a successful online learner? Here is a brief list of successful online learner qualities:

- ↗ Good with time management and can successfully manage assignments and due dates
- ↗ Works well alone
- ↗ Can read and understand material with little explanation from others
- ↗ Has motivation to succeed
- ↗ Good written communication skills
- ↗ Understand and comfortably use computers and current technology
- ↗ Can successfully interact with others online
- ↗ Clear understanding that all online instructors are not created equal

How can students prepare themselves for an online course the first time? Many colleges offer a "readiness" assessment to help students determine if this type of course is appropriate for them. Once enrolled, students should stay in contact with the instructor and take particular care not to let things slide until they get too far behind to complete the course.

Copyright © 2010 Christie Carr

Christie Carr,
Adjunct Assistant Professor
Human Development Department
Austin Community College
MA, Dev. & Adult Education, Texas State University
BA, English, San Francisco State University

*Used with permission from Christie Carr.*

# Your College Library: A Great Resource

Typical areas in the library:

- **Circulation desk.** All publications are checked out here. This is usually at the entrance of the library.
- **Reference area.** Encyclopedias, dictionaries, directories, atlases, and almanacs.
- **Book area.** Books and sometimes magazines and periodicals.
- **Audiovisual materials.** Videos, photography, audio recordings, art, and recorded music collections.
- **Computer area.** Terminals linked to Internet and college databases. These databases are reliable and can be trusted when doing research for writing papers.
- **Microfilm areas.** Microfilm materials printed in reduced size and viewed through special machines.

**Where to find help: Your college reference librarians can help you:** (They can assist you in-person, by e-mail, and many college libraries offer live chat.)

- Locate, analyze, and use information in the library.
- Use the library's many databases, which are reliable for your research projects and papers. The Internet contains both accurate and inaccurate information. The library databases contain only accurate and trustworthy information.
- Locate hard to find sources of information.
- Learn how to evaluate resources.
- Improve your research skills. Tutorials and online classes are usually available.
- Choose a research topic.
- Learn how to avoid plagiarism.
- Become familiar with citations and different documentation styles such as MLA, APA, etc.
- Know the difference between primary (original documents) and secondary sources (comments, interpretations, and writings about primary sources).
- Know how to use call numbers.
- Access loan services when what you need is not available. Books, DVDs, or whatever you are looking for may be available from other libraries and resources. Your library can borrow these and make them available to you.

Several of these ideas about the many services offered by college reference librarians came from "Frequently Asked Questions" on Austin Community College Library's website: http://library.austincc.edu.

Used with permission from Melinda Townsel, ACC Reference Librarian

# Notes

## PREFACE

1. I first heard Earl Nightingale's definition of success on his CD *The Greatest Secret in the World.* This CD is available through Nightingale-Conant Corporation 1-800-525-9000.

## INTRODUCTION

1. The two charts in the introduction are based on statistics from the U.S. Dept. of Labor and the U.S. Census Bureau. The ideas for the chart images came from: Carter, Carolyn, Joyce Bishop, and Sarah Lyman Kravits. *Keys to Success: Building Analytical, Creative, and Practical Skills.* Pearson Prentice Hall, 2012, 6–7.

## CHAPTER 1

1. Ralph Waldo Emerson (1803–1882), U.S. essayist, poet, philosopher. *Nature*, chapter 5(1836), revised and repr, 1849.

2. Carl Sandburg, "Washington Monument by Night," stanza 4, *The Complete Poems of Carl Sandburg*, rev. and expanded edition, 282 (1970).

3. Henry David Thoreau (1817–1862), U.S. philosopher, author, naturalist. Walden (1954), *in The Writings of Henry David Thoreau*, vol. 2, 356, Houghton Miffin (1906).

4. Mauer, Robert. *One Small Step Can Change Your Life: The Kaizen Way.* 21. Workman Publishing, 2004.

5. I was first introduced to the idea of the eight different goal categories by Zig Zigler at his Richer Life Course. Zig is the CEO of Zig Zigler Corporation in Dallas, Texas.

6. Maltz, Maxwell. *Psycho-Cybernetics*. Pocket Books, 1969, 32.

7. Astin, A.W., H.S. Astin, J.A. Lindholm, and A.N. Bryant. *The Spiritual Life of College Students: A National Study of College Students Search for Meaning and Purpose.* Los Angeles: Higher Education Research Institute. U.C.L.A., 2005.

## CHAPTER 2

1. Chinese proverb. Quoted in *The Columbia World of Quotations.* 1996. Number 2209.

2. Richard Bandler and John Grinder. *The Structure of Magic. Science and Behavior Books*, 1975. I believe that Bandler and Grinder made the first reference to visual, auditory, and kinesthetic learning styles.

3. Gardner, Howard. *Frames of Mind: The Theory of Multiple Intelligences. Basic Books*, 1993. Gardner is the original source of Multiple Intelligences and covers each of seven types of intelligence in chapters 5–10, pages 237–276. He later came up with an eighth type of intelligence, "Naturalistic."

4. Sternberg, Robert. *Successful Intelligence: How Practical and Creative Intelligence Determine Success in Life*. Plume, 1997, 127–128.

5. Goleman, Daniel. *Emotional Intelligence: Why It Can Matter More Than IQ*. Bantam, 1997, 43–44.

## CHAPTER 3

1. John Randolph of Roanoke-William Cabell Bruce, *John Randolph of Roanoke*, 1773–1833, vol 2, chapter 7, 205 (1992, reprinted 1970.)

2. Joseph M. Juran, pioneer of quality control, first mentioned the 80-20 rule. It is also referred to as the Paredo principle.

3. Covey, Stephen, Roger Merrill, and Rebecca Merrill. *First Things First. Free Press*, 1996, 37.

## CHAPTER 4

1. Confucius, Chinese philosopher (551–479 B.C.), Quoted in *The Columbia World of Quotations*. 1996. Number 13085.

2. Buzan, Tony. *Use Both Sides of Your Brain: New Mind-Mapping Techniques*. Plume, 1991. I believe that Tony Buzan was the originator of "mind maps" which are sometimes referred to as "idea maps" or "think links."

## CHAPTER 5

1. Alexander Pope 1688–1744. Bartlett, John. comp. 1919. *Familiar Quotations*, 10th ed.

2. The Ebbinghaus Forgetting Curve was the result of Hermann Ebbinghaus' discoveries made regarding the relationship of learning new material and how much is forgotten over time. Many Web sites contain this information. The original study material appeared in Hermann Ebbinghaus' book, *Memory: A Contribution to Experimental Psychology*, (1885). Translated by Henry A. Ruger & Clara E. Bussenius (1913). Originally published in New York by Teachers College, Columbia University. The translation can be accessed online at: http://psychology.about.com/gi/dynamic/offsite.htm?zi=1/XJ&sdn=psychology&cdn=education&tm=11&f=00&su=p897.4.336.ip_&tt=11&bt=0&bts=1&zu=http%3A//psychclassics.yorku.ca/Ebbinghaus/index.htm.

3. Pauk, Walter. *How to Study in College*. Houghton Mifflin Company, 7th edition, 2000. Walter Pauk devised the Cornell System in the 1950s and wrote about it in this book.

## CHAPTER 6

1. Attributed to William Feather-August Kerber, *Quotable Quotes on Education*, 17 (1968). Unverified.

## CHAPTER 7

1. Boldt, Laurence G. *How to Find the Work You Love*. Penguin. Arkana, 1996.

2. Bolles, Richard. *What Color Is Your Parachute?* Ten Speed Press, 1970, 2009. Richard Bolles wrote about a process known as "The System for Motivated Abilities" which was devised by Bernard Haldane.

3. Gerson, Raymond. *Create the Life You Want*. Inspirational Works. 2006, 3. The section "Career Satisfaction Improves Life Satisfaction" was adopted from this book.

4. Gerson, Raymond. *How to Create the Job You Want*. Enrichment Enterprises, 1996, 2007, 13, 14, 45–46. I wrote this book in 1996, and it is now available as a free eBook at www .successforcollegestudents.com.

5. Boldt, Lawrence. *Zen and the Art of Making a Living*. Penguin Group. 1991, 492. "The skills most wanted by employers." Original source was Michigan University Placement Services.

6. Holland, John. *Making Vocational Choices: A Theory of Careers*. Prentice Hall. 1973, 21–28. John Holland is the originator of the Six Personality Types theory.

## CHAPTER 8

1. Boldt, Laurence. G. *How to Find the Work You Love*. Penguin. Arkana, 1996.

2. Covey, Stephen. *Seven Habits of Highly Effective People*. Free Press, 1970, p. 18–19.

3. Maltz, Maxwell. *Psycho-Cybernetics*. Pocket Books, 1969, ix.

4. I got the idea for the pictures of the self-images and created a variation from a workbook that came with a CD program I purchased from Nightingale-Conant Corporation in Chicago, Illinois. The program is "The New *Psycho-Cybernetics*" by Dr. Maxwell Maltz and Dan Kennedy. Available at 1-800-525-9000.

5. Rein, Glen, Mike Atkinson, Rollin McCraty. "The Physiological and Psychological Effects of Compassion and Anger." *Journal of Advancement in Medicine,* 8.2 (1995), 87–105.

6. Cotton, Kathleen. *Expectations and Student Outcomes*. Office of Educational Research and Improvement. U.S. Department of Education. November 1989.

7. Tolle, Eckhart. *A New Earth: Awakening to Your Life's Purpose*. Penguin, 2008, p. 301–302.

8. Edward Everett Hale(1822–1909). *Respectfully Quoted: A Dictionary of Quotations*. 1989.

# Bibliography

1.  Astin, A.W., H.S. Astin, J.A. Lindholm, and A.N.Bryant. *The Spiritual Life of College Students: A National Study of College Students Search for Meaning and Purpose.* Los Angeles: Higher Education Research Institute, U.C.L.A. 2005.

2.  Boldt, Laurence. G. *Zen and the Art of Making a Living.* Penguin. Arkana. 1991.

3.  Bolles, Richard. *What Color Is Your Parachute?* Ten Speed Press, 1970, 2008.

4.  Cotton, Kathleen. *Expectations and Student Outcomes.* Office of Educational Research and Improvement. U.S. Department of Education. November 1989.

5.  Covey, Stephen, Roger Merrill, and Rebecca Merrrill. *First Things First.* Free Press, 1996.

6.  Covey, Stephen. *Seven Habits of Highly Effective People.* Free Press, 2004.

7.  Gardner, Howard. *Frames of Mind: The Theory of Multiple Intelligences.* Basic Books, 1993.

8.  Gerson, Raymond. *Create the Life You Want.* Inspirational Works, 2007.

9.  Gerson, Raymond. *How to Create the Job You Want.* Enrichment Enterprises, 1996.

10. Goleman, Daniel. *Emotional Intelligence: Why It Can Matter More Than IQ.* Bantam, 1997.

11. Holland, John. *Making Vocational Choices: A Theory of Careers,* Prentice Hall. 1973.

12. Maltz, Maxwell. *Psycho-Cybernetics.* Pocket Books, 1969.

13. Maslow, Abraham. *Motivation and Personality.* Harper Collins, 1987.

14. Mauer, Robert. *One Small Step Can Change Your Life: The Kaizen Way.* Workman Publishing, 2004.

15. Rein, Glen, Mike Atkinson, Rollin McCraty. The Physiological and Psychological Effects of Compassion and Anger. *Journal of Advancement in Medicine,* 8.2 (1995), 87–105.

16. Sternberg, Robert. *Successful Intelligence: How Practical and Creative Intelligence Determine Success in Life.* Plume, 1997.

17. Tolle, Eckhart. *A New Earth: Awakening to Your Life's Purpose.* Penguin, 2008.

# Index

*Note*: Page references followed by "*f*" refers to figures and those followed by "*t*" refer to tables.

# Other books by Raymond Gerson

Available at: http://www.upbeatpress.com

### Achieve Career Success...Find and Discover the Job You Want

Want to have a career you love and do well? This book can help! Discover your potential, a career that matches you, and learn how to get the job you want.

Available at: http://www.successforcollegestudents.com

### Create the Life You Want

Create the life you have imagined. Attract and live your dreams. You will gain insights for creating a fulfilling career, attracting the love of your life, finding a great purpose, and making a positive difference.

### How to Create the Job You Want

Create your dream career and make it happen. This book will provide you with ideas for discovering your skills and talents. Learn how to use those discoveries to create a fulfilling job even where one did not previously exist. Develop a job or business that utilizes your natural talents.

### Effective Job Search Strategies

This book contains a variety of elements for a successful job search. It includes tips on writing a resume, interviewing for a job, questions to ask during an interview, and networking strategies. A complementary resource for **How to Create the Job You Want.**

### Reaching for a Dream

This is an inspirational novel which reflects our journey to overcome obstacles to our potential. It will be easy for you to identify with the main character in this uplifting novel as he endeavors to transform his dreams into reality. You will gain motivation and ideas for fulfilling your own hopes and dreams.

### The Greatest Opportunity

Discover treasures within yourself. This is a non-fiction book which contains inspirational ideas for inner growth and personal transformation. The purpose of the book is to provide you with motivational and practical ideas for making the best use of your life.